Perfect Prepositions

Perfect Prepositions

A Real Life Guide to Using English Prepositions

Galina Kimber

iUniverse, Inc.
New York Lincoln Shanghai

Perfect Prepositions
A Real Life Guide to Using English Prepositions

Copyright © 2006 by Galina Kimber

iUniverse books may be ordered through booksellers or by contacting:

iUniverse
2021 Pine Lake Road, Suite 100
Lincoln, NE 68512
www.iuniverse.com
1-800-Authors (1-800-288-4677)

ISBN-13: 978-0-595-37577-6 (pbk)
ISBN-13: 978-0-595-82256-0 (cloth)
ISBN-13: 978-0-595-81971-3 (ebk)
ISBN-10: 0-595-37577-4 (pbk)
ISBN-10: 0-595-82256-8 (cloth)
ISBN-10: 0-595-81971-0 (ebk)

Printed in the United States of America

ACKNOWLEDGEMENTS

I wish to express my acknowledgement to Dr. J. Franke and Dr. V. Mylnikov who read through the manuscript and made valuable remarks and suggestions as to the contents and the structure of this book. I wish to thank my husband, John Evans Kimber, for reading the draft and helping me identify and address some of the shortcomings, even if I did not always accept all of advice that came my way.

THE STRUCTURE OF THE BOOK

The book consists of several sections. The introductory part explains the reasons for writing this book and for whom it is designed. Then it lists objective and subjective difficulties the author met with while preparing it and principles of organizing the contents as well as for choosing illustrative material. The terms used in the book are explained in the section 'The Structure of the Definition of the Category.' The practical part of the book contains the lists of the categories for 99 prepositions and their meanings as well as the examples illustrating them. Our research showed that the most frequently used prepositions in Modern English are the prepositions *on, at, by, for, in, of,* and *with*. An Appendix is attached at the end of the last section.

CONTENTS

Section with Prepositions and Examples

INTRODUCTION

REASONS FOR WRITING THIS BOOK

There are about 100 prepositions in the Modern English language. Their primary function is to signal or emphasize the syntactic and semantic role of notional (content) words in a phrase or a sentence. They have their own, though very abstract, meanings too. Like any other functional (relational) elements in a language, prepositions are high frequency words. However they pose more communication problems for learners of English as well as for native speakers than any other part of speech, though they are short words that seem to never change in form.

To begin with, in oral speech, being used in most of the cases in an unstressed syllable, the prepositions are pronounced fast and not very clearly. As a result of that, they are often barely distinguishable to the listener. Or take as an example the versions of some prepositions, such as: *amid* and *amidst* (variant of *amid*); *among* and *amongst* (variant of *among*); *beside* and *besides* (*besides* being an adverb). In addition, in written speech, there are circumstances when prepositions cause difficulties due to a variety of factors that I will mention later in the research. For instance, the following commonly used sentences often cause certain difficulties with non-native English speakers:

Interact with people **at school.** (or **in** school?)
He graduated high school in 1996. (or **from** high school?)
Children would starve **in the streets.** (or **on** the streets?)

Or, compare, for instance, the sentences with two different prepositions connected with one and the same verb:

He never wrote of it to anyone.
(Meaning, it didn't *occur* to him to write of it).

He <u>wrote nothing **about** it.</u>
(Meaning, he never *mentioned* it).

It takes learners time and sometimes a lot of practicing to gain 'the feeling' of what versions of the above sentences are appropriate in a particular situation. This is one of the reasons I see a reference book on prepositions is needed.

Another reason for writing this book pertains to the fact that living languages, and primarily the meanings of the words, constantly evolve over time. It's a well-known fact that dictionaries get outdated the moment they are published. So to reflect these changes, reference books describing various special phenomena in any given language, like this one, need to be updated or compiled anew on a regular basis.

That is why this book is intended to provide the user with general information about prepositions, on the one hand, and, on the other, with more specific information and ideas about the meaning and usage of one of the most dynamic parts of the speech in nearly any language—prepositions as they are used today.

FOR WHOM THE BOOK IS INTENDED

As this reference book deals with the most commonly used prepositions and presents some basic rules of usage for these functional words, it may be helpful primarily for students of English, at any level of their studies, as well as the teachers, as a source of examples for practicing with the students. Also, researchers of language may find some new ideas, regarding the meanings of the words that I tried to present in the unified form of general logical or semantic categories such as the category *'moving in some direction'*. Besides, I think that the materials presented in this book may be handy as a reference source in compiling dictionaries, grammar books and some textbooks.

I should mention here, however, that no book, this book including, can cover *all* possible cases of occurrence for a word, both in the oral and written types of speech, because any living language is an open, constantly changing system. Speech is often spontaneous so that an established traditional meaning of a word may be slightly different in a particular sentence. This book focuses exclusively on the analysis of only *one* part of speech and provides *several* examples for each usage of a preposition. That's why it has the capacity to offer *more* variants or nuances of a meaning for each preposition than, e.g., an entry in a dictionary for this preposition.

I hope that this book will assist the reader in using the language with more precision, color and vitality. There is no doubt that this book is only one effort on the part of the linguists in the continuous process of studying the semantics of form words. A further research on the subject is necessary and welcome to make sure the readers get a regular update on the usage of prepositions in Modern English.

WAYS AND DIFFICULTIES IN DEFINING THE MEANING OF A PREPOSITION

In this book we define prepositions to be a part of speech with rather abstract semantics serving to show the *relationships* between notional units of speech (words, phrases, clauses) that usually have full lexical meanings in word combinations or in sentences. A preposition expresses a relationship of the meanings between at least two parts in a sentence, and by that, between two or more *ideas*, or semantic categories.

Under *category* we understand an idea or concept, sense, essence, a term, a basic logical type of philosophical conception, a class or division in a system of classification, or a grouping.

Meaning is an interpreted goal or intent, an indication, a message. Meaning is an interpretation of something that is mostly conveyed by language or implied as an inner significance. Meanings can be looked at as linguistic embodiments of the essence of a category or rather of a group of categories in speech. Meanings can be denotational or connotational. Prepositions have primarily abstract denotational meanings.

A preposition is usually presented by a single word (*in, at, by*), sometimes by a phrase functioning as a single word (*according to, in view of*). Not all linguists include such units as well as the words *but, following, like, than* in the class of the prepositions. That is why it is not easy to delineate the exact amount of prepositions as a class or a part of speech.

Though we gave a definition of prepositions as a part of speech or class above, their individual meanings are not easy to define in every day real life occurrences as they do not always function according to a clear set of rules. In some dictionaries, the meaning of a preposition may be defined through the meaning of another preposition, a synonym, e.g. *on* means '*above* and supported *by*' as in the sentence: 'The book is **on** the table.' When two or more prepositions have the *same* meaning, when they are synonyms, they are sometimes interchangeable in their usage, which means they contain the *same* category in their meanings:

He was pleased **by/with** the answer.

However, not all prepositions have synonyms or antonyms which they may be defined by. That is why this method to find out the meaning of a preposition does not work in all the cases. I applied the *inductive method* in this research to find out the meaning of a preposition in a sentence at the syntactic and semantic levels, which means I tried to derive a meaning of a preposition primarily from the examples I gathered, not from reference books. Syntactically and semantically, all prepositions enter into relationships with *all* of the words in a sentence, but have more close, primarily semantic links, with some of them, usually a noun, a verb, or an adjective, in a phrase as a part of the sentence. For example, in the following sentence, the verb *lying* is a governing, or a head word, in the phrase *lying on the carpet*:

My cat is lying **on** the carpet.

The nominal phrase *the carpet* that follows the preposition is endocentric and may be called the *object* of the preposition **on**. Prepositions can also be part of phrasal verbs or adjectives *(depend on, aware of, happy with, proud of)*, or they can be part of an idiomatic expression. In some cases, the meaning of a preposition can be understood only from the meaning of the entire sentence, and not only from the prepositional word combination it is part of, e.g:

Voters brace **for** a runoff.

As to the role of the prepositional phrases in a sentence, they can fulfill the role of an object or an adverbial modifier, as they answer the questions, like: *which one, what kind of, how, how often, when, where, why, to what extent*, etc. They cannot be, however, the subject or the predicate in a sentence.

To show the syntactic and semantic links of a preposition with the words both on the right and on the left of it in a phrase, I underlined them in each example in the sections of the book with examples. At times, however, due to the fact that all words in sentences are interconnected and interdependent, it was hard to define the boundaries between the closer and less close links between words. For example, what should be underlined in the sentence: 'I need to brush up **on** my Math?' Should it be

to brush up on, or
to brush up on Math, or
to brush up on my Math?

For some category names in the 'practical' part of the book, there are no synonyms among the categories in the headings and in the examples themselves that are given under these headings. They are unique to some extent. That's why our principle—not to use the same word for a category name that is used in the examples to illustrate it, is sometimes violated. In other words, you cannot avoid the 'vicious circle' in defining a category so that its name doesn't repeat itself in any subcategory in the headings or in the examples I provide. So the name of the category *'focusing'*, as one of the meanings of the preposition *on,* repeats itself in the word *'Focus'* in the sentence:

Focus **on** the idea now!

This reference book deals with explaining the most common meanings of prepositions. It is a well-known fact that the meaning of any word, prepositions including, is derived from the sum of its known contexts in all forms of the present-day language. By context we mean all surrounding words, the position of a preposition in a sentence or a phrase, the communicative type of a sentence or a phrase it is used in, as well as other factors that might influence the usage of the words in speech. However, the contexts for most of the prepositions are too diverse and too numerous for making quick and simple generalizations about them.

Here are some other considerations about the objective problems linguists face while defining the semantics of words, particularly in 'form words', such as prepositions.

1)   The process of defining meanings in a language, like in all kinds of logical and spontaneous thinking that a language reflects, is associated with *categorization* of human experience and knowledge. However, a complete categorization of human knowledge has not been achieved yet. Actually, it might not be achievable at all, even in the future, due to the fact that the real world that a language reflects is in constant change so that new categories and words keep emerging in it. So languages change continually likewise.

2)   The meanings of a word are of a purely conventional value, as they are presented in reference books, e.g. in dictionaries. Different language communities all over the world do not make the same identification of one and the same object in their contact with non-linguistic reality. That's why one and the same word may have not only several separate meanings, but also lexicosemantic variants of one and the same separate meaning. The words mean only what a particular group of individuals makes them mean at a particular moment of their existence, and those meanings change with time. Thus, the meanings of most words need to be regularly redefined, or reinterpreted, or explained, both in oral practice (spontaneous speech) and in reference literature as well.

3)   The exact number of prepositions in modern English, as I mentioned before, is unknown, paradoxical as it may sound. Their number differs according to

different authors, linguistic schools, methods of defining meaning, goals of compiling reference books, etc. Besides, words not only change their meanings or develop new ones with time. They can change their status as a particular *part of speech* and transfer to another part of speech. So, that we face some borderline cases like the ones in the following sentences, where the grammatical status of the preposition as a part of speech is not clear:

> I have some Mozart, I'll put it **on** for you.
> He made his wife and children do **without**.
> I wrote down all the things he has put me **through**.
> Cats are nothing to fool around **with**.
> We <u>enjoyed our coffee with</u>…

These examples may sound not completely correct or obsolete, but they are taken out of real situations. What is *on* in the first sentence—a preposition or an adverb? In the last sentence, for instance, *with* seems to be a preposition because the phrase *coffee with* may mean 'coffee with cream', or 'coffee with milk', or 'coffee with a non-dairy creamer' and the like. So *with* still may be considered a preposition, its object (the word *cream*, for instance) is understood or implied.

The frequent omission of an object after a preposition, however, eventually turns that preposition into an *adverb*. Such a use of *with* as an 'adverb' (a preposition without an object, in this case) is taking hold in Modern English. Some more examples with the preposition *with* in this function:

> Do you want me to go **with**? (with you)
> I'll fax it to you now and you can bring it **with** (with you).
> You fix lasagna and we'll have a salad to go **with** (with it).
> Are you easy to be **with**?

A number of other words are also usable as prepositions or adverbs:

> They drove **by** the house—They drove **by**.
> He came **to** his senses—He came **to**.

Let's look at the word *above* as an example. What part of speech is this word in the sentence 'Read the *above*?' Is it part of an elliptical sentence *Read the above text* or is it a noun because an article is before it? The same in: '*The above figures.*' Is *above* an adjective here because it precedes a noun? In the phrase '*From above*' the situation is even less clear: are both words prepositions or is one word a preposition and another an adverb? To be a part of speech, a word needs to have some specific features of this particular part of speech and some research is needed to prove the status of each word in question. In the following sentence, two prepositions *up* and *until* define the adverb *recently* (instead of defining a noun or a noun phrase):

> **Up until** recently, finances have been a concern.

Another interesting situation arises, e.g., when the words *about* and *around* modify a number and again it's not clear whether they are prepositions or adverbs:

> It's **about** <u>five</u> in the morning.
> It happened **around** <u>twelve</u>.

One cannot be too sure about the status of many other words in a language. Some linguists, for instance, consider the words *pending, apropos (of), round (about), plus, via, circa, underneath, alongside (of), atop, excluding, notwithstanding, considering, barring, following, throughout, minus, than, versus, aboard, worth* to be prepositions, while some others don't. Here are some examples:

> Scientists **aboard** the research ship returned from
> a month-long voyage.

> This is a photo of Lisa and Diana, **circa** 1920.
> It's again a heart-**versus**-head situation.

We applied the following criteria in deciding whether to include a word into the class of prepositions:

> *Meaning, semantics.* Words should have their own meanings (prepositions do have their own, though very abstract, meanings). Besides they can have synonyms/antonyms and because of that be interchangeable in speech.

> *Form.* Words are considered words if they have a 'physical' expression in linguistic symbols/letters and be used separately from other language units. Prepositions are separate words and are distinguished by invariability in form and shortness.

Function. Words belonging to a class or part of speech fulfill a special role in a sentence. A preposition signals or emphasizes the syntactic and semantic role of content words. Prepositions occupy a certain position in a phrase or a sentence, usually before a noun.

Prepositions often overlap in their usage not only with adverbs but with other word classes, as well. For instance, the words *near* and *since* may function as prepositions, adverbs or conjunctions.

Prepositions as <u>a functional</u> (not a notional) <u>part</u> of speech are considered to be unchangeable and usually are not defined by any other words in the sentence. The following example, however, shows that some words (*way,* in this case) can 'add' a certain meaning to the preposition following it (probably it may be applicable only to the colloquial or inaccurate usage):

> Come to where the fun begins and continues
> **till way past** midnight.

4) Reference books usually provide a *variable* (and not the same!) *number* of meanings for any preposition. On another hand, only *one* meaning is often presented in a dictionary, which is certainly not enough in some cases. From such a definition one can get only a very general idea about the possible ways of how to use a preposition, e.g. the preposition *on.* "The American Heritage Dictionary of the English Language," for instance, gives the following definition for the first meaning of *on*: *on* = 'so as to be or remain supported by or suspended from.' We certainly need more information on the usage of *on* because, among other things, this preposition may rightly be considered the most frequently used in Modern English and we include actually 140 meanings of it in this reference book. It is designed primarily for an average user of the language, and as such it generally offers more variants of a meaning based on the examples from the present-day sources, than other reference books, including dictionaries. Providing each of many meanings of a preposition with multiple examples we try to help the readers come to a deeper understanding of these meanings 'by themselves.'

5) Different sources of information on the meanings of any word (dictionaries, reference books, grammar books, text books, etc.) define one and the same word in *different* ways by applying different *techniques,* e.g. through synonyms, antonyms or phrases consisting of generic words and more specific words, depending on the purpose, type, size of a particular reference book, as

well as author's preferences. That might cause confusion for a user as well, when he sees different definitions for the same word in different books or even only in one and the same book.

6)   A reference book or a dictionary may ascribe the *same* semantics to *different usages* of a word, so that *various* meanings of a preposition get the *same* definition. True, defining meanings is, to some extent, a subjective process, though any author naturally aspires to reach as much preciseness and unification in specifying meanings of all the words in one class as possible. Compare, for instance, the following prepositional word combinations:

> They arrived **with** bad news today.
> See that man **with** the mustache?

In the first phrase, *with bad news*, the meaning of the preposition *with* may be described as *'sharing something with someone'*, while in the second example, *with the mustache*, it has the meaning that may be defined as *'a characteristic feature'* or *'inseparable from'*. However, both prepositional phrases were listed in the above mentioned dictionary under the *same* category *'having as a possession, an attribute, or a characteristic.'* The difference is that the phrase *'bad news'* points to a temporary attribute of an object, while the word *'mustache'* to a more permanent characteristic plus the meaning of *'togetherness.'* The same can be said about the ways of defining the semantics of any preposition. For example, the preposition *in*, too, displays a rather different meaning in each of the sentences (with free word combinations and idioms) given below:

> The letter is **in** the drawer.
> We lived **in** San Francisco.
> Don't be **in** such a hurry.
> She has fallen **in** love.

As was mentioned before, several categories used as headings for a group of meanings of a preposition often overlap in their semantics. It's not easy, for instance, to distinguish the category *'a part of the day'* and the category *'a special event, happening/a particular circumstance'* in the following sentences:

> It happened **on** a night in November.
> My teacher took up the matter with
> my mother **on** open school night.

As we can see, some meanings in a preposition do overlap, or partly coincide, and it may affect the extent or level to which they are subdivided or distinguished in a particular reference book. Still, it is desirable and important to describe the notions or concepts in the words, including prepositions, in the most accurate way possible.

7)   The linguistic 'environment' or a linguistic context for a preposition in a sentence—linguistic units before and after a preposition—can be various. Prepositions relate, by their meanings, the idea of a function of notional words represented by different parts of speech: a noun (a preposition + a noun), a pronoun (a preposition + a pronoun), a verb (a preposition + a gerund), an adjective (an adjective + a preposition), or an adverb (a preposition + an adverb). The most frequently used 'object' of a preposition is a noun or a noun equivalent (a pronoun, a gerund). However, in some cases prepositions may relate to a group of words or a clause as well. In the following example the preposition *at* relates to a phrasal ellipsis:

> I sleep over **at** a friend's. (meaning:
> '*at a friend's house*' or '*at a friend's place.*')

In the following sentence the preposition *on* is linked to a verbal phrase:

> You can depend **on** my finishing the job today.

The preposition *over* governs a clause in the sentence:

> I'm concerned **over** how he can handle that.

8)   As it was mentioned before, most prepositions in a language are presented by single words (one-word prepositions), but some phrases can act as prepositions as well (complex prepositions), as in the case with the phrases '*in the event of,*' '*as a result of,*' '*in regard to,*' '*relative to*' and some others. Linguists as well as common users of a language are not completely sure whether we should consider such phrases to be a single word or a word combination (it is the so-called *stone wall* problem). Structurally, in their linguistic expression, these units are word combinations, but from the point of view of their meanings, they represent *one* notion, or idea. That's why these word combinations are considered to be *one* unit, for example, in the sentence:

We'll evaluate your credentials **relative to** your needs.

9) Some notional or content words, used in different contexts, are consistently followed by *one and the same* preposition, as in:

We *sympathize* **with** someone, him, our neighbor, everyone.

In other cases *different* prepositions can be used with *one and the same* notional word. Unfortunately, dictionaries are not always helpful on distinguishing such cases. Here are some more examples:

Broccoli is *good* **for** me. *But*:
Broccoli tastes *good* **to** me.

Food may not *agree* **with** us.
We *agree* **with** him, **with** the statements he makes. *But*:
We *agree* **to** a price, **to** a suggestion, **to** anything.

Some of the following notional words may also be used with several different prepositions: abide (by, in), accessory (of, to), accommodate (to, with), accompany (by, with), agree (with, to, on), adapt (from, to), adequate (for, to), charge (for, with), compare (to, with), concur (in, with), consist (in, of), correspond (to, with), differ (over, with), familiar (to, with), inconsistent (to, with), necessity (for, of), obvious (of, to), part (from, with), reconcile (to, with), reward (for, with), talk (of, with), transfer (from, to), unequal (in, to), use (for, of), wait (at, for, on), and others.

10) More than one preposition can be used in a phrase with the same content words in the same or slightly different situation. For instance, with the words denoting buildings or institutions, both the preposition *in* and the preposition *at* can be used with little difference in meaning as in '*in/at* the office, school, college, store,' etc. It should be mentioned here that the preposition *in* usually means '*being inside the building or institution*,' while the preposition *at* may mean '*being on the outside or near the building or institution*.' '*At*' can also have a more abstract meaning: '*being involved with the activities at this institution at some point*,' e.g.:

I found him **in** the library quietly
sitting in the back of the room.
My car is parked **at** the library.

11) With some prepositions, we might witness a new trend in Modern English which may be qualified as the substitution process of one preposition by another one in the same context. For example, nowadays the preposition *by* seems to be more often used in the word combinations that were more commonly used with the preposition *of* before, e.g.:

> The comments **by** Dr. Smith threw into question
> many of the conclusions of the study. (**of** Dr. Smith)

12) In this book the meaning of a preposition is presented by a *category* or a concept, an idea that is given as a heading, e.g. as the category *'motion.'*. A preposition may combine several semantic categories in one of its meanings. In other words, it can express similar semantic categories (overlapping) and/or different categories at the same time. For example, the prepositions expressing the idea of *'a position or place'* (*above, at, in back of, behind, below, beside, between, by, in front of, in, inside, near, next, on, over, under, underneath, to*) may, at the same time, express the idea of *'moving to some location.'* Two prepositions can even merge into one word making up a compound preposition. For example, in the words *into* and *onto*, the part *to* expresses the idea of *'moving toward a position'* while the words *in* and *on* primarily indicate *'a place or position in space'*. Or, the prepositions indicating *'location'* may simultaneously indicate the notion of *'time'*, too. There are other examples of borderline areas in thinking and language forms that embody them. Such meanings are especially difficult to define and being ascribed a category to them. In the following sentences, we cannot be absolutely sure whether there is an indication of *'time'* or *'location'* in the prepositional groups:

> I can't call you when I am **at** work.
> Get together **outside of** work!

Do the prepositional phrases in the sentences above mean *when* or *where* the actions take place, or both? In other words, should we ascribe to these examples the category of *'location'*, or *'time'* as a meaning, or both? Defining the meaning as a *double* category may be a way out in such cases. For example, we can define a meaning as *'location*/time' or *'state/condition'* as categories with an implication that both meanings are available in one and the same prepositional word combination. The notion of a double category can be applied to other prepositions, too, e.g. to the semantics of the preposition *for* as *'purpose/intention'* and *'purpose/objective'*.

13) To find out the meanings of prepositions, some procedures of transformational grammar were applied here. For instance, if several prepositional phrases, that we analyzed, answered the same question (and usually have the same part of speech as a governing word) when compared, then these examples belong to one and the same semantic group. For instance, the following word combinations answer the same question *when*. That is why these examples illustrate the usage of one and the same meaning or category:

> **On** joining us, he changed.
> **On** request, she rushed to the door.
> **On** your first order, I sent a book.

Categories in the numbered headings in the section with the examples of this book are mostly nouns or gerunds and are usually presented by *generic* words. They don't repeat themselves in the corresponding words in the examples themselves. They are synonyms to some extent, specific *sub*categories to their meanings. Usually they just govern or request the usage of a particular preposition, but sometimes, as was mentioned before, more words are involved in their 'orbit' in the sentence semantically as their meanings are interwoven. That's why it is next to impossible to say which word governs this particular preposition. The names of some categories such as the category *'advice'* are relative in the sense that, unlike the categories denoting tangible characteristics of the physical objects, they are more of the human mind's invention, very abstract in meaning, because of their broad use (anyone can give advice on anything in any situation).

14) The simultaneous use of two prepositions, or a preposition and one or more other parts of speech which makes up the so called *complex prepositions,* can combine similar or different semantic categories in their meanings. For example, in the word group *from under*, the word *under* indicates the category *'position'*, and the word *from*—*'moving from the position,'* but they function as one word. Here are some more examples with the multi-word or complex prepositions:

> She sits **across from** me, so I see her face now.
> She tried to smile at him **from across** her desk.
> No standing **ahead of** the white line (sign in a bus).
> **Along with** this exceptional rate, there's no annual fee.
> **Along with** dirty clothes, his shaggy hair made him look old.
> I have no life **apart from** his, she said.
> **Aside from** those numbers, everything else was correct.

He should have been there **as of** last night.
Check out **at around** noon, otherwise you'll pay more.
Because of these very principles, they became great.
In the morning the sun shines **in between** the drawn drapes.
He'd been walking with me **since before** S.Clara.
I will do it, I promise, but not **until after** lunch.
They stayed at my place **until after** dark.
The height of the hill is calculated **to within** an inch.

It should be mentioned here that when two prepositions stand together in a sentence they do not necessarily belong to one and the same prepositional unit. Rather they constitute two separate word combinations with two different governing words:

The mission we embarked **on over** 85 years ago, still rings true today. (embarked **on//over** 85 years ago).

15) One of the least explored fields in the semantic relationships between speech units that include prepositions are words (or phrases?) we see in the following sentences:

Can you give us the student-**to**-teacher ratio?
One-**on**-one relationships are a primary focus right now.
Many small animals are kept '**behind**-the-scenes'.
We want to please you with **up-to**-the-minute deals.

I can also mention here as an issue for a possible interest on behalf of the linguists the *repetitive* use of one and the same preposition, evidently for the purpose of emphasis alongside with adding some more information with the subsequent prepositional phrase. Usually the prepositional phrase is repeated twice:

Enjoy Holiday Magic: from shopping **to** dining **to** entertainment!
The plane flew from Sydney **to** Fiji, **to** Canton Island, **to** Honolulu, **to** San Francisco.
Shopping **after** work **after** dark is becoming the order of the day.

16) Prepositions are predominantly short words. Long compound prepositions like *alongside, throughout* are rare. Short words, as is well known, usually are hard to hear in a spoken language because they are less stressed or even unstressed, especially when they occur at the end of a sentence or a phrase.

Besides, if a sentence is too long, the listener may be unsure of what was at the beginning of that sentence or forget it, as well as what kind of a relationship the preposition used at the *end* of the sentence or a phrase has with the preceding words. Here are some examples:

> They need looking **after**.
> What are you going to shop **for**?
> I had several friends one of whom I grew to care **for** deeply.
> I wish I knew which magazine her article appeared **in**.
> As I alluded **to** before, the joy is dead.
> How many people can I count **on**?
> We need tools to work **with**.
> Where'd you run off **to**?

17) As was mentioned before, some prepositions are highly predictable, one can easily guess them if they happen to be omitted from a text. Still, one should be careful in omitting prepositions because in some circumstances one can end up in confusing styles or even in misunderstanding the message. Here are some examples (sentences like these primarily belong to the colloquial style):

> Are you home? (**at** home).
> Life is crazy these days. (**in** these days).
> What color cloth do you like? (color **of** the cloth).
> What size shoes does your son wear? (size **of** shoes).
> Let's stop running red lights! (**past/through** red lights)
> Shop the Haight Street! (**on** the Haight Street)
> I suggest biking the Bay Bridge. (**across** the Bay Bridge)
> Student enrollment in schools rose 1% the past two years.
> (**in** the past two years).

In many cases prepositions are omitted after the verbs denoting *mental* or *speech activities*:

> Think Thanksgiving!
> Don't think kennel, think shrines!
> They are talking career, not job.
> We're talking a major makeover now.
> You are talking a big-time transformation.
> Try telling that to a partner.
> We read it cover to cover.

> People write me that the diet is easy to follow.
> They all are crying unity.

The frequent occurrence of such cases nowadays shows that though they might belong primarily to the sphere of oral speech (sometimes colloquial informal style), we may at the same time consider them already to be a standard element of the language structure as well. Consider also the difference in the following sentences that seem to be alike in meaning used with and without a preposition:

> He blows **on** the old trombone. (with a preposition)
> He can play the violin and the piano. (without a preposition)

Less evident on what might have been omitted are the following two sentences:

> The demo is now over (Meaning: **with** the demo).
> Where are the kids (Meaning: **at** what place)?

18) Prepositions can 'provoke' omitting a word in a phrase. There may be a hidden notional word that seems to be skipped like the words *some* or *more*:

> Give **of** your time to the homeless.
> (*some* of your time/*more* of your time. Compare with:
> Give your time to the homeless).

> I slipped the jacket **on** and tiptoed out of the house.
> (*onto* myself)

19) Due to the fact that in many cases it is hard, and at times even impossible, to distinguish between a *free* phrase and an *idiomatic* combination of words, and that this distinction does not make any big difference for a user in everyday communication acts either, this book does not discriminate between the free and bound or idiomatic usage of the words. The illustrative material covers to some extent both of them, though emphasis is made on the free word combinations. Many recognized or traditional idioms include prepositions whose correct use is not always 'logical' or predictable and that may be confusing for a user, e.g.:

> We search **for** something. *But*:
> We are in search **of** something.

When the meaning of a preposition does not follow any pattern or logic in usage, it must be learned together with the surrounding words as a vocabulary unit:

> It's **about** time, don't you think?
> Congratulations **on** the purchase of your home.
> He is never **on** time, sorry to say that.

20) The process of classifying or categorization of the examples, and through that figuring out or extracting the meanings of the prepositions themselves, may be hampered in a situation when it is unclear whether a *preposition* governs some word or is *governed* by the word before or after it in a sentence or a phrase. Generally prepositions precede the words which they 'govern' and which are sometimes called their objects. In most of the sentences the phrasal stress makes the meaning of the preposition rather clear. In some sentences, however, the logical emphasis can be shifted from the words preceding a preposition to the words after it, which makes it difficult to decide what the governing word is. Compare the following examples:

> He is <u>in a real hurry</u> **for** bread. *But*:
> He is in a real hurry **for** <u>bread</u>.
> I went to the store **for** <u>milk</u>. *But*:
> I went <u>to the store</u> **for** milk.
> Voters <u>brace</u> **for** a runoff. *But*:
> Voters brace **for** a <u>runoff.</u>
> That is an idea ready **for** <u>discussion</u>. *But*:
> That is an idea <u>ready</u> **for** discussion.

In such cases, one cannot be sure which word the preposition 'belongs' to or depends on: the preceding word(s) or the one(s) that follows it. To some extent it is a question of the degree of interdependence of the words, of obligatory or optional usage of an object as a complementation to a preposition. We face almost the same situation in a prepositional group comprised of a preposition and its modifier, e.g. the words '*immediately*' and '*right*':

> We left home *immediately* **after** lunch.
> It happened *right* **in** front of the fountain.

The same can be said about the preposition *to* preceded by the word '*back*'. As they are often used together, the question arises whether the word '*back*' as an adverb is an emphasis to the meaning of the preposition *to* or the main semantic element in a new compound preposition '*back to*' as in the sentence:

Please mail this card **back to** Senior Center.

21) By saying that a particular preposition has a particular meaning in a prepositional phrase, I mean that this preposition matches the meaning of a particular *category*, and in a specific example it enhances, to some extent, the meaning of a word combination of which this preposition is a part. So we talk more of the meaning of a *word combination* rather than the meaning of an isolated preposition matching the meaning of the corresponding category.

22) Most of the reference books illustrate the meaning of a word only by a *single* example, usually in the form of a phrase, sometimes a sentence. By doing so, the compilers may give a subjective, if not a biased, presentation on the semantics of a word and lead the reader in a specific direction in understanding the meaning of a speech unit. Besides, in real life, a particular user may never face a case illustrated by such a single example in a phrase. That is why *multiple* examples on the meaning of a word, especially in the context of a complete sentence, which is our approach here, might present a more objective situation and allow the readers to make conclusions about the meanings of the prepositions on their own, too. The amount of the examples on each usage of a preposition in this book may reflect:

a) The importance of a particular meaning of a preposition in question among all its meanings, from the point of view of how easy it can be comprehended. For instance, the meaning 'moving in the direction' for the preposition into as in the sentence: 'The balloons flew into the sky,' is easier to understand than the meaning 'being/getting interested' as in the sentence: 'She is not into basketball any more.'

b) The frequency of the usage of this particular preposition. In the examples above the category 'moving in the direction' is more often used than the category 'being/getting interested'. Some prepositions are restricted in their frequency of use, especially foreign borrowings like the words circa, versus.

SOURCES AND PRINCIPLES FOR CHOOSING EXAMPLES

Keeping in mind that multiple examples, presented in a wide array of genres both in publications and oral presentations, may show certain patterns of the word usage by a broad group of users much better than a single example from a single source, we followed some of the principles in picking up our illustrative materials for the preposition usage in this book:

1. Providing examples that reflect the contemporary usage of words and deal with everyday situations. To achieve this objective, the illustrative material was taken from both oral and written sources. Since an accurate record of the language phenomena as they are used today is crucial, emphasis was made on the word combinations used primarily by mass media: newspapers, radio talks, TV shows, as well as flyers and leaflets. Some examples we found in everyday live conversations that reflect the speech habits of well-informed speakers, writers, politicians, journalists, actors, teachers, etc. And the reason for using mass media sources is that, on the one hand, nearly every member of a modern society reads newspapers or listens to the radio and watches TV daily, which to some extent standardizes the language used by millions of readers, listeners and viewers. On the other hand, while everyday news publications, for instance, give a vivid idea of major events all over the world, they do it through dynamic and very often innovative use of contemporary language. At the same time, mass media represent broad and diverse groups of people who may use different styles of the same language. Some of the prepositions belong to the formal style (*amidst, apropos, pending, notwithstanding*), some to the informal style (*than*). Some of them are used almost exclusively in the written speech (*via*). This book deals with both styles.

2. Defining each individual meaning in the terms of semantic or logical categories that allows a high degree of unification in the presentation of the meanings of all the prepositions.

3. Presenting the meanings of each preposition in the examples in typical, recurrent, high frequency contexts in a frame of a sentence (not a word combination).

4. Trying to avoid the so-called 'vicious circles' in defining the meanings of words, by not using the prepositions themselves as the names for the categories that define their generic meaning. It is not a desirable situation when the meaning of a word, e.g. the meaning of the preposition *outside* is defined

in a dictionary entry for this preposition as '*on the outside of*' which is an example of tautology.

5. Trying to provide as many examples for a single *notional* word, before which a preposition is used, as possible. That's why there are more examples in some cases than in others which reflects the frequency in the usage of this or that preposition, e.g. the preposition *on* is one of the most often used prepositions nowadays. For some high frequency content words many examples are given, e.g., for the words '*school*' and '*office*'. In some cases, I as well included several examples for one preposition used for notional words that are semantically related to a high frequency word, e.g. the word *school* (*academy, college, institute,* etc.) as they belong to the same semantic group. Here are some examples (the words 'to *enthuse*' and the expression 'to *be enthusiastic*' are in the same semantic field):

> to <u>enthuse</u> *over/about* something and
> to <u>be enthusiastic</u> *over/about* something

6. Presenting the sentences in the section on the examples in such a way so that the headings and subheadings for individual meanings in a preposition begin with a more common or simple category and proceed to a more complex one.

7. Following the rules of economy/brevity in expression and trying to record the meanings of the prepositions in a short, precise, easily understood manner.

8. Trying to present the names of all headings and subheadings or the names of the semantic categories and subcategories for all the prepositions discussed in the book, in a *unified* form. So one can find the category '*motion*' among the meanings of the preposition *on* as well as among the meanings of other prepositions, e.g., the preposition *in*.

To fix a precise definition of a word meaning, it is necessary to consider its form and the linguistic context as well as the extra-linguistic circumstances under which it is to be interpreted by the user. For achieving this goal, several approaches or methods and techniques were used:

a. Applying the *inductive* method based on many observations of the 'raw material' in the form of the examples in the natural flow of speech with the goal of finding out how the language 'mechanism' works. The fact that these observations are repeatable shows they are correct.

b. Using *thesauri*, including online dictionaries, for finding out synonyms and antonyms for both prepositions and notional words used with them.

c. *Comparing* definitions of the meanings for a preposition in different reference books as well as comparing the meanings of the words in the examples taken from publications and oral sources.

d. Comparing *multiple cross-definitions* of two or more synonymous prepositions in one and the same or several dictionaries for detecting common and different elements in their meanings.

e. Applying *transformational grammar* rules, e.g. the substitution procedure. In some cases the combination of methods or procedures was applied to properly subdivide the meanings in one word.

f. *Checking* the meanings of prepositions through the procedure of asking questions to the prepositional groups. For instance, alternative questions with the conjunction *or* were asked in order to find out synonyms and antonyms for a particular preposition.

g. Using *native speakers' expertise* to verify the correctness of each sentence.

h. Using *common sense*, or intuition, in selecting a meaning, which naturally is used by any researcher to make conclusions, if intuition doesn't conflict with observation.

THE STRUCTURE OF THE DEFINITION OF THE CATEGORY

Under the *definition* of the (sub)category we understand a semantic analogue, a synonymous word or expression, serving as a short and exact explanation or interpretation of the meaning of a given preposition as well as the process of identification of the meaning in a particular example that follows. For instance, one of the meanings of the preposition *around* is defined as the semantic category '*approximate time*' (the definition) as it is presented in the example: 'Check out **around** noon.'

A semantic category (in a numbered subheading) is usually presented as a word (a noun or a gerund) or a phrase consisting of a noun or a gerund with their modifiers. One category can sometimes be expressed by two synonyms (two nouns or gerunds) as in the case of the category '*detecting/finding*.' The category '*speech*,' can be presented in the subcategories '*an oral speech*' and '*a written speech*,' that is, in more specific meanings. The same we find in almost any other category (generic word), e.g., for the category '*emotion*' and subcategories '*a positive emotion*' and '*a negtive emotion.'* In the names of the categories and subcategories, words are generally presented in the singular form, e.g. as the category *'source'* (not 'sources').

It should be mentioned that definitions are always relative as to their contents (meaning) as well as to the linguistic way they are presented in reference literature. They depend on the goals of a book, the kind of potential readers, the numbers of sources covered, time of writing, author's preferences, etc. So, an entry or the total amount of the examples that provide the entire information for one preposition in this book will differ in content and length from that for another preposition.

A capitalized word after a number representing a category as one of the meanings of a preposition in the set of the examples is a definition or a *generic* meaning of this preposition. These words are basic semantic categories and in some cases subcategories showing more specific or detailed meanings. We accept the idea that all words in a language can be explained through the meanings of each other, however distant these meanings may seem to be from one another. Actually, all meanings of prepositions are identified either through synonyms or synonymous expressions, i.e. words or word combinations with more or less proximity to the ideas expressed in the original (main) meaning of the preposition. The preposition itself is a kind of a 'nuclear meaning' in this situation, and the words explaining or interpreting it, are at different semantic distances away from it.

The hierarchy of meanings or subcategories to a category for each particular preposition is based in most cases on the principle 'from a more concrete, specific meaning to a more abstract and/or figurative one.' That can be seen in the following examples:

The ball flies **across** the field. (a concrete meaning)
She came **across** some valuable old books. (an abstract meaning)

He did all the work **on** his own. (a concrete/abstract meaning)
She was **on** her own since then. (an abstract meaning)

The meaning of a preposition (concrete or abstract) is determined, among other things, by the presence of the determiners before a notional word such as an article, a pronoun, or a numeral. In the majority of cases, I have presented the most frequently used meaning first, though sometimes the criteria mentioned above were conflicting. One or more subsequent meanings may be derived from the previous or following meanings. This is because they might be very close in their semantics and hard to distinguish. That is why I tried to present them in a logical order. For instance, the category *'a job place'* precedes the category *'a teaching job'* in the subheadings for one of the meanings of the preposition *at*.

In the section on the examples, the capitalized word, e.g. '*FOR*', is followed by the word '*indicates*', by a *number* for each semantic category (1, 2, 3…) and by the examples. So the heading '*FOR indicates*' includes the meaning of the preposition '*FOR*' itself and that of the words on the left and/or on the right of it. For instance, the category '*time*' (a point, a period/duration, or an event) is assigned not only to the preposition '*FOR*' or any other preposition itself, but to the notional leading word like the words '*last*', '*festival*', '*to live*' and the like that contain this category (implicitly):

> **During** *the festival* we made recordings.
> The talks *lasted* **for** two days,
> They will *live* here **for** a year.

Below is an example of the entry for one of the meanings of the preposition *above*:

4. *AN AMOUNT GREATER, HIGHER THAN/MORE THAN/EXCESS*

Your baggage was **above** the weight limit.

Here number "4." indicates that there are three other entries before this subheading. The line "*AN AMOUNT GREATER, HIGHER THAN/MORE THAN/EXCESS*" is the subheading itself. The sentence: "Your baggage was **above** the weight limit." is an example illustrating the meaning of the category 4. The forward slash (/) in the line with the semantic category in it means "*or*". It shows there is a larger semantic difference in the meanings of the words in that line (subheading) than in the case where the words following each other are separated by a comma (,). In other words, a comma shows that the lexical meanings corresponding to the categories of the prepositions are very close or synonymous. At the end of the list of all the entries for a preposition, I provide synonyms and/or antonyms to the meanings of the preposition in question, if any.

I hope that this book will assist the reader in using the language with more precision, color and vitality. There is no doubt that this book is only one of the efforts on the part of the linguists in the continuous process of studying the semantics of form words. Additional research is necessary to make sure the readers get a more and more objective picture and an update on the usage of prepositions in Modern English.

ABOARD/ON BOARD indicate:

1. BEING ON A VEHICLE, LOADED, SHIPPED/IN TRANSIT

    We met each other **aboard** the ship.
    They married **aboard** a cruise ship in Hawaii.
    I will be sick **aboard** this vehicle.

2. PLACING, MOVING IN, INTO

    I am loading equipment **on board** the truck now.
    Don't put too much **on board** the truck today.

    Synonyms: *0*
    Antonyms: *0*

ABOUT indicates:

1. BEING AT SOME PLACE AROUND, IN THE VICINITY/NOT FAR, NEAR

    Kids were **about** the house at that time.
    The idlers're hanging **about** the door of the house.
    All sorts of toys were **about** this place.
    I left my book somewhere **about** the house.
    I am curious about goings on **about** the city.

2. BEING ACTIVE/BUSY AT SOME PLACE/EMPLOYING

    I was busy **about** my work.
    He was a man of all work **about** the Office.
    Bustle (hurry up) **about** it!

3. BEING ON ALL SIDES, ALL AROUND

    We were sitting **about** the fire.
    The twilight was closing **about** me.
    If you look **about** you, you'll see everything you want.
    I found a beautiful garden all **about** me.
    Notes were scattered **about** the room.

4. MOVING IN NO PARTICULAR DIRECTION/HERE AND THERE

He walked restlessly about the room.
She wandered about the park.
People wandered about the streets.
I moved about Paris by myself today.
He tossed the toys about the floor.
My baby crawls about the house.
Why are you tearing about the streets
in this improper manner?
Alex wandered about town for an hour.

5. MOVING AROUND

The earth moves about the sun in 365.26 days.
I'll put my arm about your neck.

6. BEING CLOSE, NEAR IN TIME/APPROXIMATE TIME

It was about noon. About time!
He will be along about four.
About how old were you when you came here?
About May people receive graduation invitations.

7. A REFERENCE, SUBJECT/CONCERNING

It's about money and your attitude.
What are their services all about?
The crisis is not only about the system.
Was he about the new project?
Chess is about struggle, about not giving up.
I should see somebody about a job.
Make no mistake about it.

8. THINKING, CONSIDERING/A DOUBT

I began brooding about healthy food.
I could guess about her to a degree.
We commiserated about love.

He <u>deliberated</u> **about** <u>the public good</u>.
He <u>was</u> very <u>preoccupied</u> **about** the trip.

9.   AN UNDERSTANDING/POSSESSING INFORMATION

She <u>had misconceptions</u> **about** <u>my country</u>.
It might be one of <u>the wrong concepts</u> **about** <u>the system</u>.
He <u>is</u> highly <u>knowledgeable</u> **about** <u>money matters</u>.
People <u>are often misled</u> **about** <u>this</u>.
I don't <u>know</u> **about** <u>heaven</u>, but I lived
through something already.

10.   SEARCHING/DETECTING

<u>Find out</u> **about** <u>the schedule.</u>
How do <u>we go</u> **about** <u>getting data on salaries</u> elsewhere?
<u>Join us to learn</u> **about** <u>pain management.</u>

11.   AN ORAL SPEECH/A SHORT CONVERSATION

Everyone <u>spoke</u> **about** <u>it</u> in whispers.
<u>Anything you want to talk</u> **about,** Jack?
Mental expert <u>testifies</u> **about** <u>the criminal</u>.
We <u>joke</u> **about** <u>it</u> down at work.
He was <u>mumbling something</u> **about** <u>guilt</u>.

12.   A WRITTEN SPEECH

<u>A</u> new <u>book</u> **about** <u>kids' behav</u>ior is on sale.
The article <u>carried information</u> **about** <u>the fire</u>.
Read <u>those statements</u> **about** <u>the role of women in society</u>.
Two <u>paragraphs</u> **about** <u>it</u> don't quite get to my point.
<u>The news broke</u> **about** <u>the people</u> being cloned.

13.   COUNSELING, CONSULTING

Dad <u>taught me a lot</u> **about** <u>life</u>.
I can <u>advise you</u> **about** <u>what you need to do</u>.
You'd better <u>see a doctor</u> **about** <u>that cough</u>.
Try to <u>be more exact about</u> **the timing**.

14. INQUIRING, QUESTIONING, CHECKING

She is very curious **about** it all.
Examiners will continue to quiz applicants **about** it.
I asked him what was so great **about** that place.

15. A CONNECTION/APPLICABILITY TO AN INDIVIDUAL

If you could change one thing **about** yourself,
what would it be?
He can never use this title **about** himself.

16. AN ASSUMPTION, VIEW, CONVICTION

We have strong opinions **about** TV.
They differed **about** the origins of species.
Keep your wits **about** you.
I may be wrong **about** that.
It's time to get serious **about** your memory.
A good rule of thumb **about** humor is
that if you have to explain it, it flopped.

17. AN EVALUATION, COMPARISON

It was **about** the same situation.
What is important **about** your experience?
Reflect on everything that was positive **about** the last year.

18. AN APPROXIMATE SIZE, POSITION

The rosebush is **about** my height.
It's **about** a mile from here.
The tree was **about** the same hight as the house.

19. BEING IN THE ACT, PROCESS

We went **about** our business.
While you're **about** it, please clean the room.

20. A CAUTION, ALERTNESS

My mom always <u>warned me **about guys**</u> like him.
<u>Warn her **about** not getting involved</u> with strangers.

21. A POSITIVE PERCEPTION

<u>Are you very pleased **about** it?</u>
She <u>was happy **about** that stuff</u>.
He was <u>excited **about** the game</u>.
We <u>were excited **about** our success</u>.
I always <u>get emotional **about** that old tree</u>.

22. AFFECTION

<u>There is something I love **about** him.</u>
<u>Work out your feelings **about** love
and commitment.</u>

23. A CAUSE, SOURCE OF AN EMOTION/CONDITION

<u>She was all I cared **about**</u> in life.
<u>That's what I love **about** the South.</u>
What do you <u>like **about** this person?</u>
<u>Sorry **about** that!</u>

24. A NEGATIVE EMOTION

<u>I started feeling bad **about** it.</u>
Lately I've been <u>feeling discouraged **about** my job.</u>
What do I <u>hate **about** this award?</u>

25. A NEGATIVE EMOTIONAL STATE/DISTRESS/NERVOUSNESS

We <u>are so worried **about** her</u>.
She and her Dad must <u>be upset **about** it</u>.
I'm <u>concerned **about** their inexperience</u>.
I should <u>be uneasy **about** you</u>.
She <u>felt no anxiety **about** us</u>.

26. AN APPREHENSION/A STATE OF ALARM, PANIC

There's nothing to fear **about** aging.
We fret **about** bad cholesterol.
He had moments of despair **about** their future.

27. BEING IN A STATE OF UNCERTAINTY, UNDECIDED

I was hesitant **about** giving up single life.
Some parents are insecure **about** their authority.
I am not sure **about** the statute of limitations.

28. AN ATTITUDE

He is very careful **about** money.
Some are a lot more casual **about** it.
There's no way to kid myself **about** that car.
That's what I think **about** emigration.

29. A POSITIVE ATTITUDE

He enthuses **about** milk and cheese.
He urges them to be candid **about** her.
I've never felt this way **about** anyone.

30. A NEGATIVE ATTITUDE

They were tight-lipped **about** the case.
She was so ready to take offence **about** nothing.

31. A WAY PEOPLE BEHAVE

Do something **about** it right now!
What did they do **about** these people?
We commiserated **about** the rocks and
shoals of romance.
These women hang **about** the baby.

32. A NEGATIVE BEHAVIOR

I confronted her **about** this.
Just don't be a brat **about** it!
What are they quarreling **about**?
It unfits you to argue **about** business.
I complain **about** the noise coming in the night.
They lied **about** the date of their marriage.
What do you have to cry **about**?
He fidgets **about** the garden.
Kids often brag **about** things they
are feeling nervous about.

33. AN INTENTION, PLAN

I was **about** to observe wildlife here.
We were just **about** to strart.

34. A POSSESSION/BELONGINGS

She had a lot of jewelry **about** her.
Have you got your watch/any money **about** you?
She lost nearly all she had **about** her.

35. AN INNATE, PERMANENT FEATURE

There is no arrogance **about** him.
What was there remarkable **about** their children?
We are just plain people with no nonsense **about** us.
There was a gentleness and simplicity **about** her.
There is something pathetic **about** my grandad.
You feel a certain well-to-do air **about** the man.
He had a smack of sea **about** him.

36. A TEMPORARY STATE

We are wary **about** profits.
There is too much odour **about** cheese.

She <u>was agog</u> **about** <u>her husband.</u>

Synonyms: *around, close to, concerning, near, of*
Antonyms: *0*

ABOVE indicates:

1. BEING AT A HIGHER LEVEL/A LOCATION, POSITION HIGHER THAN

   Trees frequently <u>grow **above** a wall</u>.
   <u>The whistle blared **above** their heads.</u>
   <u>His head and shoulders were **above** the rest.</u>
   <u>The village is **above** the sea level</u>, it's safe.

2. BEING VERTICALLY UP FROM THE SURFACE BELOW

   The dark clouds <u>were **above** all fields</u>.
   <u>The moon was **above** the top of the mountain.</u>
   I <u>looked at the starry sky **above** me</u>.
   I feel <u>sword of Damocles **above** my head</u>.
   <u>I need that light **above** my head.</u>
   He was <u>hiding in the penthouse **above** her office.</u>

3. BEING HIGHER THAN THE NORM

   Today's <u>temperatures will be **above** zero</u>.
   <u>The air pressure was **above** normal.</u>

4. BEING SUPERIOR IN RANK, CLASS, ORDER

   <u>Is the rank of Major General **above**</u>
   <u>the rank of General?</u>
   He believes he <u>is **above** the law.</u>

5. MOVING TO A POSITION HIGHER THAN/OVER SOMETHING

   The plane was <u>flying **above** the clouds</u>.
   Several kites are <u>flying **above** the beach</u>.

6. PLACING AN OBJECT TO A POSITION HIGHER THAN/OVER SOME-
    THING

>   Shelves were added **above** the sink.
>   He tried holding my book **above** his head.
>   I raised my arms **above** my head.

7. NOT BEING ABLE TO COMMIT EVIL THINGS

>   He would never lie, he is **above** that.
>   A hero should be far **above** the fray.
>   Our mother is not **above** helping out
>   when we're busy.
>   The policemen should be **above** dishonesty.
>   She has always been **above** petty intrigue.
>   He put principles **above** expediency.
>   Everyone should be **above** falsehood, but
>   particularly those who are set over others.

8. BEING BEYOND A CIRCUMSTANCE/A STATE

>   They are **above** slander, I know that.
>   She didn't kill, she is **above** suspicion.

9. BEING SUPERIOR IN MENTAL CAPACITY

>   Kyrill's intelligence is **above** average.
>   He is head and shoulders **above** the others in math.
>   Sometimes he rises **above** my level,
>   sometimes he falls below it.

10. BEING GREATER, MORE THAN/AN EXCESS, INTENSITY

>   Such subjects are **above** me.
>   Your baggage was **above** the weight limit.
>   A person is a senior citizen if he is 65 and **above**.
>   Over and **above** my salary, I get commission.
>   She asked it, her tone slightly **above** freezing.
>   There's something **above** and beyond us
>   in every wedding.

11. GOING, REACHINNG BEYOND THE LEVEL/BEING ABOVE THE AVERAGE

It was a shot that was heard **above** the music.
Go **above** and beyond ordinary fundraising!
Be strong and rise **above** the circumstances!
We have the ability to float **above** ourselves.

Synonyms: *atop, before, below, over*
Antonyms: *beneath, within*

ACCORDING TO indicates:

1. AN AUTHORITY/SOMETHING AS STATED, SHOWN, INDICATED

According to a friend, she died of a stroke.
According to statistics, it is the most densely
populated country.
According to the map, we have 30 miles to go.

2. ABIDING/AN AGREEMENT, CONFORMITY

The young people acted **according to** the rules.
The list of names is arranged **according to** the alphabet.

3. A PROPORTION

They will charge you **according to** weight.
We will charge you **according to** the water used.

Synonyms: *0*
Antonyms: *0*

ON ACCOUNT OF indicates:

1. A REASON, CAUSE

He had to resign **on account of** his health.
They've raised their prices **on account of**
higher labor costs.

2.   AN ACTIVITY FOR THE SAKE OF

> We didn't get <u>divorced **on account of** the kids</u>.
> He didn't <u>leave home **on account of** his disabled wife.</u>

Synonyms: *as, for, due to*
Antonyms: *0*

ACROSS indicates:

1.   BEING ON THE OTHER SIDE

> He <u>lives **across** the US</u>.
> They <u>live **across** the Bay</u>.
> We <u>lived **across** the river</u>.
> She <u>lives **across** the road from us</u>.
> <u>A criss-cross of channels was cut **across** the site</u>.
> <u>It was far away **across** the meadow</u>.
> The group <u>was right **across** the hills</u>.

2.   BEING EVERYWHERE, ALL OVER

> <u>A search was conducted **across** a wide area</u>.
> <u>The bridge **across** the river</u> was ruined by the quake.
> Do you like <u>the new wallpaper plastered **across** the screen</u>
> of the computer?
> <u>Keep the napkin folded **across** your lap</u>.
> The book highlights <u>the best artists **across**</u>
> <u>a wide range of styles</u>.
> I <u>worked **across** all industries and age groups</u>.

3.   MOVING FROM ONE SIDE TO ANOTHER

> <u>The army sped **across** the country</u>.
> They <u>rolled quietly **across** the border</u> (in the car).
> I <u>walk **across** the village</u> every morning.
> They were <u>marching **across** the field</u>.
> <u>Draw lines **across** the paper first!</u>

4.   MOVING BACK AND FORTH/IN ALL DIRECTIONS

The skaters glided **across** the ice.
The teacher walks **across** the front of the room.
He stomped **across** the kitchen floor with his boots.
You will move the mouse **across** a flat surface.
Use short strokes, moving **across** your teeth.

5.   MOVING FROM ONE SIDE TO THE OTHER SIDE ABOVE THE SURFACE

The plane raced **across** the sky.
Traffic hummed **across** the Bay Bridge.
Cars go **across** the bridge with the same speed.
Learn to glide **across** the street, and then **across** the river.
The book flew **across** the table.
A flaming splinter of wood explodes **across** the room.
We should control capital flight **across** the borders.
He leaned **across** the table.

6.   MOVING THROUGH/REACHING

I cut **across** the lawn.
We always cut **across** the square on our way home.
He pointed **across** the rock-strewn meadow to a shepherd's hut.
The diagnosis has varied **across** time.
There was a stiff breeze blowing **across** the river.
A stiff wind was blowing **across** the small island.
The thought flashed **across** his mind.

7.   FINDING AN OBJECT BY CHANCE

I ran **across** some interesting facts.
Recently I came **across** this quote of the scientist.
She came **across** some valuable old books.

8.   MEETING ACCIDENTALLY

I ran **across** him in the City yesterday.
Eva came **across** her old friend at the store.

9. INCLUDIIING ALL/COMPRISING EVERYONE, ALL OBJECTS

Management <u>increased salaries **across** the board</u>.
It's actually <u>a larger message that I want to get **across**</u>.
This is <u>a problem that reaches **across** all </u>socioeconomic<u> classes</u>.
This <u>research will cover schools **across** the entire nation</u>.

Synonyms: *over, through*
Antonyms: *along*

IN ADDITION TO indicates:

1. A THING, ITEM ADDED

He <u>bought a boat **in addition to** his collection</u> of kayaks.
They <u>built a tower **in addition to** the flat landing</u>.

2. A SUMMATION/BEING ATTACHED

I <u>broke my arm **in addition to** all my troubles</u>.
He <u>lost his ability to move **in addition to** it</u>.

Synonyms: *with*
Antonyms: *without*

AFTER indicates:

1. A TIME DIVISION/SPECIFIC TIME PAST THE HOUR

<u>It's ten minutes **after** two</u>.
It happened <u>a couple of minutes **after** midnight</u>.

2. HAPPENING AT A LATER TIME/BEING SUBSEQUENT IN TIME

<u>Let's go there right **after** class</u>.
<u>**After** a while, she fell asleep</u>.
<u>There was no stopping me **after** that</u>.
<u>**After** the mile, we mounted and spurred</u> again.

3. FOLLOWING CONTINUOUSLY/REPEATING/KEEPING DOING CEASE-
LESSLY

> Day **after** day they waited for him.
> I watched them time **after** time.
> I really cannot spend dollar **after** dollar in repairs.
> He took pictures of everyone, roll **after** roll.

4. BEING NEXT TO/BEHIND A PLACE, ORDER

> Close the door **after** you, please.
> The letter *G* comes **after** the letter *F.*

5. TAKING CARE/LOOKING, SEEING

> Eva was looking **after** my cats in my absence.
> Who is looking **after** your Grandmother?

6. BEING LOWER IN ORDER, RANK, IMPORTANCE

> I placed **after** my friend in the aptitude test.
> You placed yourself **after** your friend.

7. A RESULT/CAUSE

> They fired me **after** the big mistake I made.
> **After** the car accident, she got disabled
> and was put on SSI.

8. A SEARCH/LOOKING FOR/AN OBJECTIVE

> Are you going **after** a book?
> I am going **after** the mail.
> Jack is going **after** his medicine at the pharmacy.
> I am **after** a part-time job.
> She doesn't seek **after** fame.

9. A PURSUIT, CHASE/HARRASSING

> They are <u>running **after** the robber</u>.
> My dad really <u>went **after** me</u> that afternoon.
> <u>My mother constantly went **after** her</u>.
> <u>The silent killer can be **after** him.</u>

10. REQUESTING/INQUIRING

> Whenever we meet, <u>she asks **after** you</u>.
> They <u>inquired **after** his son</u> over the telephone.

11. CRAVING, LONGING, DESIRING/ASPIRING

> <u>He is **after** your heart.</u>
> <u>They are only **after** money.</u>
> They <u>are **after** big money</u>, no doubt about it.
> He <u>was **after** power</u>, no doubt about it.

12. AN AVERSE SITUATION/HAPPENING REGARDLESS OF

> They<u> are still friends **after** all their differences.</u>
> <u>**After** all the work we did</u>, the management
> still turned it down.

13. IMITATING, COPYING/MODELING IN THE STYLE OF

> <u>The painting seems to be done **after** Picasso.</u>
> <u>Satirical stories **after** A. Buchwald were kind of passive.</u>
> <u>I didn't take **after** my mother.</u>

14. A COMMEMORATION, HONOR/CALLING, NAMING IN HONOR

> They <u>named their daughter **after** the poet</u>.
> I am <u>named **after** the spice</u> of nourishment.
> Three out of five <u>babies are named **after** relatives</u>.
> <u>*Onto* is formed **after** the analogy of *into.*</u>
> <u>The province is called Normandy, **after** the Normans.</u>

15. A CORRELATION/ATTITUDE

> She is a singer **after** my own heart.
> He is a pastry cook **after** my own heart.

> Synonyms: *behind, in back of*
> Antonyms: *before*

AGAINST indicates:

1. BEING VERY CLOSE/A PHYSICAL CONTACT/TOUCHING

> His elbow rested **against** one of the counters.
> **Against** the walls stood various boxes.
> A book was propped up **against** a bowl of apples.
> My bicycle was propped **against** the tree.
> The tent abuts **against** a blank wall.

2. BEING OUTLINED, PROJECTED, DISTINCT

> **Against** the sky was the mountain, dimly visible.
> A tiny light **against** the line of mountains was our station.
> The painting looks nice **against** the white wall.

3. A BACKGROUND

> The little sail stood out **against** the pink sky.
> The red roof was bright **against** the rainless blue.
> I liked dark colors **against** her fair skin.

4. PLACING AN OBJECT TOWARDS ANOTHER OBJECT VERY CLOSELY

> Move the bookcase up **against** the door!
> I placed the small table up **against** the wall.

5. PRESSING FORCIBLY TO ACHIEVE A CONTACT

> I pressed my hat **against** my breast.
> The cat rubs her head **against** my hand.

6. CLASHING FORCIBLY AT THE PHYSICAL CONTACT

    The boat had run **against** a rock.
    The rain was beating **against** the window.
    Winds came up and pushed the ice **against** the levee.
    In places the water dashed **against** their knees.
    I pushed the chair back hard **against** the table.

7. ACHIEVING A BALANCE/REPOSING, RELAXING

    I reclined **against** the wall.
    She leaned her hand **against** my shoulder.
    The book was resting **against** her breast.
    Sit down, huddle **against** the rocks, relax.
    Exhausted, he leans **against** the tree.

8. MOVING IN THE OPPOSITE DIRECTION

    He thought he would be safe going **against** the traffic.
    She crossed **against** a red light into a path of the streetcar.
    It's not easy to row **against** the current here.

9. A COMPARISON/CONTRAST

    We stack our parents' lives **against** our own.
    She must be weighing my skin tone **against** hers.
    Our success **against** them depended on information.
    We should not measure ourselves **against**
    some ridiculous ideal.

10. A NEGATIVE ATTITUDE/BEING CONTRARY, ADVERSE, PROHIBITED

    Public hugging is **against** the law here.
    Laws **against** domestic violence should focus
    on the abuser.
    Authorities push **against** using hormone pills.
    It's a slam **against** their deceased parent.
    The allegations **against** him were made in May.
    They advise **against** censorship.

11. AN OPPOSITION/RESISTANCE

We <u>are **against** higher taxes</u>.
Couldn't we <u>take action **against** them</u>?
He could never <u>argue **against** her</u>.
Those girls <u>believed **against** belief</u>.
Use all your will power <u>to fight **against** the habit</u>.

12. A CLASH OF INTERESTS

<u>There was another witness **against** him</u>.
He was compelled <u>to stay **against** his will</u>.
<u>It is dangerous to go **against** the majority</u>.
Luck appeared <u>to be **against** him</u>.

13. A REBELLION/ATTACK, BATTLE

<u>Struggle **against** fate is tough.</u>
They <u>raise a mutiny **against** the president</u>.
<u>Crimes **against** people</u> accounted for 28%
of incidents.
This is <u>an outrage **against** any civilian law</u>.
<u>His reason revolted **against** it.</u>

14. ANTICIPATING A PROBLEM

They <u>bought insurance **against** floods.</u>
The doctor <u>vaccinated the baby **against** colds</u>.
Seniors will <u>get shots **against** the flu</u> on Friday.
<u>Store grain **against** the possibility of a bad harvest.</u>
<u>They had no provision **against** rain.</u>

15. A PROTECTION, SHELTER/SAFEGUARD, DEFENSE

<u>Protect the weak **against** the strong.</u>
The public <u>are cautioned **against** pickpockets</u>.
<u>I secured myself **against** all intrusion.</u>

16. A COMMERCIAL TRANSACTION/PAYMENT RECEIVED IN EXCHANGE

> Enclosed is a check for $ 55 against my bill.
> He drew a check against his bank balance.
> We can raise cash against our accounts receivable.
> Write a check against this account.
> The carload of canned meat against order *N* 2 has arrived.

> Synonyms: *regardless of, toward*
> Antonyms: *for*

AHEAD OF indicates:

1. DOING SOMETHING IN ADVANCE, EARLIER THAN

> We arrived ahead of the others.
> They tried to get the tickets ahead of us.
> You have to go ahead of us.

2. A SUPERIOR, ADVANCED POSITION

> We are well ahead of you in that field.
> Who is ahead of us in teaching methods?

> Synonyms: *before, prior to*
> Antonyms: *behind*

ALONG indicates:

1. A POSITION, LOCATION/BEING CLOSE

> Motels are usually found along major roads.
> The trees along the 6th Avenue were planted in May.
> The remains of more than 80 pyramids have been
> found along the Nile.
> Along the walls there's an unusual hedge.
> Now you can see birch trees along the avenue.

2.   MOVING CLOSE, BY THE SIDE/BEING PARALLEL TO

> I walked **along** the road.
> We often walked **along** that sidewalk.
> They walked **along** the path hand in hand.
> The dog ran back and forth **along** the creek bank.
> We have rowed **along** the shore for two hours.
> The plane had flown out for a trip **along** the coast.
> To open the letter, tear **along** the perforation.

3.   A CORRELATION, CONFORMITY, ACCORDANCE

> The group split **along** party lines over this issue.

4.   BEING TOGETHER

> We, **along** with the staff of the Park, helped
> solve the problem.
> My wife and I, **along** with her siblings, were
> invited to a dinner party.
> The information **along** with the questions it raises,
> is useful to school administrators.

> Synonyms: *at, by, near*
> Antonyms: *0*

ALONGSIDE indicates:

1.   BEING BY THE SIDE, NEAR/ON ONE SIDE

> The ship lay **alongside** the pier only at night.
> Huge posters were seen **alongside** the picket line.

2.   MOVING BY THE SIDE

> See the lights put **alongside** the road?
> Many palm trees were planted **alongside** our street.

> Synonyms: *at, close by*
> Antonyms: *0*

AMID (ST) indicates:

1. BEING PART/IN THE MIDDLE OF A SITUATION

    She got lost **amidst** all the confusion at the airport.
    The dogs were <u>walking **amidst** the debris</u> of
    the ruined buildings.

2. AN UNFAVOURABLE ENVIRONMENT/CIRCUMSTANCE

    A beast is <u>rising **amidst** many people</u> and multitudes.
    <u>Tensions are felt **amid** preparations for convention.</u>
    <u>The conference opened **amid** restrained optimism.</u>
    <u>There were warnings **amid** the optimism </u>at the meeting<u>.</u>

    Synonyms: *amongst, between*
    Antonyms: *0*

AMONG (ST) indicates:

1. BEING IN THE MIDDLE/SURROUNDED BY

    <u>What does a little girl feel **among** adults?</u>
    He <u>was the most talented **among** his peers</u>.
    We do outreach work **among** the local people.
    There's <u>a lemon tree **among** birches</u> in the backyard.
    <u>An emergency worker stood **among** flames and</u>
    <u>the debris</u> of the jet.

2. BELONGING TO A GROUP OF MORE THAN TWO/BEING INCLUDED

    You <u>are **among** the fortunate.</u>
    <u>There is much disagreement **among** economists.</u>
    <u>This dish is popular **among** the Latino people.</u>
    <u>He never was **among** the wealthy.</u>

3. BEING ASSOCIATED, CONNECTED

    <u>**Among** their strengths is an obsessive curiosity.</u>
    <u>He drifts **among** the broken threads of memory.</u>

4.   DISPERSING/SHARING

Distribute all items of this clothing **among** yourselves.
Divide the books **among** the members of your family.

5.   A CHOICE/DIVISION

Decide on five courses **among** all those the school offers.
Among chores, grocery shopping is the worst.

6.   A MUTUAL EFFORT, JOINT ACTION

Kids often fight **amongst** themselves.
We sometimes quarrel **among** ourselves.
They reached an agreement **among** themselves.
Traveling **among** a group of tourists,
he watched her closely.

Synonyms: *amid(st), between*
Antonyms: *0*

APART FROM indicates:

AN EXCLUSION/EXCEPTION

The paper was good **apart from** a few spelling mistakes.
Apart from a few scratches, the car was undamaged.

AROUND indicates:

1.   MOVING, ROTATING IN A CIRCULAR DIRECTION/MAKING A CIRCLE

How many planets rotate **around** the Sun?
The Earth moves **around** its axis in 24 hours.
He stepped **around** the car into the street to inspect it.
Two horses moved slowly **around** the circus arena.

2.   SURROUNDING, ENCIRCLING

See the trees **around** the field?
Around each word the teacher drew a circle.
I don't like that belt **around** your waist.
He tightened the scarf **around** his neck.
She put her arm **around** my neck.

3.   PUTTING, PLACING AN OBJECT IN DIFFERENT DIRECTIONS/RAN-
DOMLY

Pass platters of food to each other **around** the table.
Jeff was tossing the ball **around** the room.

4.   MOVING HERE AND THERE, RANDOMLY, THROUGHOUT/WITHIN

Tourists were ferried **around** town by buses.
Don't walk **around** the city late at night.
Walk **around** the neighborhood you wish to live in.
Browse **around** the site and you'll find an answer.
What do you hang **around** the house in?
Leon showed us **around** his house and garden.

5.   BEING EVERYWHERE, IN ALL AREAS, ALL OVER

We have many new plants **around** the Center.
There are rumors **around** the city about the strike.
People standing **around** the room were talking in soft voices.
Press Freedom Day is established by them **around** the globe.
The conversation buzzed **around** him.
I had things to do **around** the house.

6.   BEING NEAR, IN THE IMMEDIATE VICINITY/ON ANOTHER SIDE

Do not smoke **around** gasoline.
She lives **around** Norfolk.
The Church is just **around** the bend.
The Community Bank is **around** the corner.
The intersection is just **around** the curve.

7.   BEING CLOSE TO SOMEONE/STICKING TOGETHER

      She never wants <u>to be **around** me anymore.</u>
      <u>He was the only male I was raised **around.**</u>

8.   A STATE

      They <u>felt nervous **around** him.</u>
      What should I do <u>to be more comfortable **around** her</u>?
      He <u>was</u> very <u>cautious **around** those people.</u>

9.   AN APPROXIMATE TIME

      I <u>woke up **around** seven.</u>
      <u>Check out at **around** noon.</u>
      Do you usually <u>snack</u> heavily **around** <u>bedtime</u>?
      <u>Family gatherings **around** the holidays</u> are large and noisy.
      The development of <u>cerebral dominance is</u>
      firmly<u> established **around** puberty.</u>

10.   BEING, BECOMING A CENTER/BASIS

      <u>Organize thoughts **around** separate ideas.</u>
      The society was <u>built **around** the belief in democracy.</u>
      We need <u>to plan **around** this.</u>

11.   AVOIDING, BYPASSING, OVERCOMING

      Try <u>to find a way **around** an obstacle.</u>
      The kid <u>got **around** the difficulty</u> somehow.
      How <u>to get **around** these difficulties</u>?

                Synonyms: *about, near, near by*
                    Antonyms: *far from*

AS indicates:

1. A ROLE/CAPACITY/FUNCTION

    He always <u>enjoyed acting</u> **as** <u>a mediator</u>.
    She <u>worked</u> **as** <u>a substitute teacher</u> there.
    <u>I dressed</u> **as** <u>Santa Claus.</u>

2. BEING THE SAME, SIMILAR

    On this issue, <u>they thought</u> **as** <u>one</u>.
    She <u>was light</u> **as** <u>a feather</u>.
    <u>I couldn't recognize him</u> **as** <u>John.</u>

    Synonyms: *like*
    Antonyms: *unlike*

AS FOR/TO indicates:

1. REFERENCE/WITH REGARD TO

    We are <u>puzzled</u> **as to** <u>how</u> it happened.
    As for <u>re-evaluation of your papers</u>, it'll take a week.
    As for <u>me</u>, I don't trust you

2. CORRELATION, ACCORDANCE TO/IN THE ROLE OF

    Those <u>chosen</u> **as to** <u>ability to do math</u> are invited to the test.
    As to <u>their readiness to help</u>, we'll let you know.
    As to <u>what we found out</u>, it's not relevant.

    Synonyms: *regarding, about*
    Antonyms: *0*

ASIDE FROM indicates:

1.   AN EXCEPTION

> **Aside from** <u>a mild fever</u>, the patient feels fine.
> **Aside from** <u>her being small</u>, she is strong.

2.   AN EXCLUSION

> **Aside from** <u>John,</u> everybody was present.
> He can eat everything **aside from** <u>meat</u>.

> Synonyms: *over and above, as well as, beyond, besides*
> Antonyms: *0*

AS OF indicates:

THE STARTING POINT IN TIME

> The regulations <u>are valid **as of**</u> September 1st.
> **As of** <u>the middle of April last year</u>, a new law was in effect.

> Synonyms: *with, since*
> Antonyms: *0*

AT indicates:

1.   AN ASTRONOMICAL, GEOGRAPHICAL COORDINATE, DIRECTION

> **At** <u>the zenith of the sky we saw</u> pink clouds.
> The sail gradually <u>**disappeared at** the horizon</u>.

2.   BEING SOMEWHERE IN THE NATURAL ENVIRONMENT

> Fishing boats <u>are **at** sea</u> for ten days.
> Did you <u>have fun **at** the beach</u> today?
> Jack snorkeled **at** <u>Ocean Beach</u>.
> The boy drowned while swimming **at** <u>a beach in Kauai.</u>

It's not dangerous <u>to fly</u> <u>at high altitudes</u>.
I had a chance <u>to stand</u> <u>at the top of the mountain</u>.

3.   BEING NOT CLOSE/FAR AWAY

My home <u>is</u> <u>at a considerable distance</u> from here.
Our uncle always <u>keeps us</u> <u>at arm's length</u>.

4.   A RELATIVE POSITION ON A SCALE/EQUIVALENCE

Try <u>to change laws</u> <u>at the local, state, or federal level</u>.
The question of <u>jobs</u> <u>at livable wages</u> was seen as key.

5.   A NAME OF A LARGE CITY AS THE FOCUS OF ACTIVITIES THERE

He participated in <u>the swimming event</u> <u>at Athens</u> (the Olympics).
Who will <u>rule</u> <u>at Rome and</u> <u>at Byzantium</u>?

6.   A NAME OF LARGE CITY WHEN AN AIRPORT, STATION THERE IS OF
INTEREST

I <u>got off the plane</u> <u>at Madrid</u> (at the airport in Madrid).
They had <u>to get out</u> <u>at Moscow</u> (at a r/w station in Moscow).

7.   A NAME OF ANY CITY WHEN A UNIVERSITY THERE IS OF INTEREST

I'm <u>a faculty member</u> <u>at the University of California</u> <u>at Berkeley</u>.
He <u>is</u> <u>at the University of California</u> <u>at Los Angeles</u>.

8.   A NAME OF A SMALL/MIDDLE-SIZED SETTLEMENT

She mentioned <u>stopping</u> <u>at Petalluma</u>.
We enjoyed a few hours <u>on the beach</u> <u>at Coney Island</u>.

9.   A LOCATION, PLACE WITHIN A SETTLEMENT

Macy's <u>stores are</u> <u>at Union Square</u>.
There's <u>a cafe</u> <u>at United Nations Plaza</u>.

10. A PART OF A STREET

Shall we turn at that corner?
The bus driver parked his bus at a street corner.
The truck stopped at the first intersection.
We'd picnic at the side of the road.
I saw his car in its parking space at the curb.

11. A HOUSE NUMBER IN AN ADDRESS

Come to the office at 21 Gough Street.
We lived at 1223 44th Ave in San Francisco.

12. A STOP FOR MEANS OF TRANSPORTATION/DEPOT

Exit the train at Glen Park station.
The train called at all small stations.
They alighted at the terminal.

13. BEING IN A MAGNIFICENT/IDEAL PLACE

I worship only at the altar of science.
We have your best interests at heart.
To be at a place like that is a real treat.

14. BEING CLOSE TO A VERTICAL SURFACE/ANOTHER OBJECT

A lemon tree was at the back of the house.
Our trash is picked up weekly at the rear of our home.
If the manager is not available at a building, talk to tenants.
Don't stand at that window, they can see you.
Who has left the package at the door?
She listened at the key-hole.

15. BEING AT A PRECISE LOCATION, PLACE/POSITION/POINT

I often sleep over at a friend's.
We provide services at two residences.
We were invited to have dinner at his home.
That ceremony at my house lasted an hour.

We <u>met</u> <u>at Smith estate</u> three years ago.
I <u>saw some spots</u> <u>at the center of the page</u>.
<u>At the top of the stairs</u> he paused.

16. A STOPPING PLACE/ROAD HOUSE/LODGE

We <u>stayed</u> <u>at a motel</u> in New York.
He <u>checked in</u> <u>at Astoria Hotel</u>.

17. BEING CLOSE TO A DEVICE/USING A TOOL

I <u>was</u> <u>at the wheel</u> for eight hours running.
I saw it while <u>standing in line</u> <u>at the register</u>.
<u>Be</u> <u>at your computer</u> and have the manual available.
He spoke to me <u>standing</u> <u>at the blackboard</u>.
<u>The ball went right for the man</u> <u>at bat</u>.

18. BEING CLOSE TO, USING A PIECE OF FURNITURE

They can <u>sit with us</u> <u>at the table</u>.
Dad was <u>asleep</u> <u>at his desk</u>.
<u>At the piano</u> there was a tiny girl sitting.

19. A PLACE FOR A SOCIAL EVENT/ACTIVITY

We <u>were</u> <u>at the supermarket</u>.
<u>The ceremony will be performed</u> <u>at City Hall</u>.
The bimonthly <u>meeting was held</u> <u>at the Church</u>.
A computer <u>lab is located</u> <u>at the Community Center</u>.
<u>Signs</u> <u>at airports</u> are very helpful to drivers.
<u>A ten-year old</u> <u>at summer camp did it</u>.
<u>Turn left</u> <u>at the gas station</u>.

20. A WORKPLACE

<u>The doctor's</u> <u>at the hospital</u> now.
I can't call you <u>when I am</u> <u>at work</u>.
She is not sure <u>he is still</u> <u>at work</u> now.
This is the only time <u>I'm not</u> <u>at the office</u>.
Her <u>work</u> <u>at the factory</u> was a part-time job.

He works at the lab, she works at the conservatory.
Research was conducted at the aquarium.
We'll volunteer at a soup kitchen.
Stayed at his post that day, he did.
There is a massive book dumping at the public library.
You'll meet the author at the Children's Book Division.
Sign up at the Courtesy Counter first.

21. AN EDUCATIONAL INSTITUTION AS A WORKPLACE

He teaches at a prep school.
I will volunteer at the school.
He is a visiting scholar at UC Berkeley.
He teaches at Portland State University.
He works at the Children's Center.
She taught at various workshops.

22. STUDYING, BEING WITH A SCHOOL AS A STUDENT

We do learn some skills at school.
Now this is becoming a problem at day care.
He majored in computer science at Wesleyan University.
These students are guaranteed a place at a UC campus.
At the Institute he studied child psychology.
He never was late at school.
I was never good at school.
Pick him up at school.

23. AN ENTERTAINMENT, RECREATION CENTER/BEING A SPECTATOR, AUDIENCE

I saw it at the Galaxy Cinema.
They eat a lot of popcorn at the movies.
The movie raked in millions at the box-office.
Forget about buying candy at the movies these days.
He is invited to star at La Scala.
We play an hour of tennis at an indoor court.

24. A PLACE FOR TRADING, SELLIING, PURCHASING

> He <u>sold it **at** auction</u>.
> You can <u>buy scones **at** the baker's</u>.
> Is there <u>anything you want **at** the store</u>?
> What can one <u>buy **at** that Farmers' Market</u>?
> Horses were <u>bought and sold **at** the market or horse fair</u>.
> We <u>picked up our rings **at** a downtown jeweler</u>.
> <u>**At** one boutique</u> I was shown a wedding dress.
> She <u>bought a pair of jeans **at** the yard sale</u>.
> <u>The sellout will be **at** Embassy Suites.</u>
> I <u>see her **at** a beauty shop</u> sometimes.
> I'll <u>meet you **at** Macy's</u>.

25. A PLACE FOR FOOD CONSUMPTION

> Describe <u>experiences you had **at** a restaurant</u>.
> On our vacation last year, we <u>ate lunch **at** TacoBell</u>.
> He complained about <u>inedible food **at** the hospital cafeteria</u>.
> As he <u>orders **at** the snack bar</u>, we are chatting at our table.
> You can listen to <u>music played **at** the outdoor cafes</u>.

26. STAYING AT A HEALTH INSTITUTION

> Both my <u>babies arrived safely **at** the hospital</u>.
> <u>Some stay **at** the Center</u>, sobering up overnight.
> He was <u>operated **at** the new hospital</u>.

27. A PART OF THE BODY/BEING ON THE BODY

> <u>The gray **at** my temples</u> can tell you much about my life.
> He used to sit here, <u>legs crossed **at** the ankles</u> or <u>**at** the knees</u>.
> Her <u>suit pulls **at** the armpits</u> when she gives me a hug.

28. AN PRECISE, EXACT AGE

> <u>**At** 6 months many children cry</u> at the sight of a stranger.
> <u>Your child needs shots **at** 6, 12 and 15 months.</u>
> <u>He was 6" tall **at** maturity.</u>
> <u>**At** 56 years of age</u> we retired.

At 80 she still works.
His death came **at the ripe age of 83**.

29. A BEGINNING POINT/A CLOSING POINT, BOUNDARY

At the end of each chapter you'll find assignments.
At the outset of the story the hero is returning home.
The lighthouse stood **at the head of a** small island.
He was **at the head of the business**.
Whose name is **at the bottom of the list**?
They got **at the end of the long line of tourists**.

30. A PART OF THE DAY/A PRECISE MOMENT

Turn on television **at 6 o'clock**.
I'll be done with my project **at midday**.
I have to be at lunch **at noon**.
He is out, he is **at lunch.**
The ceremony took place **at sunset** in their home.
I'll call you **at noon or at night**.
The bill was due **at midnight**.

31. AN ACTIVITY AT A PARTICULAR TIME

He takes a baby aspirin **at bedtime**.
Solicitors usually call **at dinnertime**.
At lunch he told us about it.

32. A TIME AS THE FOCUS OF INTEREST

At times he would talk to himself.
Go to fast food places **at peak hours**.
A rental fee is payable **at class**.
Write to our Mom **at every opportunity.**
If you go there **at off-hours**, you
might run into trouble.

33. AN EVENT, ACTIVITY AS THE FOCUS OF INTEREST

No one raised this question at the meeting.
At appointments you can ask all the questions.
At each visit he'll give you a preview of what to do.
Success at dating is something everyone can learn.
At the lectures he would talk a lot about it.
It's always fun to eat at a baseball game.
See the sign, 'Caution, slow: children at play'?
He stays in the classroom at recess.

34. AN EVENT, SITUATION AT A SPECIFIC TIME

She was pregnant, it turned out at the autopsy.
I hope to see you at my graduation.
They came at the time of the famine.
At the court hearing, no mention was made of that.
They rushed to help, but he was dead at the scene.
At the opening night of the film I saw many friends.
We're going home at Christmas.
The contract expires at year's end.

35. A STATE/CONDITION

I am never at fault.
Those fellows are at fault.
She is completely at home with her new duties.
I am at a great disadvantage, as I've no experience in the field.
I am not at liberty to give you this information.
He was always busy at some scheme.
He died last week, he's at rest now.
You're at risk of catching the flu.
We stood aghast at our danger.

36. THE CAUSE OF A STATE, REACTION

I was shocked at the news.
He was disappointed at my failure.
I was aghast at what had happened.

37. A SITUATION, CIRCUMSTANCE

The whole fleet was at anchor.
We argued about the novel at hand.
Use constructive criticism about the points at issue.

38. AN EXTENT, A HIGH DEGREE IN VALUE/MAXIMUM

She can work as a secretary at best.
The old actor was at his best yesterday.
We can pay you $2,000 at the most.
I visit the place twice a day at the least.
We'll see each other the next day at the latest.
The battle was at its highest.
A marriage without trust is no marriage at all.
The population increase is at an all-time high.
One should be involved in one's daily life
and the world at large.

39. A CRUCIAL POINT/CRITICAL SITUATION

We live at the very edge of our means.
His inexperience left him speechless at crucial moments.
I am at my limit with money, I am rather at sea.
She is at the end of her rope.
Human lives were at stake, but he didn't know that.
When we think we fail at love, we may just be succeeding.

40. MOVING IN THE DIRECTION, TOWARD/APPROACHING

He climbed cautiously at the window.
Some visitors exited at the rear gate that night.
People prostrated at his feet.
He jerked his head at the sea.
Now let me at that food.

41. REACHING THE POINT/LOCATION, TARGET

They arrived at the house at 2 pm.
We arrived at our destination that night.

He <u>showed up later</u> **at** <u>the studio</u>.
I didn't <u>get back</u> **at** <u>my parents'</u>.

42. PLACING AN OBJECT/INDIVIDUAL IN A PARTICULAR PLACE

<u>Put the wand</u> **at** <u>the TV set.</u>
She <u>sat us</u> **at** <u>a table</u> inside her home.

43. AN OBJECT AS THE FOCUS OF AN ACTIVITY

She <u>tugged</u> **at** <u>my arm</u>.
He <u>snatches</u> **at** <u>the jacket</u>.
<u>A drowning man catches</u> **at** <u>a straw.</u>
I <u>tore</u> **at** <u>the seams</u> I had stitched.

44. AN ACTIVITY TOWARDS A LIVING BEING/HANDLING

<u>Anger can eat</u> **at** <u>you.</u>
He also <u>made a pass</u> **at** <u>her.</u>
Radio shows were <u>directed</u> **at** <u>housewives</u>.
She <u>slid a package of popcorn</u> **at** <u>me</u>.
She <u>threw a stone</u> **at** <u>the dog</u>.
The dog <u>rushed</u> **at** <u>the bull</u> in time.
He <u>waved a gun</u> **at** <u>them</u>.
I would <u>like to set your mind</u> **at** <u>rest</u>.

45. AN ACTIVITY TOWARDS AN OBJECT/HANDLING

<u>The man banged</u> **at** <u>the door.</u>
He <u>munched</u> **at** <u>the cheese and crackers</u>.
He should <u>keep</u> **at** <u>it by all means</u>.
<u>You have to work</u> **at** <u>it</u>.

46. AN ATTACK ON A SINGLE OBJECT

They were <u>throwing stones</u> **at** <u>a tin can</u>.
The boat seemed like <u>a horse making</u> **at** <u>a fence</u>.

47. BEING AGGRESSIVE/ATTACKING SOMEONE

He burst out **at** her.
The other guy slashed **at** me.
He struck **at** one of them.

48. AN ATTEMPT AT DOING/TRYING TO ACT

He tried his hand **at** it.
They had a few tries **at** the guy.
He did not make any effort **at** hiding his attention.
I had had another shot **at** it.
I was **at** the pains to protect him.

49. USING AN OPPORTUNITY

His heart leapt **at** the idea.
She jumped **at** the chance to meet him.
I jumped **at** the idea and the offer.
It'll give us a better chance **at** long-term survival.
I don't make aim **at** popularity.

50. PLANNING, HAVING IN MIND/BEING INVOLVED

I intend to go **at** my profession in earnest.
He'd probably been **at** this for years.
How many readers do you have **at** this magazine?

51. AN ABILITIY, SKILL

He was quick **at** learning.
She is very good **at** her job.
The girl is very good **at** music.
Jack has always been good **at** math.
Though he is only 10, he's skilled **at** playing chess.
Is the new method effective **at** finding viruses?
They are terrible **at** planning parties.
He is fairly adept **at** computers.
Leon is handy **at** garden work.

52. BEING AN EXPERT/THE HIGHEST DEGREE OF EXPERTISE

You <u>are a whiz</u> <u>at</u> <u>political strategy</u>.
He is <u>a master</u> <u>at</u> <u>keeping it simple</u>.

53. A FEELING, EMOTION ABOUT SOMEONE/CAUSE OF THE EMOTION

She <u>wonders</u> <u>at</u> <u>him</u>.
I am <u>surprised</u> <u>at you</u>.
She <u>marvelled herself</u> <u>at her own wisdom</u>.
You'll be <u>amazed</u> <u>at what you can do</u>.
We <u>marveled</u> <u>at her poise</u>.

54. A FEELING, EMOTION ABOUT SOMETHING/CAUSE OF THE EMOTION

You used <u>to thrill</u> <u>at that</u>.
I was <u>sorry</u> <u>at their mishap</u>.
Did he <u>rejoice</u> <u>at the victory</u>?
He was <u>puzzled</u> <u>at the technical terms</u>.
He was <u>delighted</u> <u>at being free</u>.

55. A NEGATIVE FEELING ABOUT SOMEONE

I've been <u>furious</u> <u>at my husband</u>, too.
I still <u>feel mad</u> <u>at her for saying yes</u>.
She is <u>impatient</u> <u>at her sister's behavior</u>.
She was <u>bitter</u> <u>at him</u> because he married another woman.
I <u>lost my temper</u> <u>at his persistence</u>.

56. A NEGATIVE FEELING ABOUT SOMETHING

She is <u>often angry</u> <u>at something</u>.
They were <u>annoyed</u> <u>at the commercials</u>.
I was <u>embarrassed</u> <u>at becoming the center of attention</u>.
He <u>relieved his anguish</u> <u>at being isolated</u>.
I was <u>revolted</u> <u>at these changes</u>.
He <u>grew irritable</u> <u>at this silence</u>.
He was <u>vexed</u> <u>at the incident</u>.
They <u>seemed hurt</u> <u>at that</u>.

57. A SOURCE, CAUSE OF A FEELING

Everybody experienced shock at the verdict.
She trembled at the thought of his returning.
He rang the bell shivering at the clang it made.
He groaned at his helplessness.

58. AN ATTITUDE TOWARDS AN OBJECT/HUMAN

Jack is always at my side.
It shouldn't be left at the mercy of the court.
I used to turn up my nose at guided tours.

59. A CONDUCT, BEHAVIOR

He nodded at me, smiling.
He laughs at me for my ignorance.
He snapped his fingers at the baby.
Why are you frowning at me, Jack?
She stuck out her tongue at him.
The neighbors are at it again.
He beamed at me.

60. A CAUSE OF THE CONDUCT

I turned at the sound.
Cats jump at noises.

61. A WAY TO WATCH, OBSERVE OBJECTS/HUMANS

I looked at them distractedly.
He just goggled at me.
Her eyes strained at him.
I glanced at my dad.
He peered at her out of the corner of his eye.
They winked at each other shrewdly.
I stood agape at her.
He squinted at us.
The baby smiled at his mother.
Stop grinning at me!

62. A VERBAL BEHAVIOR

> She <u>shouted at the kids</u>.
> Boy, <u>he sure yelled at you</u>.
> They <u>scream at her</u> for the least thing.
> He would <u>nag at his wife</u> for that.
> She <u>grumbled at his punctuality</u>.
> <u>Questions came at us</u> from all sides.
> I began <u>firing questions at him</u>.
> They <u>started swearing at me</u>.
> He <u>grunted at her</u>.

63. TRYING TO UNDERSTAND/DISCOVER INFORMATION

> See if you <u>get at the facts</u>.
> <u>Get at the bottom of this.</u>
> There is no need <u>to guess at the matter</u>.
> I could only <u>guess at his reaction</u>.

64. A CHOICE/PREFERENCE

> He could <u>change it at will</u>.
> <u>See us at your convenience</u>.
> You <u>have plenty of time at your disposal</u>.
> <u>I am at your service.</u>

65. AN ADVICE

> We <u>applied for the job at your recommendation</u>.
> <u>At his suggestion</u>, I went to the sea that summer.

66. ASKING/CLAIMING

> Can you <u>do it at the client's request</u> now?
> He <u>joined the Army at his father's demand</u>.

67. A WAY, MANNER IN DOING THINGS

> He went off, <u>almost at a run.</u>
> It's not <u>learned at a parent's knee</u>.

I can tell you <u>what she is at a glance</u>.
I'll learn <u>how to beat the casino at its own game.</u>
The point is <u>to make a living at what you love.</u>
He keeps <u>doing work at the leading edge.</u>
<u>Call us at the number</u> shown on your card.
<u>I picked up two magazines at random.</u>
<u>Winning at blackjack</u> is not that easy.
<u>Sample it at no risk</u> whatsoever.

68. ESTIMATING VALUE/CHARGE, PAYMENT

The furniture was <u>sold at cost price</u>.
You can <u>get nice things at a low cost.</u>
The airline <u>has one seat left at the good fare.</u>
Samples are <u>offered at no charge.</u>
You can <u>buy clothes at great savings.</u>
He <u>sold his car at a clear profit.</u>

69. A UNIT OF MEASUREMENT

I <u>bought tomatoes at 30 cents a pound.</u>
I <u>bought eggs at $1.00 a dozen.</u>
<u>At normal level</u> the water is 9 feet deep.

70. A VELOCITY, ACCELARATION

They <u>chased him at a high speed.</u>
Defensive driving means <u>driving at a safe speed.</u>
When they <u>speak at a normal speed</u>, we understand them.

71. A CHANGE IN THE STATE AT A POINT IN TEMPERATURE

<u>Does paper burn at 350°F?</u>
Water <u>boils at 100 degrees Celsius.</u>
<u>Ice melts at zero degrees Celsius.</u>

Synonyms: *on, near, to, about, in, in front of, upon*
Antonyms: *away from, far from, off*

ATOP indicates:

BEING ON/ABOVE AN OBJECT/OVERHEAD/HIGHER

> **Atop** a magic mountain there is a cabin.
> Now he started building homes **atop** the hill.

> Synonyms: *at, above, beyond, on, over*
> Antonyms: *below, down*

IN BACK OF indicates:

1. A POSITION, BEING IN THE REAR, BEHIND

> There was a secret room **in back of** the house.
> There is a garage **in back of** the City Hall.

2. A SUPPORT

> I am **in back of** you all the way in this matter.
> He was **in back of** the drug dealers, unfortunately.

> Synonyms: *after, afterward, behind, following*
> Antonyms: *In front of*

BECAUSE OF indicates:

3. A CAUSE, REASON

> He resigned **because of** ill health.
> The Center was closed **because of** lack of funds.
> I didn't come to any conclusion **because of** lack of evidence.

> Synonyms: *considering, due to, in view of*
> Antonyms: *0*

BEFORE indicates:

1. THE TIME EARLIER THAN, PREVIOUS TO

    He worked there **before the war**.
    I knew it **before** he said it.
    Like his father **before him** he had an eye for a face.
    He wanted to cross the border **before** daybreak.
    He worked **before** dawn.
    We went for a bath **before** breakfast.

2. THE FUTURE PERIOD OF TIME/BEING IN STORE/HAVING TIME

    His whole life lies **before** him.
    He was a man with no future **before** him.
    This I must settle first, **before** anything else.
    He hoped to return **before** another year.
    There are several options **before** you.

3. BEING IN FRONT, IN THE PRESENCE/FACING

    She gets nervous **before** an audience.
    He'll speak two days **before** students at that school.
    He collapsed on stage **before** a packed house last night.
    He felt at a loss **before** such accusations.
    He presented himself **before** us.
    He stared **before** him.

4. BEING AHEAD/HIGHER IN RANK/HIERARCHY

    There are only two people **before** me in my class:
    I got the third highest grade.
    My sister was always **before** me in everything we did.

5. A PREFERENCE, PRIORITY

    We'll always choose work **before** play.
    I always think of my family **before** myself.
    Some doctors put profit **before** patients.
    He loved her **before** himself.

6. BEING/GOING UNDER JURISDICTION

> Jack <u>was summoned</u> **before** <u>the judge.</u>
> They <u>were summoned</u> **before** <u>the court.</u>
> I have <u>to appear</u> **before** <u>the court</u> today.

7. MOVING AHEAD

> <u>A car drove up</u> **before** <u>that house.</u>
> He <u>knelt</u> **before** <u>her</u> for the first time.

Synonyms: *ahead, in front of, prior to*
Antonyms: *after, behind*

IN/ON BEHALF OF indicates:

1. A BENEFICIARY OF AN ACTION

> Her <u>ex-husband didn't speak out</u> **in her behalf.**
> We <u>raised money</u> **on behalf of** the earthquake <u>victims.</u>

2. BEING ON THE PART OF/AGENT

> The guardian <u>signed the contract</u> **on behalf of** <u>the minor child.</u>
> <u>We support that stand</u> **on behalf of** <u>journalists</u> everywhere.

Synonyms: *0*
Antonyms: *0*

BEHIND indicates:

1. BEING IN BACK, IN THE REAR

> <u>We were</u> **behind** <u>you.</u>
> **Behind** <u>each dune were other dunes.</u>
> <u>I shut the door</u> **behind** <u>me.</u>
> He <u>walks with his hands</u> **behind** <u>his back.</u>
> We <u>all talk</u> **behind** <u>people's backs.</u>

2.   BEING BEYOND/ON THE OTHER, FATHER SIDE

The dog is **behind** the door.
They were **behind** prison bars.

3.   BEING IN THE BACKGROUND/MOVING THERE/BEING HIDDEN, CONCEALED

The moon was **behind** the clouds.
He was invisible now **behind** his paper.
You can't see the roof **behind** the trees.
Some reader assumed other motives **behind** our list.
Get **at** the truth **behind** the headlines.
Behind your every word is a lie.
What's **behind** all this?

4.   SUPPORT, HELP/BEING AT THE BACK/FOUNDATION

There was truth **behind** what she was saying.
Who were the men **behind** the war?
The leaders have the army **behind** them.
With Newton and Darwin **behind** us, we'd learned all about
the fundamental workings of the universe.
I stand **behind** my statement and concern.
The guy has a lot of money **behind** him.

5.   BEING INFERIOR, NOT UP TO THE LEVEL, LESS ADVANCED THAN

He was **behind** the other students.
Some countries are **behind** us in technological development.

6.   BEING LATER THAN/BEHIND SCHEDULE

Everybody was **behind** schedule.
Mother was always fidgety when father was **behind** time.
I am always **behind** the times.

7.   THE TIME THAT HAS BEEN PASSED, LEFT/DISTANCING AWAY

> <u>Their worries are</u> **behind** <u>them.</u>
> Her <u>concern about money is</u> **behind** <u>her</u> now.

8.   MOVING TOWARD THE REAR

> Let's <u>hide</u> **behind** <u>that bush.</u>
> Two trucks <u>pulled up right</u> **behind** <u>the car.</u>
> She <u>comes</u> **behind** <u>his chair.</u>

9.   BEING A SOURCE

> <u>The Commission is</u> **behind** <u>most of the projects.</u>
> <u>He is behind all the plots.</u>

10. DEPARTING, ABANDONING/TAKING ONE'S TIME

> <u>He left a pregnant 18-year-old</u> **behind** <u>him.</u>
> He had <u>lagged</u> **behind** <u>them</u> to chatter to a friend.
> He had <u>fallen</u> **behind** <u>the other workers</u> so as not
> to participate in the conspiracy.
> They fell back, <u>leaving their dead</u> **behind** <u>them.</u>

> Synonyms: *after, following, in back of*
> Antonyms: *ahead, in front of*

BELOW indicates:

1.   BEING BENEATH, UNDERNEATH/AT A LESSER ELEVATION, LOWER
POSITION

> They <u>detected another layer of paint</u> **below** <u>that one.</u>
> Fish were <u>seen two feet</u> **below** <u>the surface</u> of the water.
> <u>The country lies</u> **below** <u>sea level.</u>

2.   BEING FATHER ALONG THAN

> Our <u>boat was found two miles</u> **below** <u>the village.</u>
> <u>The barn is a mile</u> **below** <u>the settling.</u>

3.   TEMPERATURE LESS THAN

At night, it was 20 degrees **below** zero.
They stayed away from school when it was 40° **below** zero.
This spring temperatures were **below** the average.

4.   PRICE LESS THAN

I will be moving and sell everything **below** cost.
Here you can purchase some items **below** cost.
They sell jewelry **below** cost.

5.   BEING LOWER IN LEVEL, CLASS, RANK THAN/HIERARCHY

His knowledge of history is **below** average.
Her performance was **below** excellence.
Many rank human beings **below** other animals.

6.   BEING UNWORTHY, UNSUITABLE, UNBEFITTING

They are really **below** our notice.
To talk to you is **below** his dignity.

7.   MOVING UNDERNEATH, BENEATH/TOWARD A LOWER PLACE

The sun slowly sank **below** the horizon.
Logs floated **below** the old wooden bridge.
He hit me **below** the knee.

Synonyms: *beneath, underneath, under*
Antonyms: *above*

***BENEATH* indicates:**

1.   BEING BELOW, UNDER

A coal mine **beneath** this hill is out of operation.
Nobody knew about a lake **beneath** this city.
Asphalt feels good **beneath** my sensibly shod feet.
We stood on the riverbank **beneath** a birch-tree.

2. BEING COVERED

> The earth lay **beneath** the blanket of snow.
> **Beneath** the carpets, the floor was molding.

3. BEING HIDDEN, CONCEILED

> The tears are just **beneath** the surface of the laughter.
> I couldn't see the face **beneath** the mask.

4. MOVING BELOW, UNDER

> They walked **beneath** the moon, hand in hand.
> The girls crouched **beneath** their dripping umbrellas.
> We sink **beneath** the burden of parenthood.
> The apple-trees bend **beneath** the clusters of rich fruit.
> He paced **beneath** the awed gaze of the girls.

5. BEING AT A LOWER LEVEL IN CLASS, PLACE/STATUS/PRICE

> A corporal is **beneath** a sergeant in rank.
> He thinks us **beneath** him.

6. BEING UNDER THE FORCE, CONTROL, INFLUENCE

> Dad was a rigid disciplinarian towards all **beneath** him.
> He was inconsiderate of those who were **beneath** him.

7. BEING UNWORTHY/UNBEFITTING

> He felt it was **beneath** him to ask for a promotion.
> They turn down those jobs because they think the jobs
> are **beneath** them.
> Such petty behavior is **beneath** me.
> It's **beneath** his dignity to lie.
> I think the offer **beneath** contempt.

Synonyms: *below, under*
Antonyms: *above, over*

BESIDE indicates:

1. BEING BY THE SIDE OF, NEXT TO, AT

    I sat **beside you**, remember?
    The site we'd picked was **beside a waterfall**.

2. BEING ADDITIONAL

    Many creatures living **beside** man live in communities.
    He takes some vitamins **beside** medicines.
    You finally committed to something **beside** work?

3. COMPARIING

    Chemistry seemed easy to me **beside** physics.
    This proposal seems to be more reasonable **beside** the other.
    Beside him other students seemed to be less smart.

4. BEING IRRELEVANT/UNRELATED

    That remark was **beside** the point.
    So anything I feel or want or do is **beside** the point.

5. BEING ON THE EQUAL LEVEL, FOOTING

    He earned the place **beside** the best performers in the business.
    She played chess **beside** the champions.
    Your offer seemed quite reasonable **beside** the other two.
    I saw his car double-parked **beside** their car.

6. A STATE, FEELING

    He was **beside** himself when he learned his car was stolen.
    I was **beside** myself with joy on learning the news.

Synonyms: *at, by, near, next to*
Antonyms: *far from*

BESIDES indicates:

1. BEING ADDITIONAL

    Besides physics, you will study two more subjects.
    You don't want to know anything else **besides** sports!

2. BEING OTHER THAN/EXCLUSION, EXCEPTION

    Everybody **besides** him participated in the outreach work.
    Nothing mattered for her **besides** money.

    Synonyms: *apart from, beyond*
    Antonyms: *0*

BETWEEN indicates:

1. A CONNECTION BETWEEN TWO OBJECTS

    We needed a railroad **between** the two cities.
    There are two bridges **between** the city and the country side.
    It's about **between** here and San Francisco.

2. BEING INTERMEDIATE IN SPACE

    Greater London is **between** Essex, Kent, Surrey, Berkshire, Buckingham and Hertfordshire.
    She splits her time **between** homes in California and France.
    There's another way to move **between** programs.

3. SEPARATING OBJECTS

    Avoid sweets **between** meals.
    In packing china, be sure to place paper **between** the plates.
    He was speaking **between** his set teeth.

4. AN INTERVAL IN TIME

    It happened **between** 1 and 2 o'clock.
    Give me a call **between** 4 and 5 o'clock.

5. A SHARED ACTIVITY, COMBINED EFFORT

    We'll get the job done **between** us.
    How much money did they raise **between** them?
    This conversation passed **between** us.
    She gasped **between** the kisses.

6. A COMBINED OWNERSHIP

    They have only a few dollars **between** them.
    He wants Sue, and her family, and even more
    kids **between** them.
    Did they always split the profits **between** them?
    Let's keep this secret **between** ourselves.

7. A CHOICE, OPTION

    It costs **between** 3 and 5 dollars.
    Their upbringing alternated **between** strict
    supervision and utter neglect.
    Choose **between** living here and living abroad.

8. A DISTINCTION/DIFFERENTIATING

    Where is the difference **between** standard language and slang?
    There are distinct differences **between** New York and Dallas.
    Where is the line **between** the wrong and insane mind?
    This is a difference **between** the present and the past generation.

9. A DISAGREEMENT, CONTRADICTION, DISCREPANCY

    They are **between** two fires.
    There's been a controversy **between** the members
    of the committee.

10. AN ANALOGY, COMPARISON/RESEMBLANCE, AFFINITY/CONTRAST

    I accept the fact of the disparity **between** the two approaches.
    There is a resemblance **between** the two stories.

11. MOVING/PLACING/INTERFERING

Slide the floss **between** your teeth.
People always cross the street **between** moving vehicles.

Synonyms: *amid, among, within*
Antonyms: *0*

BEYOND indicates:

1. BEING ON THE FAR SIDE/THE OTHER SIDE/THE FAR DISTANCE

My people live **beyond** sea.
The post office is just **beyond** the barber-shop.
The parking lot is **beyond** the stadium.

2. MOVING FARTHER THAN

You have to go **beyond** the railroad station.
He tossed the ball **beyond** the line.
Though faded and worn **beyond** her years, Mom looked great.
The bus doesn't go **beyond** this junction.
We cannot go **beyond** the written agreement.

3. A TIME LATER THAN, AFTER

The meeting lasted **beyond** midnight.
I don't have any plans **beyond** next week.
He arrived at our house an hour **beyond** the set time.
The sisters are sitting **beyond** their usual hour.

4. AN ADDITION

I don't know what to say **beyond** I'm sorry.
They will provide basic education **beyond** high school.
There is life **beyond** grade school.

5. BEING OUTSIDE THE LIMITS

    The woman he loves is forever **beyond** his reach.
    Jack's father found the boat stranded **beyond** help.
    Unfortunately, your files are **beyond** retrieve.
    It's an evil **beyond** remedy.

6. CROSSING A BOUNDARY/GOING OUTSIDE THE LIMITS

    Travel **beyond** the ordinary!
    Thousands of teachers go **beyond** typical fund-raisers.
    He supported his children **beyond** the age of 18.
    You know how to move **beyond** small talk.
    Move **beyond** rage right now!

7. EXPANDING, PROLONGING

    They extend their powers **beyond** what is needed.
    He became rich **beyond** his wildest dreams.

8. AN EXTREME SITUATION, STATE

    It was **beyond** words.
    She's already **beyond** the call of reason.
    It's **beyond** my ability to solve that problem.
    It's **beyond** our expectations.

9. AN EXCLUSION

    The actress asked for nothing **beyond** peace and quiet.
    He asked nothing **beyond** supporting his new program.
    We saw nothing **beyond** what had been stated.

10. CERTAINTY

    I had the symptoms, **beyond** all mistake.
    It is clear **beyond** quesiton to everyone now.
    Her honesty is **beyond** all questions.

11. BEING SUPERIOR, EXCLUSIVE

He <u>sings beautifully,</u> **beyond** <u>compare.</u>
<u>Her performance was</u> **beyond** <u>any other that I've ever seen.</u>
Her company would <u>be to me</u> <u>a treasure</u> **beyond** <u>price.</u>
<u>You are wise</u> **beyond** <u>your years.</u>

Synonyms: *above, after, outside, over, past*
Antonyms: *inside, next to*

BUT indicates:

AN EXCLUSION

<u>Everyone</u> **but** <u>me had a hard time.</u>
<u>They all are done with the project</u> **but** <u>him.</u>
She <u>packed everything</u> **but** <u>her books.</u>
We <u>found everything</u> **but** <u>the letter.</u>

Synonyms: *without*
Antonyms: *0*

BUT FOR indicates:

A CONDITION

But for <u>her help</u>, I couldn't have passed the exam.
But for <u>the storm</u>, they would never meet each other.

Synonyms: *0*
Antonyms: *0*

BY indicates:

1. BEING NEAR, CLOSE, NEXT TO/CONNECTING OBJECTS

Our farms <u>were down</u> **by** <u>the river.</u>
You'll <u>find the letter</u> **by** <u>my bed.</u>

The mixing bowls <u>are **by** the fridge</u>.
I can <u>see my mother **by** the phone</u> in the kitchen.
The piano has always <u>been **by** the window</u>.
He always <u>sits **by** the door</u>.

2.   MOVING BEYOND, PAST WITHOUT STOPPING

She <u>walked **by** me</u> without even saying hello.
He <u>passed **by** my house</u> without looking up.
The bus <u>went right **by** the corner</u> where I wanted to get off.
We <u>drove **by** New York</u>, but we didn't go into the city itself.
You can <u>fly to Boston **by** way of New York City</u>.
<u>Sneak up **by** the teacher's desk!</u>

3.   PASSING THRHOUGH

He <u>entered **by** one of the windows</u>.
We <u>brushed **by** the guards</u>.
She <u>entered **by** the lower gate</u>.
We <u>came **by** the back road</u>.
Please <u>leave **by** the center doors</u>.

4.   MOVING PAST/DROPPING IN, AT A PLACE

Please, <u>go **by** the grocery store</u> and pick up a carton of milk.
<u>Come **by** our office</u> on Monday.
<u>I stationed myself **by** the table.</u>
<u>Put the wand **by** the TV set.</u>

5.   NOT MOVING ANY MORE

I <u>stopped **by** his place</u> to pick him up.
Please <u>stop **by** the front office</u> to pick up your papers.
Just <u>stopby the kiosk</u> at any large store.

6.   A DIRECTION WITH POINTS OF THE COMPASS

<u>South **by** southeast is the right direction</u>.
He said they were <u>sailing north **by** northeast</u>.

7. MOVING DOWN/OCCUPYING A PLACE

He took his seat **by** the driver.
Nobody sat down **by** her.
They regained their seats **by** the fire.

8. A CONNECTION, LINK

They are siblings **by** blood.
The responsibility entailed **by** me.

9. BEING BORN OF/INTO A FAMILY

I have one son **by** my first marriage.
My ambition is to have a child **by** him.
She had hard times raising her daughter **by** a baseball star.
His wife has a child **by** her second husband.

10. A POINT, PERIOD IN TIME/HAPPENING DURING SOME TIME

Sleeping **by** day made him feel better.
By day we swim, cook, breakfast, explore caves.
He made the last trip **by** night.
By moonlight the ocean must be ravishing.

11. A PROXIMITY IN TIME/HAPPENING NO LATER THAN/DEADLINE

Complete the report **by** the end of the week.
He'll come back home **by** January.
Come here **by** 1:30 p.m.

12. GETTING A COMPENSATION FOR A FIXED PERIOD OF TIME

She works **by** the day.
We get paid **by** the week.

13. A RATE, EXTENT, AMOUNT, DEGREE

Onions and carrots are sold **by** the pound.
They got letters **by** the hundreds.

Reduce your taxes **by** thousands of dollars.
Citizens have been voting **by** the millions.

14. FOLLOWING A PRINCIPLE, HABIT

I will abide **by** what I said.
He seems bound **by** honour rather than **by** love.
At least some people live **by** illusions.

15. AN INSTRUCTION, DIRECTION

We will abide **by** your decision.
Some people do abide **by** this rule.
Customers should abide **by** the closing time of a store.
Even when no one is watching you, try to play **by** the rules.
He is not bound **by** California's criminal laws.

16. A PREFERENCE, SELECTION/DECISION

You begin **by** choosing two books.
I'll stand **by** my reply, though.

17. A CLAIM, REQUIREMENT, WILL

By popular demand, here's my traditional column.
By popular request, he will instruct you again on that subject.
It was quite **by** his wish that I went there.

18. AN ANALYSIS/OPINION

Judging **by** the pictures, you could guess he's ill.
By her own account, everybody was having a great fun.

19. A REASON

What do you mean **by** that?
What did he mean **by** his remark?

20. AN EDUCATIONAL BACKGROUND

My parents <u>are engineers **by profession**</u>.
He <u>was a biologist **by training**</u>.

21. AN AGENT PERFORMING AN ACTION

San Francisco <u>was overrun **by goldminers**</u>.
I am <u>amazed **by people**</u> who write to you about it.
The ruins of the temple were <u>overgrown **by jungle**</u>.
He was <u>washed off the deck **by** a huge wave</u>.
Your <u>paycheck is being eaten up **by taxes**</u>.

22. AN AGENT PERFORMING AN ACTION AS AN ADDITIONAL INFORMATION

We <u>followed the cross-examination **by the judge**</u>.
I meant <u>protection</u> for companies <u>**by intelligence services.**</u>
<u>The decision **by the legal team**</u> was never made.
<u>A ruling **by the Supreme Court**</u> is expected in June.
<u>Massages **by** Terry are popular</u> in the community.
They suggested <u>a visit **by the physicist**</u> to Boston.
I was reading <u>a manuscript **by a friend**</u>.
He feels lonely because of <u>abandonment **by a friend**</u>.
He had always sought <u>the validation **by genius**</u>.

23. A SOURCE OF AN EMOTION, STATE

He had been <u>possessed **by an idea**</u>.
Don't let them <u>be shocked **by my present**</u>.
We all <u>are made stupid **by fear**</u>.
<u>He is a loner **by nature**</u>.

24. A TOOL, NSTRUMENT, DEVICE

The bird was <u>killed **by a bullet**</u>.
Corn is <u>reaped **by reaping machines**</u>.
He <u>shaped his course **by the compass**</u>.
<u>What's the time **by your watch?**</u>

25. A FORCE/SOURCE OF ENERGY

The house was <u>heated by low pressure steam</u>.
Most of the vehicles are <u>driven by fossil fuel.</u>

26. A WAY, METHOD OF PERFORMING AN ACTION

We <u>learn a lot by doing</u>.
Sorry, I <u>did it by mistake</u>.
He <u>found the way out by chance</u>.
Many discoveries are <u>made by accident</u>.
I'll <u>visit the the doctor by appointment</u>.
<u>Learning poems by heart</u> develops memory.
My mother <u>washes linen by hand</u>.
You cannot <u>pay by check</u>, only <u>by money order</u>.
How <u>to earn daily bread by the pen</u>?
They <u>win by having the highest score</u>.
They <u>installed a new order by force</u> of arms.
The car is <u>taken by force or threat</u>.
They <u>addressed me by the name</u>.
He <u>won the election by only a couple of votes.</u>
Enrollment is <u>permitted by consent of the instructor</u>.

27. A SOURCE OF INFORMATION/VERIFYING IDENTITY

I can <u>tell by your face</u> that you are tired.
He had <u>to be identified by his clothes</u>.

28. A SEQUENCE OF OBJECTS, EVENTS

The kids <u>left the room one by one.</u>
They were <u>persuaded little by little</u>.
We'll <u>learn</u> the technique <u>step by step</u>.
You can just <u>go ahead day by day</u>.
I <u>studied the report page by page</u>.

29. MEANS OF COMMUNICATION/MEDIA

We may <u>invite guests by telephone</u>.
I can <u>send a message by fax or by phone</u>.

They usually <u>answer an invitation by mail</u>.

30. MEANS OF CONVEYANCE, VEHICLES

We can <u>go to Europe by air or by water</u>.
They can be <u>reached by a short bus ride.</u>
I will <u>go downtown by the streetcar</u>.
You can <u>go to Berkeley by BART</u>.
The city <u>is an hour south of here by car</u>.

31. BEING ALONE, ACTING WITHOUT HELP

I need <u>to be by myself</u>.
<u>Do it by yourself</u> for a change.
<u>The child can't dress by himself.</u>

32. A MATH OPERATOR (MULTIPLICATION/DIVISION SIGN)

<u>Multiply 4 by 6 to get 24.</u>
<u>Divide 10 apples by 5.</u>

33. SEIZING, GRASPING, CATCHING/HOLDING

I <u>grabbed him by the arm</u> and wouldn't let go.
<u>Seize him by the collar</u>, if you can.
I was <u>leading my son by his hand</u>.
Someone <u>pulled me by the shoulder</u>.

34. A BENEFICIARY/ACTING ON BEHALF OF

<u>The company has done very well by its employees.</u>
<u>They are doing very well by their children.</u>

Synonyms: *about, according to,* in, *close to,*
near, of, past, through, towards with
Antonyms: *Away from*

IN CASE OF indicates:

A CONDITION

> **In case of** emergency, call 911.
> **In case of fire,** they'll be transferred to a residential hotel.

> Synonyms: *0*
> Antonyms: *0*

CLOSE TO indicates:

1.   A NEARNESS, PROXIMITY IN SPACE

> Golden Gate Park **is close to** where we live.
> The radio station **is close to** the border.

2.   A NEARNESS/PROXIMITY IN TIME

> It was **close to** midnight when they at last called us.
> It was **close to** the spring when the fog set in.

> Synonyms: *around, about, near*
> Antonyms: *far from*

CONCERNING indicates:

A REFERENCE/CONNECTION

> Your request **concerning** a new fan is being
> handled by our specialists.
> The question **concerning** the roof repair was raised again.

> Synonyms: *about, regarding*
> Antonyms: *0*

CONSIDERING indicates:

TAKING INTO ACCOUNT

<u>**Considering** her poor condition</u>, we should delay the trip.
<u>**Considering** the new price raise</u>, I can't afford it.

Synonyms: *in view of*
Antonyms: *0*

CONTRARY TO indicates:

BEING DIFFERENT FROM, OPPOSITE TO

<u>**Contrary to** all predictions</u>, he won the race.
<u>**Contrary to** the weather forecast</u>, there were scattered showers.
<u>**Contrary to** popular belief</u>, this insect is harmless.

Synonyms: *in accordance with*
Antonyms: *0*

DESPITE indicates:

AN OPPOSITION, CONTRAST

<u>**Despite** all her troubles</u>, she got her award.
<u>**Despite** two kids,</u> my marriage was on the rocks.
<u>**Despite** good intentions</u>, you just can't stick with it.
The professionals <u>practice all summer **despite** the heat</u>.
<u>**Despite** my unlisted number,</u> someone called.
I love him <u>**despite** all his faults</u>.

Synonyms: *in spite of, notwithstanding*
Antonyms: *0*

DOWN indicates:

1.   BEING AT THE FARTHER END/LOWER LEVEL

> They <u>lived **down** the street</u>.
> They <u>had a big gas spill **down** the road</u>.
> <u>The bathroom was **down** the dark hallway.</u>

2.   MOVING TO A LOWER LEVEL

> The cart <u>rolled **down** the hill</u>.
> I love <u>walking **down** that lane</u>.
> He intentionally <u>fell **down** those stairs</u>.
> <u>Cold chills went **down** my spine.</u>
> <u>The skirt fell **down** her hips.</u>

3.   MOVING ALONG THE COURSE

> <u>Floating **down** the river</u> takes less time to reach the village.
> She <u>escorted her daughter **down** the aisle.</u>
> <u>The coin rolled **down** the pavement.</u>
> He <u>looked up and **down** the block</u>.
> <u>Tears were rolling relentlessly **down** her face.</u>
> <u>Tears poured **down** her face.</u>

4.   MOVING FROM A HIGHER-NUMBERED STREET TO A LOWER-NUM-
     BERED

> You <u>go **down** to 14th Avenue from 42nd Avenue.</u>
> <u>Strolling **down** to 5th Street</u>, he made up plots for his new books.

Synonyms: *below, into, of, through, upon, under*
Antonyms: *up*

DUE (TO) indicates:

1.   A CAUSE/BEING CAUSED BY

> **<u>Due to</u>** <u>his carelessness</u>, we lost a valuable customer.

The film was <u>lost</u> **due to our negligence**.
We were <u>late</u> **due to the storm**.
Creditors have rejected you **due to your lack of a credit history**.
<u>The cancellation of the concert</u> in the stadium <u>was</u> **due to** the rain.
Due to <u>fire safety requirements</u>, spaces are limited.
The class has been <u>discontinued</u> **due to** <u>lack of participation</u>.
<u>Breakages are</u> always **due to bad packing.**

2. BEING PAYABLE, OWED

<u>How much money is</u> **due** them?
The amount of <u>money</u> **due** <u>me</u> was insignificant.

3. GOING DIRECTLY, IN THE DIRECTION

Now they will <u>sail</u> **due** <u>north</u> for several days.
Due <u>east, in the direction of his home,</u> I saw
an enormous blaze.

Synonyms: *as, for, in view of*
Antonyms: *0*

DURING indicates:

1. ENTIRE LENGTH OF TIME OF AN ACTION

<u>Much happened to him</u> **during** <u>the war.</u>
She <u>has</u> one <u>job</u> **during** the day and <u>another</u> **during** <u>the evening</u>.

2. WITHIN A PARTICULAR PERIOD OF TIME

He was <u>born</u> **during** <u>the blizzard</u>.
She <u>cried</u> **during** <u>the</u> last <u>sermon</u>.

Synonyms: *0*
Antonyms: *0*

EXCEPT indicates:

AN EXCLUSION

> Everybody left the office **except** me.
> All of us realized it **except** Kevin.
> Everyone **except** me cheered.
> Nothing will result from the rule **except** confusion.
> They re-scheduled everyone **except** themselves.

Synonyms: *but, without*
Antonyms: *include*

FACING indicates:

BEING ON THE OTHER SIDE, OPPOSITE

> There is a mirror **facing** the door.
> This was the only high-rise **facing** the hill.

Synonyms: *contrary, opposite*
Synonyms: *like*

IN FAVOR OF indicates:

1.   A SUPPORT, APPROVAL/CHOICE, PREFERENCE/ADVANTAGE

> The court decided **in favor of** the plaintiff.
> He talked **in favor of** joining the club.
> He is **in favor of** cleaning the playground just now.

2.   A BENEFIT

> We'll write a check **in favor of** a charity.
> I make regular donations **in favor of** the Center.

Synonyms: *for, to*
Antonyms: *0*

FOR indicates:

1. TRYING TO GET SOMETHING/TAKE HOLD/GRASP AN OBJECT

    He reached for her hand
    He reached his hand out for his glass.
    We sent for sandwiches and coffee.
    I ran for the bus but couldn't catch it.

2. TRYING TO OBTAIN A COMPENSATION/BENEFIT

    Do they volunteer or work for wages?
    I would work for free, for money, or for a meal.
    It's not like I don't work for my allowance.

3. EXPECTING/ANTICIPATING/A PROSPECT

    Trouble is lying in wait for them around the next curve.
    She was watching for a bus.
    Both cats followed me downstairs hoping for a snack.
    He is hoping for a manslaughter conviction instead of murder.

4. AN INTENTION/OBJECTIVE/RIGHT

    He always aims for active diplomacy.
    Early in the race he contended for a lead.
    An assassin often argues for history
    by committing his crime.
    This allowed for immediate investigation.

5. AN INTENDED RESULT OF AN ACITON/AN EXPECTED BENEFIT

    He just filed for bankruptcy.
    She is returning to school for her master's degree.
    Board the plane bound for success.
    There's no penalty for using the device.

6. A REQUEST, CLAIM

    They can bargain for benefits now.

This recipe calls **for** a pound of tomatoes.
I hear myself scream out **for** freedom.
Decide what you really want, and go **for** it!
Pick up a career and go **for** it.
Girls go **for** a guy because they like him.
I saw children hungry **for** knowledge.

7.   A DEMAND

He pushes **for** the childcare bill in the Senate.
They stopped him and asked **for** money.
Don't argue **for** a lower price on anything.

8.   TRYING TO ACHIEVE A SPECIFIC PURPOSE

What do you do **for** exercise?
Dig inside yourself **for** the answers.
When my pain acts up, I go right **for** my pill.
Adjust your mask **for** a snug fit.
He went **for** the doctor.

9.   TRYING TO REACH A DESTINATION, POINT/DIRECTION

He started **for** Mexico City.
We are leaving **for** Nicaragua.
He headed **for** the border.
She headed **for** the phone.
They were heading **for** the library.
They left **for** home about an hour ago.
The ball went right **for** the man at bat.
I reached **for** his shoulder to stop him.
Now **for** the coffee house!

10. A DISTANCE

Jack used to walk **for** miles.
The beach stretched **for** several kilometers.
They roamed in the forest **for** a mile or so.

11. MEETING PEOPLE FOR MEALS, DRINKS

Go to a restaurant **for** lunch.
She invited me over **for** dinner tonight.
He meets them **for** a cup of coffee.

12. MEETING PEOPLE FOR SOCIALIZING

I remember her returning **for** a reunion.
All of them will be in town **for** the annual convention.
They insisted we drop by **for** a visit.

13. AN OPINION

For one thing, we can't afford it.
For all I know, it might be the only house.
For all I can tell, we ought to be cautious.

14. A STAND, ATTITUDE, PRINCIPLE

They died **for** their country.
Were they **for** or against the proposal?
We stood **for** quality in everything.
Nobody is **for** higher taxes.
One should always stand up **for** his or her rights.

15. SEEKING/TRYING TO FIND

We have searched **for** proof in vain.
Look hard **for** mistakes in all the papers.
What mistakes do you still have to watch out **for?**
They will check the file **for** errors today.
She choked **for** words in French.
He groped blindly **for** his papers.
Arrange **for** a counselor to meet with the family

16. EXAMINING/SEARCHING/BEING ALERT

Keep an ear out **for** that project.
Analyze the styles **for** similarities and differences.

Have students listen **for** specific information.

17. TAKING CARE

During the holidays, you'd better watch out **for** your pets.
Watch out **for** the pills Grandpa is taking.

18. INQUIRING, GETTING INFORMATION/KNOWLEDGE

People were hungry **for** news.
Her quest **for** the truth is understandable.
Please read the documents **for** more information.
Reading **for** study or work develops your skills.

19. A DESCRIPTION, DEFINITION, CLARIFICATION

We need some explanation **for** finding a place.
We find it hard to account **for** her ignorance.
The kid had to account **for** the loss of the key.

20. LOOKING FOR A POSITION, JOB, OCCUPATION

I have applied **for** several jobs.
She tried out **for** girls' basketball.
Run **for** the office, the time couldn't be better!

21. WORKING FOR A BUSINESS/BEING WITH

He is a human resource specialist **for** a bank.
He is a representative **for** a major marketing organization.
He is a security guard **for** the Main Library.

22. A COMPETITION/RIVALRY

Who is the third candidate **for** the presidency?
A second language is important in competing **for** good jobs.
Pressure **for** gasoline price increased.

23. GETTING PREPARED FOR A JOB, OCCUPATION

> He was <u>trained **for** the ministry</u>.
> Who <u>trains recruits **for** soldiers</u>?
> He had <u>gone in **for** journalism</u>.

24. GETTING TRAINED AT A PLACE FOR STUDIES

> <u>To enroll **for** fall classes</u>, you'll need your ID.
> <u>Registration **for** classes</u> starts at 8 o'clock.
> We <u>signed up **for** a one-day workshop</u>.
> <u>Have you applied **for** credit?</u>
> <u>High school students bound **for** college</u> tend to volunteer.

25. A FUTURE ACTIVITY/PROJECT, PLAN

> He was <u>preparing **for** battle</u>.
> <u>The hospital is slated **for** closure.</u>
> <u>Her plan **for** 'communiversities'</u> is thought-provoking.
> That <u>is an idea ripe **for** discussion</u>.
> Always <u>be ready **for** changes</u>!
> <u>The company is up **for** sale.</u>

26. A DECISION/SELECTION

> He <u>opted **for** a part-time job</u>.
> Originally he <u>headed **for** a career in medicine</u>.
> <u>Is there any preference **for** admissions?</u>
> People will often <u>go **for** the opposite of what they want</u>.
> We don't do business with them any more,
> we <u>closed our market to them **for** Canada</u>.
> <u>It will be **for** the judge to decide.</u>

27. INTENDING TO BUY SOMETHING

> He <u>went to the store **for** bread</u>.
> I'd better <u>shop **for** groceries</u> before the stores get crowded.
> You'll have time <u>to shop **for** souvenirs</u>.
> <u>Send **for** our book</u> today!

28. A DESIRE, HOPE TO GET, OBTAIN SOMETHING

He was <u>impatient **for** a raise.</u>
<u>They wish **for** a particular result.</u>
Humans <u>long **for** peace and happiness</u>.
She is <u>desperate **for** attention and help</u>.
Now <u>who's **for** a taco?</u>
<u>Care **for** some wine?</u>

29. HAPPENING DESPITE, NOTWITHSTANDING/HOWEVER, YET

<u>**For** all that</u>, she is nice.
<u>**For** all her experience,</u> she can't find a way out.
<u>**For** all the difficulties</u>, it was a valuable experience.
He can't solve the problem, <u>**for** all the math he's studied</u>.
<u>**For** all her crudeness</u>, Mary had a nice personality.

30. A FUNCTION/TASK

Why don't you <u>take him **for** a model</u>?
<u>A good spot **for** watching the parade</u> is that hill.
<u>Learn about secrets **for** finding love.</u>

31. AN OBJECTIVE, PURPOSE

<u>Consult a specialist **for** help.</u>
<u>They petition **for** acceptable reasons.</u>
He <u>called her</u> the next day <u>**for** a date</u>.
<u>**For** assistance, call the given number.</u>
Many <u>turn to the computers **for** answers</u>.
I am <u>shopping **for** a hobby</u>.
They are <u>fair game **for** criticism</u>.
They <u>promote a new concept **for** health care</u>.
We stacked logs <u>**for** our winter's fire</u>.

32. A CAUSE, MOTIVE

On hearing the news, <u>I jumped **for** joy</u>.
They met at the end of <u>his hospital stay **for** severe war injuries</u>.
He was <u>expelled from the college **for** his improper activities</u>.

I <u>choose my friends</u> **for** <u>their good looks</u>, <u>my acquaintances</u> **for** <u>their good characters</u>, and <u>my enemies</u> **for** <u>their good intelligence</u> (O. Wilde)

33. A SYMBOL, REPRESENTATION

<u>Red is</u> **for** <u>stop.</u>
<u>The picture is</u> **for** <u>silence.</u>

34. A PART OF A NAME OF AN INSTITUTION/KIND OF AN INSTITUTION

They <u>joined the Institute</u> **for** <u>Policy Studies.</u>
<u>Funding came from the American Center</u> **for** <u>Wine.</u>

35. BEING (IN) APPROPRIATE, (NOT) GOOD

<u>He was no match</u> **for** <u>her.</u>
<u>Neither plan is expedient</u> **for** <u>the moment.</u>
<u>To qualify</u> **for** <u>admission</u>, you must have a Master's Degree.
<u>We are handy</u> **for** <u>that</u> kind of a job.
<u>The day was too hot</u> **for** <u>riding.</u>

36. A FOUNDATION, GROUNDS

He gets a ticket **for** speeding.
The road is closed **for** repairs.
<u>Prisoners were released</u> **for** <u>lack of evidence.</u>
<u>There is no legal basis</u> **for** <u>such opinion.</u>
<u>You have no cause</u> **for** <u>jealousy.</u>

37. A BENEFICIARY/ACTING IN THE INTERESTS OF

We <u>provide a lot of services</u> **for** <u>seniors.</u>
You <u>know what's right</u> **for** <u>you.</u>
I <u>bet you're happy</u> **for** <u>them</u> now.
<u>Would you mind spelling your name</u> **for** <u>me?</u>
<u>Make a name to yourself and</u> **for** <u>us,</u> too!
I'm going <u>to give a speech</u> **for** <u>the candidate.</u>
<u>I have a question</u> **for** <u>you.</u>

38. AN EXCEEDING CAPACITY

I am too pretty to settle **for** him.
She's too intelligent **for** the work she's doing.
This suggests something too important **for** the phone.
He was spry **for** his advanced age.
He's very tall **for** his age.

39. A LONG PERIOD OF TIME, THE LENGTH OF TIME

My family has been here **for** generations.
They were lovers **for** life.
Margarita left **for** good.
The baby plays happily **for** long stretches at a time.
We lived in New York **for** two years.
He could read it **for** hours.

40. A SPECIFIC POINT IN TIME

He has a temporary job **for** today.
I had an interview **for** 2 o'clock.
They had no clothes **for** winter.
What to anticipate **for** 2010 and beyond?
Where do you plan to go **for** summer vacation?
The date was fixed **for** a Tuesday.
For an instant, he almost shuddered.

41. HAVING AN ABILITY/BEING CAPABLE TO DO SOMETHING

Readers must figure out the answers **for** themselves.
He is old enough to fend **for** himself.
It was hard **for** me to understand the problem.
Rooting is a natural instinct **for** pigs.

42. HAVING A SKILL, PROFICIENCY/A SENSE, TALENT

She is competent **for** this kind of work.
He has a knack **for** happy phrases.
He had a natural aptitude **for** outdoor games.
One has a capacity **for** both fury and forgiveness.

I have no turn **for** such things.
I had a very marked bent **for** mathematics.

43. AN ATTITUDE/CONDUCT

He has a new appreciation **for** life.
It was nice **for** you to remember my birthday.
It was bad **for** her to write this letter.
Take no care **for** your dignity, and you are gone.
That was the beginning of self-respect **for** me.
I tried **for** irony one more time.

44. APPRAISING/ENCOURAGING

Well, good **for** them.
Hurray **for** you, kids!
Lucky **for** him!
You cheered **for** my career, then say I work too much.

45. A POSITIVE SENTIMENT, EMOTION/BEING SENSITIVE

I share your enthusiasm **for** great history.
Have some feeling **for** the poor.
For a moment, he ached **for** her again.
She was homesick **for** Argentina.
Thank you **for** presenting the other side of this issue.
Weather to die **for!**

46. AN AFFECTION, FONDNESS

He showed more affection **for** their babies.
Her love **for** her son was overwhelming.
Don't fall **for** this temptation.

47. A NEGATIVE FEELING/DISLIKING

He has contempt **for** her.
I have no taste **for** popular art.
I don't go **for** those novels.
He demonstrated complete contemp **for** that.

We <u>knew about his disdain **for** that man.</u>
I <u>grieved **for** all of them</u>.

48. AN APOLOGY/REGRET, REMORSE

<u>Sorry **for** being late</u>, Mom.
<u>Alas **for** freedom!</u>
<u>I held deep regrets **for** missed opportunities.</u>
Will I <u>be responsible **for** more unnecessary pain</u>?

49. AN INNER STATE

<u>Am I at risk **for** osteoporosis?</u>
<u>The grain was ripe **for** harvest.</u>
<u>It's terribly hot **for** this time of year.</u>
<u>It still isn't very cold **for** January.</u>

50. AN EXTERNAL STATE/CIRCUMSTANCE

I <u>lacked **for** nothing</u>.
He <u>is in a real hurry **for** bread</u>.
She <u>was pressed **for** time</u>.

51. CALLING, GIVING A NAME IN HONOR OF SOMEONE

The girl is <u>named **for** grandmother</u>.
The street is <u>named **for** a labor leader</u>.

52. A CORRELATION, PROPORTION/CORRESPONDENCE

Everybody <u>knows that **for** a fact.</u>
<u>You'll see their behavior **for** what it is.</u>
<u>It took one step back **for** two steps forward.</u>
<u>Images compensate **for** the loss of reality.</u>
The kid <u>repeated it word **for** word</u>.
<u>Our conduct will speak **for** itself.</u>
He is <u>eligible **for** death penalty.</u>

53. A MISTAKEN IDENTITY

I was usually taken **for** a Greek.
She is often mistaken **for** an actress.
I hate being mistaken **for** a teenager.

54. A CHANGE/REPLACEMENT, SUBSTITUTE

Every icon stands **for** some object.
They seek a successor **for** the ailing Prime-Minister.
I made the mistake, but she took the blame **for** me.
She left him **for** Robert.
A pill cannot substitute **for** good eating habits.
I'd like to do something **for** a change.

55. A RESTITUTION, REMUNERATION

Exercise can help compensate **for** that.
We were rewarded **for** what we had done.

56. BEING ACCOUNTABLE, ANSWERABLE, OBLIGED

Who is liable **for** injuries?
Nobody is liable **for** damages in this fire.

57. A TRADE, EXCHANGE, REFUND

He sold three items out **for** cash.
He gave legal advice **for** small fees.
How to get mutual funds **for** free?
They exchanged copper **for** gold.

58. AN EQUIVALENCE IN A FINANCIAL EXCHANGE

I bought all the dolls **for** a dollar.
She received a check **for** several hundred dollars.
The plumber sent me a bill **for** fifty dollars.

59. A PAYMENT

> I paid $10.00 **for** a ticket.
> How much will I have to spend **for** books?
> What do you charge **for** your service?
> You may be charged **for** the call.

> Synonyms: *at, because of, during, from, out, over,*
> *through, throughout, to, toward, with*
> Antonyms: *against*

FROM indicates:

1.   A STARTING POINT IN SPACE, PLACE/A POINT OF DEPARTURE

> They took a train running west **from** Denver.
> **From** where I stood, I could see her.

2.   A DISTANCE

> The station is several minutes walk **from** here.
> My home is five miles **from** my office.
> I never surf farther than half a mile **from** shore.

3.   A DIRECTION

> The suspect approached the victim **from** behind.
> Do it with the mouse or **from** the keyboard.
> I lifted my eyes **from** the book.

4.   A STARTING POINT FOLLOWED BY A BORDERLINE/LIMIT

> The topics can vary **from** simple *to* complex.
> The ladies surveyed me **from** tip *to* toe.
> The salary may range **from** $10 *to* $15 per hour.

5.   A PLACE FROM WHERE SOMETHING IS TAKEN, REMOVED

> She pulled her keys **from** her pocket.
> The mayor ordered them to remove the poor **from** sight.

It was enough to drive him **from office**.
He was excluded **from membership** last year.
He was dismissed **from his service**.
I brushed the tears **from my eyes.**

6.   A PLACE FOR GETTING, OBTAINING THINGS/SOURCE

Take these books **from the library**.
You can rent a car **from our agency.**
The company develops drugs **from tropical plants**.
I reap the success **from my efforts.**
Morality comes **from the way** people live.
No profits might accrue **from the deal.**

7.   AN INDIVIDUAL AS A SOURCE OF GETTING, OBTAINING THINGS

He leased the house **from her** for one year.
He demanded money **from us.**

8.   AN INDIVIDUAL AS A SOURCE OF A FEELING, STATE

I remember humiliation **from my Dad**.
She will not be lacking in support **from me.**

9.   A FEELING AS A SOURCE OF A STATE

He has suffered **from jealosy**.
I was crying **from rage.**

10.   A PLACE FOR BUYING THINGS

They purchase flowers **from local markets**.
I bought oranges **from a street vendor.**

11.   GOING, MOVING AWAY/LEAVING

He slipped **from his room**.
I met him running **from my room.**
Mitchel walks home **from school.**
She ran away **from home** at 16.

He leaped **from** the car.
I separated **from** my husband last year.

12. ESCAPING/DISTANCING

He was running **from the police.**
I got to get away **from this unsafe place.**
He broke away **from** her on some vague pretext.
The cat made his escape **from the box.**
All the froth and fury of that has faded **from**
my memory.

13. FREEING/RELEASING

It meant liberation **from slavery** for them.
Our son-in-law was exempt **from mobilization.**
It redeems us **from our selfishness.**
A sob broke **from her.**

14. PROTECTING/SAVING

He saved the artist's name **from oblivion.**
Dolphins saved sailors **from drowning.**
The trellis was some protection **from the dust.**
That doesn't prevent relapses **from occurring.**
It kept her **from** being bothered by bad guys.
The spray protects wood **from molding.**

15. DISTRACTING/STOPPING/AVOIDANCE

Kids will refrain **from this behavior.**
I could hardly restrain **from crying.**
I dissuaded him **from the trip.**
He discouraged his son **from getting married.**
Something kept me **from doing it.**

16. SEPARATING/PARTING

Laws prohibit felons **from serving on juries.**
He was totally estranged **from the world.**

Keep them **from making the same mistake**.

17. RELAXING/RESTING

We retired **from business**.
He retired **from public life**.
I abstained **from drinking wine.**

18. AN EDUCATIONAL INSTITUTION/BACKGROUND

He received his law degree **from the University** of California.
Suzanne got her degree **from the University** at Berkley.

19. A PLACE OF ORIGIN/ETHNIC BACKGROUND

He comes **from Russia**.
She is **from the north** of the Philippines.

20. A SOURCE, ORIGIN OF KNOWLEDGE/EXPERIENCE

Not all people learn **from their mistakes**.
From the new evidence, Mason must be guilty.
Well, I speak **from experience**.
You can infer it **from her own words**.
You'll be hearing **from us** soon
All I need is a little pep talk **from our leader**.
From my parents I inherited a love of music.

21. GETTING, TAKING ADVANTAGE

Everyone can benefit **from that discussion**.
You would profit **from regular reading**.

22. A CAUSE

My eyes were watery **from crying**.
Many kids faced death **from starvation**.
My face had turned red **from the hot water**.
I want to see the jungle when it's wet **from rain**.

The poor girl fainted **from** hunger.
I suffer **from** neglect.

23. AN ILLNESS, AILMENT/CAUSE OF AN ILLNESS

They died **from** cancer.
Grandma suffered **from** heart disease.
So far, no one was cured **from this deadly disease.**

24. A REASON

We often eat **from** fear or excitement.
He broke down **from** extended overwork.

25. DISTINGUISHING/DISCRIMINATING/A DIFFERENCE

You should know right **from** wrong.
I differ **from** you.
They are different **from** us.
It was hard to tell friend **from** foe.

26. A BEGINNING, STARTING POINT IN TIME

The theory dates **from** 385 B.C.
I knew him **from** childhood.
We were friends **from** grades four to six.
From that morning on, she started fasting.
Several years **from** now, you won't recognize the city.
We will start in four minutes **from** now.
Prom is a month **from** today.

27. TAKING AWAY/DEDUCTING

Three **from** six leaves three.
Five **from** ten leaves five.

Synonyms: *of, out of, due to*
Antonyms: *to*

IN FRONT OF indicates:

BEING AHEAD, BEFORE

> He never blushed in front of her.
> Lisa never felt shy in front of that group.

Synonyms: *before*
Antonyms: *behind, in the rear of*

IN indicates:

1. BEING INSIDE, WITHIN/AT A LOCATION

> I usually study in quiet places.
> This is a place in which you belong.
> Who are those people in the background?
> Now I am in uncharted territory.

2. BEING WITHIN THE LIMITS, INSIDE A LIMITED SPACE

> In one map, you see that two states have changed places.
> She didn't want him in there (in the room).
> How many stripes are there in the flag?
> Smooth any wrinkles in the clothes.
> I've got some brochures in my purse.
> See the bibliography in the back of the book.
> He knew it without looking it up in the dictionary.

3. BEING INSIDE THE BODY

> I scratched myself in the eye.
> Sometimes a piece of food gets caught in the throat.
> A vein in his temple began to throb a little faster.
> He says you have eyes in the back of your head.
> In the bend of the elbow you may feel tense.
> She felt her heart pound in her chest.
> He occupied a special place in her heart.
> He felt the heat in his cheeks.

4.   HAVING SOMETHING ON THE BODY/WEAR ING

I let the cat <u>settle</u> <u>in my lap</u>.
<u>The tall woman</u> <u>in the overcoat</u> is my ex.
<u>That little man</u> <u>in glasses</u>, do you know him?
They were <u>dressed</u> <u>in full gear</u>.

5.   BEING (NOT) AVAILABLE

Ask what the future <u>has</u> <u>in store</u>.
My dog <u>eats everything</u> <u>in sight.</u>
<u>The library system lacks</u> <u>in bookshelving.</u>
He's <u>lacking</u> <u>in the sense of humor.</u>
<u>I had a magazine photographer</u> <u>in attendance.</u>
<u>In her absence</u> I'd <u>arrived</u> <u>at certain conclusions.</u>

6.   A POINT IN THE COMPASS/DIRECTION

This spice <u>is common</u> <u>in the East</u>.
All his kids <u>live</u> <u>in the West</u>.
<u>Pay attention to the</u> <u>in-bound traffic</u>

7.   A MEDIUM, ENVIRONMENT/NATURE

We can <u>see</u> the <u>comet</u> <u>in the night sky</u> in April.
The adults <u>who are afraid</u> <u>in water</u> can learn
swimming at our club.
Don't <u>stay</u> <u>in the sun</u> too long.

8.   A WEATHER CONDITION

I <u>walked</u> to school <u>in the rain</u>.
The curtains <u>moved</u> gently <u>in the wind</u>.
They <u>shivered</u> <u>in the moist air</u>.
Don't <u>go out</u> <u>in the wet</u> without rubbers.

9.   A CONTINENT/ISLAND/MOUNTAIN/WATER BASIN

<u>Life is different</u> <u>in the island.</u>
Where did she <u>live</u> <u>in Australia</u>?

He <u>taught math</u> in a village <u>in the Philippines</u>.
Do bears <u>live</u> <u>in the foothills, grasslands, or mountains</u>?
Quito is <u>located</u> <u>in the Andes</u>.
We <u>picked up</u> a couple of <u>mushrooms</u> <u>in the glade</u>.
My parents <u>were</u> still <u>in the field</u>.
<u>No fishing</u> <u>in this lake</u>!

10. BEING INSIDE A PLANT

The nightingale was <u>singing</u> <u>in the rosebush</u>.
The blossoms are <u>blooming</u> <u>in the trees</u> in my backyard.
<u>You couldn't sleep in a tree</u>, could you?

11. A COUNTRY, STATE, PROVINCE

Linda <u>spent three weeks</u> <u>in Australia</u>.
They <u>live</u> <u>in a country</u> known for its wines.
I <u>live</u> <u>in the East Bay area</u>.
The newlyweds <u>live</u> <u>in Hawaii</u>.
Right here, <u>in the Bay Area</u>, <u>he wrote</u> five books.

12. A CITY, TOWN/COMMUNITY

I used to <u>live</u> <u>in Mexico City</u>.
<u>Are there any post offices</u> <u>in the neighborhood?</u>
We <u>live</u> <u>in the Sunset district</u>, and she <u>lives</u> <u>in Richmond</u>.
There are two <u>university campuses</u> <u>in Riverside</u>.
I saw them <u>walking</u> <u>in the park</u>, hand in hand.
You can <u>ice skate</u> <u>in a rink</u> now.

13. A SQUARE/STREET

<u>The statue</u> <u>in the main square</u> <u>symbolizes love</u>.
I especially <u>enjoy the shopping</u> <u>in Union Square</u>.
He <u>spoke with a reporter</u> <u>in the central market</u>.
Children will not <u>starve</u> <u>in the streets</u>.
<u>What's going on in SoMa?</u> (South of Market.)
<u>He leaves his truck</u> <u>in the driveway</u> all day.

14. MEANS OF TRANSPORTATION

I could <u>pick</u> you <u>up</u> <u>in the car</u>.
They <u>traveled</u> <u>in the same</u> <u>bus</u> all over Egypt.
<u>In his seat</u> <u>in the back row</u>, <u>he felt uncomfortable</u>.

15. A BUILDING/RESIDENCE/ROOM

My parents <u>lived</u> <u>in a small rancho</u>.
They were <u>married</u> <u>in their own home</u>.
<u>Our next class is</u> <u>in the science building</u>.
I <u>stood</u> <u>in the doorway</u> dripping wet.
You'll <u>see film clips</u> <u>in class</u>.
<u>Are you</u> still <u>in the shower</u>?

16. A PIECE OF FURNITURE/DEVICE

<u>The boy stayed</u> <u>in bed</u> until two.
I <u>lay</u> <u>in bed</u> pretending to be asleep.
My cat is <u>asleep</u> <u>in my chair</u>.
<u>Relax</u> <u>in a chair</u>.
Our skates <u>were</u> <u>in the back seat</u>.
Animals cannot <u>see</u> themselves <u>in the mirror</u>.

17. MOVING INSIDE, ENTERING/PASSING THROUGH

The coin <u>landed</u> <u>in the street</u>.
<u>Don't stop</u> <u>in the intersection</u>.
Who should get <u>to park</u> <u>in the garage</u>?
Let's <u>go</u> <u>in the house</u>.
She is <u>coming</u> <u>in the door</u> right now.
I walked <u>in the front door</u>.
I let the cat <u>settle</u> <u>in my lap</u>.

18. PLACING AN OBJECT INSIDE

I <u>put a quarter</u> <u>in her hand</u>.
I <u>threw the letter</u> <u>in the wastebasket</u>.
We <u>threw a couple of pennies</u> <u>in the fountain</u>.
It'll get sticky if you <u>put</u> too much <u>water</u> <u>in rice</u>.

I put the suitcase in the back.
Our things were put in the backseat.
Dip the pastry brush in cold water.
How about planting the tree in this spot over here?
They put innocent people in prison for years.
He raised a finger in the air.
He wrote "Nice" in the margin of my paper.

19. A PUBLIC PLACE

Business people usually stay in hotels.
He stayed in the hospital for several days.
We stopped to eat in a restaurant.
She began to spend hours in galleries.
Sitting in an airport lounge, we talked about kids.
I observed an incident in a shop.
I was in a local houseware store.

20. A WORKPLACE

He is working in a law office next summer.
Please talk to Ann in the front office.
He leaves home to work in a drugstore.
We used to wait on the tables together in a restaurant.
She taught art in junior high school.
A professor in the anthropology department said that.

21. BEING RESPONSIBLE, ACCOUNTABLE

Who is the person in charge now?
They found it difficult to be in charge.
The officer in command didn't know that.
Who will speak in honor of the event?

22. BEING EMPLOYED

I am no longer active in the profession.
To stay competitive in the job, upgrade your skills.
We work in low-paying jobs.
We make headway toward parity with men in the workplace.

23. AN OCCUPATION/FIELD OF THE ACTIVITY

Some friends work in sales.
In television, the star is king.
She appears in movies and plays.
He knows all the subtleties in the latest fashions.
They make money in stock market and real estate.
They are involved in sports.
He holds a first-degree black belt in judo.
His life in politics is full of weird situations.

24. GETTING INVOLVED/PARTICIPATING

I need your help in resolving a problem.
They enlisted in the experiment.
Many hurry to enroll in the citizenship classes.
She tried to engage them in discussions.

25. BEING INVOLVED IN AN ACTIVITY AT A SPECIFIED TIME

She's in conference now.
I am terribly sorry, but he is in a meeting.
Thomas is in a meeting, too.
Later, in debate, they described all those devices.
I am sure he is in class now.

26. ALL THE PEOPLE/POPULATION

Learn your rights in today's complex society.
One should work hard for his place in the sun.
A healthy diet eliminates the need for medicine in people.

27. BELONGING TO A GROUP/ASSOCIATION

I have never belonged in Hollywood.
That country reported a 42% rise in enrollees.
There are a lot of people I know in the math community.
Loss of muscle is associated with disability in the elderly.
In infants, too much water dilutes their sodium levels.
Decay is responsible for most tooth loss in adults.

Wrinkles appeared reduced <u>in some women</u>.
<u>Problems</u> <u>in a marriage</u> <u>are</u> a two-way street.

28. A PLACE FOR STUDYING, AN EDUCATIONAL INSTITUTION

Subjects <u>taught</u> <u>in school</u> include Science.
She <u>is</u> still <u>in school</u>, I think.
I <u>am a year behind</u> <u>in school</u>.
Ask students why they <u>were not</u> <u>in school</u>.
<u>I was not a great student in school.</u>
I always <u>do well</u> <u>in school</u>.
<u>Activities</u> <u>in school</u> generate friendships.
There's <u>a real nice guy</u> <u>in our school</u>.

29. A PARTICULAR KIND OF A SCHOOL

Our daughter <u>is</u> <u>in preschool</u>.
<u>In the public school</u> <u>they teased her</u>.
His two daughters <u>are</u> <u>in grade school</u>.
This class is <u>taught</u> <u>in high schools</u>.
<u>It just gets more difficult</u> <u>in middle and high school.</u>
While I <u>was</u> <u>in junior high</u>, we lived in a rouchy apartment.
Two of our sons <u>are</u> <u>in college</u>.
Think about the next year of <u>instruction</u> <u>in our university</u>.

30. A LEVEL/YEAR OF STUDYING, TRAINING

My son <u>is</u> now <u>in first grade</u>.
<u>In the fourth grade I decided</u> I would be a nurse.
When I <u>was</u> <u>in sixth grade</u>, we started calling her "mother".

31. A TRAINING, CLASS/INSTRUCTION

<u>In this course</u>, <u>you will learn</u> how to write business letters.
What I <u>learn</u> <u>in this seminar</u> can be helpful in everyday life.
<u>To spend time</u> <u>in a recovery program</u> is a must.

32. A FIELD OF INSTRUCTION, TRAINING/EDUCATION

He <u>has a master's</u> <u>in International Business</u>.

He majored in Physics.
Few students were trained in neuro-linguistics.
He is occupied in the study of butterflies.

33. AN INFORMATION, KNOWLEDGE

Those are nice ideas in theory, but the timing is way off.
These people were mentioned in prophecy.

34. AN ABILITY/EXPERTISE/PROFICIENCY

He is good in writing songs.
Those who apply for this job will vary in skills.
I am next to Helen in math.
Meditation assists in the development of intuition.

35. AN EMPHASIS/ASSUMPTION, VIEW, BELIEF

In the first place, she is right.
Parents might guess in their child's decision to go to college.
They seldom, if ever, concur in an opinion about anything.
I am wrong in saying he is smart.

36. A WAY IN EXPRESSING ONESELF/SPEAKING

He said it in a rude tone of voice.
The baby is sick and they speak to each other in a whisper.
She said it in her throaty voice.
He spoke in a quiet voice about the liberal tradition.
We were speaking in whispers.

37. A TYPE OF COMMUNICATION/A TONGUE

What language did they sing the songs in?
I showed him letters in both English and Russian.
He took a poet's joy in the language.

38. A STYLE OF COMMUNICATION, LANGUAGE

Consult a lawyer and put it in writing.

Try <u>to interpret the pictures</u> <u>in words</u>.
<u>Write the answers down</u> <u>in block letters.</u>
I can <u>make a poem</u> <u>in iambic pentameter</u>.

39. A TYPE OF COMMUNICATION/MASS MEDIA

<u>A red envelope came</u> <u>in the mail.</u>
I <u>received this notice</u> <u>in the e-mail</u>.
<u>In the TV series</u>, what color was his hair?

40. A FEATURE, TRAIT, ATTRIBUTE OF AN INDIVIDUAL

<u>She has a good mother</u> <u>in her.</u>
They don't <u>resemble</u> <u>one another</u> <u>in looks or personality</u>.
My sister and I <u>differ</u> from each other <u>in appearance</u>.
We <u>have something</u> <u>in common</u>—love of the Opera.

41. A FEATURE, TRAIT, ATTRIBUTE OF AN OBJECT

The beauty <u>consists</u> <u>in the simplicity</u> of the style.
<u>The crime scene is rich</u> <u>in evidence.</u>
<u>The city is rich</u> <u>in history.</u>

42. A STAGE OF LIFE/LIFE SPAN, LIFETIME

<u>Be happy</u> <u>in the moment!</u>
Be with children <u>similar in age to yourself</u>.
Kids <u>ranging</u> <u>in age</u> from 2 to 8 died in fire.
<u>In the second year of life</u> the child learns to speak.
He <u>hit fame</u> <u>in his twenties</u> with his first novel
<u>She had been a famous beauty</u> <u>in her youth.</u>
She <u>was a lady</u> <u>in declining</u> <u>of her years</u>.
He <u>died</u> <u>in his prime</u>.

43. A PHYSICAL STATE OF AN INDIVIDUAL

The baby appears <u>to be</u> <u>in pain.</u>
My stomach <u>was</u> <u>in knots</u> when I rode home.
His cancer <u>is</u> <u>in remission</u>.

44. AN EMOTIONAL STATE, CONDITION OF AN INDIVIDUAL

Yes, we have a lady in distress here.
Archeology lets you stand in awe.
If in doubt, don't do it.
As I am writing this, I am in tears.
She was in a vengeful mood.
I sent it in the hope that you'll respond.
Can you afford to retire in comfort?
His eyes narrowed in confusion.

45. AN EMOTIONAL STATE, CONDITION OF A GROUP OF PEOPLE

The whole campus is in mourning.
Many people are in a rush to set up sites on the Internet.
The nation is in an uproar after the elections.
Everyone else is in turmoil.

46. A FEELING/AN EMOTION/A REACTION

She exclaimed it in delight.
Kids will delight in new picture books.
A crowd of children watched it in horror.
My body was trembling in anger.
I am deeply in love.
She, too, turned her head in shame.
He resigned in humiliation yesterday.
Everyone would gaze in secret envy.

47. A CHANGE IN A SITUATION/STATE, CONDITION

Try to fit in with the requirements of my class.
I stopped dead in my tracks.
Want to get in shape?
He lost his child in death.
We have a life cycle that ends in death.
Get the system in operation as soon as possible.

48. A WAY, MANNER IN DOING THINGS

> They always <u>do things in a big way</u>.
> He <u>apologizes in a rare manner</u>.
> <u>She is an artist in her own right</u>.
> When you <u>work in a pool</u>, you build a nice team.
> I <u>looked at my watch in irritation</u>.
> <u>Invite</u> guests <u>in person</u>.
> Kids could <u>sleep in the nude</u>.
> <u>She took my hand in an awkward handshake</u>.
> At a Price Club you <u>buy things in bulk</u>.
> <u>It's like chasing your tail in circles</u>.
> <u>Fold the paper in half</u> lengthwise.
> Just mention it <u>in passing</u>.

49. A CONFORMITY, CORRESPONDENCE, ACCORD

> Her behavior <u>was not in line</u> with company policy.
> His work <u>was not in step</u> with the avant-garde.
> Her words <u>were in a sharp contrast</u> with her behavior.
> I am hoping <u>to fit in a long weekend</u> in Oakland this spring.
> We silently <u>nodded in agreement</u>.
> We <u>are very close in our aspirations</u>.

50. AN ATTITUDE

> I <u>accept</u> Picasso <u>in good faith</u>.
> Father is <u>in complete denial</u>.
> Happiness <u>consists in wanting</u> what you have.
> She received the news <u>in icy silence</u>.
> This information is used in way that may <u>result in abuse</u>.
> You can <u>be there in spirit</u> at least.

51. A TRUST/ACCEPTANCE

> I believe <u>in fun class, not in drudgery</u>.
> <u>Believe in yourself</u>. <u>Have faith in your own abilities</u>!
> She <u>has faith in his judgment</u>.
> That day he <u>confided in me</u>.

52. A TYPE, MANNER OF BEHAVIOR

Please don't persist in ringing the bell.
They are mule-stubborn in their pursuit of the news.
She looked him in the eye and shook her head.
Be careful in doing the thing.

53. A DANGEROUS BEHAVIOR/HURTING, INJURING, DAMAGING

I wanted to pop her in the nose.
I was hit in the knee several times.
The ball hit the man in the head.
He was shot twice in the chest.

54. A ONE-TIME SITUATION/EVENT

I had to drive a car in real life, in real traffic.
I almost got killed in a car accident.
We are not sure how we did in the elections.
He asked him questions in cross-examination Sunday.
They died in a fire at their group home.
Three people were killed in the explosion.
He performed in concert with the Boston Pops.

55. A CURRENT SITUATION/CIRCUMSTANCE

The talks are in a stalemate.
The government is in debt.
The economy is in crisis already.
Call 911 for crimes in progress.
He will be in contract with us.
Court is in session, please remain silent.
The kitchen will be in use Monday afternoon.
The rules have been in place since the agency opened.
The scanner has not been in use since then.
The party is in danger of losing its voters.
His clothes are always in fashion.
Reach out to others who you sense are in need.
Your skills will be in demand.

56. A TIME OF YEAR/A SEASON

My son was born **in the spring time**.
We have no fog **in the winter** here.

57. A PERIOD OF TIME/DURATION

It's the best concert **in years.**
He was finished **in less than an hour**.
He has not worked steadily **in the last five years**.
Finally she was smiling as she hadn't **in months.**
In a single day, a season seemed to have slipped past me.
Make healthy meals **in minutes.**
It can be done **in ten minutes**.
You must journey **in time** back to 1800.
Some tasks you accomplish **in the next few weeks.**

58. A PARTICULAR TIME PERIOD/BEFORE THE INDICATED MOMENT, POINT

I provide them with comfort **in times** of need.
In that time, people headed for the mountains.
In ancient times people didn't know what 'honor' meant.
In the aftermath, he has suffered terribly from his guilt.
The container is full early **in the week.**
She's been medically screened earlier **in the day.**
In this exclusive evening he'll reveal his secret.
They were going to do it to your house **in the night**.
It happened **in the seconds after** he fell with fatal wounds.
In the final year I must write and defend a thesis.
We are always **in time for the meetings**.
We talked it over, waiting **in line** to pay for our purchases.
I sing really well **in the shower.**

59. A MATERIAL

They put a statue **in bronze** in front of the hotel.
You can buy a sculpture **in clay**.
The note is written **in pencil.**
Do you have the capacity to print **in color**?

60. A COMPOSITION

Buildings and developments <u>are</u> <u>varied</u> <u>in design</u>.
He liked <u>fabric</u> that <u>fell</u> <u>in luxuriant folds</u> in that painting.
The stone was <u>split</u> <u>in two</u>.
Choose <u>foods high</u> <u>in nutrition</u> and <u>low</u> <u>in sugar</u>.
This article is <u>based</u> <u>in part</u> on a presentation.

61. A TYPE OF MONEY/PAYMENT

She <u>got thousands of dollars</u> from Dad <u>in cash</u>.
<u>How much did you get</u> <u>in change?</u>

62. A RATIO

At this store, only <u>one</u> <u>in six people work</u> full time.
My husband <u>is one</u> <u>in a million</u>.

63. A QUANTITY

The Minister said, <u>letters came</u> <u>in thousands.</u>
The people <u>came</u> to the city <u>in great numbers</u>.

64. A FINANCIAL TRANSACTION

You can <u>purchase</u> the car <u>in equal payments.</u>
They <u>paid</u> him <u>in kind</u>.
They <u>give away millions of dollars in cash</u>.
He is ordered <u>to pay $25 a month</u> <u>in back pay.</u>
He was ordered <u>to pay $2,000</u> <u>in fines</u>.
I <u>receive $140.00</u> <u>in food stamps</u>.
The robbers <u>stuffed a plastic bag with $1 million</u> <u>in chips</u>.
They <u>sold</u> $<u>500 million</u> <u>in goods and services</u> over the Internet.

65. A PURPOSE/OBJECTIVE

They <u>send</u> you <u>in search</u> of other books by this writer.
An offering will be <u>received</u> <u>in support</u> of our meetings.

66. A REASON/CONSEQUENCE

He <u>did it</u> **in protest.**
It was <u>followed</u> **in pursuit.**
<u>This letter is</u> **in a follow up to** your recent screening at the checkup center.
Metabolism provides <u>the energy</u> that <u>results</u> **in** movement.
He just <u>shook his head</u> **in reply.**
He <u>inclined his head</u> **in** brief salutation.

67. A PROPORTION/MEASUREMENT/DEGREE

The water there <u>was</u> only <u>two inches</u> **in depth.**
<u>The field increases</u> **in width.**
Disk capacity <u>is measured</u> **in bytes.**
<u>The room was bare</u> **in the extreme.**
My <u>intentions were serious</u> **in the extreme.**
The firefighters <u>saved only one</u> **in ten.**
The wash is <u>beneficial</u> **in reducing tooth decay.**

Synonyms: *of, with, on*
Antonyms: *out, out of, outside of*

INSIDE (OF) indicates:

1. A LOCATION, BEING WITHIN LIMITS/INDOORS

My cat likes to stay **inside** <u>the house</u> all the time.
I found some old letters **inside** <u>the trunk.</u>
I was <u>trapped</u> **inside** <u>your brain</u>.

2. BEING WITHIN SOMETHING ELSE/CONCEALED, HIDDEN

Inside <u>me lives a little girl</u> who was completely free.
When you <u>were</u> **inside** <u>Mommy</u>, I was happy.

3. BEING, STAYING WITHIN TIME LIMITS

I'll <u>finish the letter</u> **inside of** <u>an hour.</u>
He'll be <u>done with the deal</u> **inside of** <u>a week.</u>

4.   PLACING AN OBJECT INSIDE ANOTHER OBJECT

> I reached **inside** my pocket.
> He put the wrong key **inside** the keyhole.

Synonyms: *within, in, into*
Antonyms: *outside, out*

INSTEAD OF indicates:

SUBSTITUTING/BEING IN PLACE

> **Instead of** going to the concert, we went to the beach.
> **Instead of** eating red meat you can eat beans.
> We argued for probation **instead of** prison.
> Talk to her **instead of** pointing your finger at her.

Synonyms: *0*
Antonyms: *0*

INTO indicates:

1.   MOVING IN THE DIRECTION OF A MEDIUM

> The balloons flew **into** the sky.
> When we emerged **into** bright sunlight, he collapsed.
> She flipped the coin **into** the air.
> The fire in the fireplace crackled **into** the night.
> And out **into** the rain I went.
> Kids were jumping **into** the water.
> Three people fell **into** the water.
> They fell **into** a big pile of mud.

2.   RELOCATING/A DIRECTION FOR MIGRATING

> On the morning, I would cross **into** Texas.
> A large part of the population is crowded **into** provincial towns.
> We have had this problem since moving **into** our house.
> They moved **into** a new apartment.

3.   MOVING INSIDE, ENTERING (PART OF) A CITY/BUILDING

He went into the house.
I considered forcing my way into the house.
She rushed me into the park.
You dash into a gas station to consult a map.
I walk into my office intending to boot up my e-mail.
She's walking into the room.
I saw her go into the conference room.
We're getting into the shower.

4.   MOVING INSIDE A VEHICLE/STARTING IT

He slipped nervously into his car.
The guy pushed me into the streetcar.
He shoved the car into gear and pulled away.

5.   RESERVING A ROOM AT A LODGE

He booked into the same hotel again.
I'd check into a motel, shower and put on fresh clothes.

6.   PLACING AN OBJECT INSIDE SOMETHING

She puts some cheese into her shopping cart.
Put your handkerchiefs into the washing machine!
He strapped himself into the booster seat.
He burrowed back into his chair.
She pulled him gently into her arms.
My mother tucked me into bed.
Dump unused stuff into a plastic bag.
Plug it into the socket.
They pressed two or three shillings into my hand.
He dug his hands into the pockets of his vest.
The mailman stuck some letters into the black mailbox.
He'd driven that car of his into a tree.

7. INSTILLING IDEAS/TEACHING

    Devotion has been <u>bred **into** me</u>.
    Loyalty has been <u>drilled **into** us</u>.

8. ALTERNATING, SUBSTITUTING

    <u>She helped him **into** his coat.</u>
    I <u>changed out of my wedding dress **into** jeans and a T-shirt.</u>
    I saw her <u>struggle **into** that dress</u> and smiled.

9. INCLINING, TENDING TOWARD/RELYING

    She <u>leaned **into** the shoulder</u> of her brother.
    I <u>leaned **into** my husband's shoulder</u>, crying.

10. COLLIDING WITH AN OBJECT

    The car <u>ran **into** a tree</u>.
    Her sports car <u>crashed</u> head-on **into** a van.
    They <u>crashed **into** the bridge</u>.

11. RUINING, DAMAGING

    The commissions <u>eat **into** your return</u>.
    The taxes will <u>eat **into** your earnings</u>.

12. MOVING THE EYES IN THE DIRECTION

    He <u>stared **into** the fire</u>.
    <u>Look **into** the tired eyes</u> of your wife.
    She <u>leveled her eyes</u> ominously **into** his.
    I <u>gazed off **into** the setting sun.</u>
    He <u>smiles **into** the mirror</u>.

13. ADDING

    He <u>wrote</u> a new character **into** the play.
    I can <u>plug</u> this arsenal of words **into** any answer.

14. BROADENING, GETTING BIGGER, EXTENDING

A job can expand into a full-fledged career.
The parade stretched out into several hours.

15. FALLING APART/SPLITTING

The mirror broke into two pieces.
She cut the cake into six pieces.
Cut the cheese into four squares.
Species do not fall easily into categories.
We eventually split into camps.

16. A DIVISION IN MATHEMATICS

Five into ten is two.
Four goes into eight twice.

17. BEING/GETTING INTERESTED

She is not into eating butter.
He is into physical fitness.
I am not into doing morning exercises.
He is into vegetarianism, she is into yoga.
He is not into reading poetry, but his roommate is.
She is into shopping always early in the season.
All kids of that school are into football.
I get into novels involving conspiracies.
Some people get into music.
Paul is into telescopes.

18. GETTING INVOLVED IN AN ACTIVITY

Get your son into a regular play group.
Get into class the first day of school!
Any review will help you put it into perspective.
He never ventured into political discussion.

19. GETTING INFORMATION/STUDYING

The police went <u>to check</u> **into** <u>the situation</u>.
The lawyer promised <u>to look</u> **into** <u>our case</u>.
The legal officer is <u>looking</u> **into** <u>the matter</u>.
They gave us <u>insight</u> **into** <u>child abuse</u>.

20. BEGINNING AN ACTIVITY/STARTING A CAREER, AN OCCUPATION

I was so happy that <u>I broke</u> **into** <u>a song</u>.
They've <u>gone</u> **into** <u>business</u> for themselves.
Some college graduates <u>go</u> **into** <u>banking</u>.
We <u>hired</u> him **into** <u>the office.</u>
They are still waiting to be <u>sworn</u> **into** <u>office</u>.
He was <u>drafted</u> **into** <u>the army.</u>
Why would any sane person <u>go</u> **into** <u>politics</u>?
They did try <u>to break</u> **into** <u>movies</u>.

21. GUIDING/TRYING TO CONVINCE, PERSUADING

I <u>talked</u> her **into** <u>going to</u> New York.
The book will <u>steer</u> you **into** <u>a new eating pattern</u>.
Brokers <u>talk</u> you **into** <u>giving up control</u> over prices.
He did <u>coerce</u> her **into** <u>complying</u> with the rules.
He tries to <u>entice</u> me **into** <u>something</u> resembling romance.
They are <u>pressuring</u> us **into** <u>buying</u> more stuff than we need.
You <u>smooth-talk</u> a young couple **into** <u>buying</u> this car.

22. FORCING, PRESSING

Although I resisted, we were <u>pushed</u> **into** <u>opening gifts</u>.
Each of us was <u>pressed</u> **into** <u>work</u> as housekeeper and cook.

23. CHEATING/LYING

He has been <u>fooled</u> **into** <u>thinking</u> that I loved him.
Don't be <u>duped</u> **into** <u>donating</u> to people who don't need help!
We do sometimes <u>buy</u> **into** <u>the advertised ideas</u>.
They <u>wormed their way</u> **into** <u>big business</u>.
They <u>bribe their way</u> **into** <u>power</u>.

24. TRANSLATING INTO ANOTHER LANGUAGE

They have to <u>translate</u> it **into English**.
The article was <u>translated **into two languages**</u>.

25. PRODUCING A RESULT/CONSEQUENCE

He will <u>get **into** trouble</u>.
I <u>breathe life **into** everything</u> I touch.
<u>The pieces all fall **into** place</u>.

26. MEETING SOMEONE BY CHANCE

<u>I ran **into** her</u> at the fundraising.
You can walk out your front door and <u>run **into** your friends</u>.
Then we <u>ran **into** a buddy of ours</u> and lost track of the time.

27. SOMETHING THAT HAPPENS INCIDENTALLY

He <u>chanced **into** the exhibit's opening day</u> with his kids.
I <u>chanced **into** the store</u> before it was closed.

28. BEING SUITABLE/EQUIVALENT

Hopefully you don't <u>fall **into** this category</u>.
How does humanity <u>fit **into** the future</u> of the Universe?
I have to somehow <u>fit **into** the new environment.</u>

29. BRINGING INTO CONFORMITY

We <u>bring</u> the laws <u>back **into** line</u> with the values of our people.
The parties <u>entering **into** agreement</u> have been at war for a year.

30. IMPLEMENTING, ACCOMPLISHING INTENTIONS

Who <u>signs bills **into** law</u>?
<u>Transform</u> your dreams **into reality**!
<u>An idea can be made **into** invention.</u>
<u>Transform</u> your idea from a dream **into solid success**.
<u>Transform</u> your fear **into action**.

31. CHANGING ABEHAVIOR, CONDUCT

What's gotten into you?
Come **into** your own.
Gradually work **into** a new meal pattern.
Integrate humor consciously **into** your life.
He has just gotten **into** the habit of nodding absently.
He felt himself slipping back **into** old habits.
They went **into** a furious huddle.
She broke **into** a bright smile.

32. CHANGING THE SOCIAL STATUS

And out **into** the world I went.
He was baptized **into** the Mormon Church.
She dances **into** the future.

33. CHANGING THE FINANCIAL STATUS

Should you be putting your money **into** bonds?
How to convert the money you waste **into** a fortune?

34. CHANGING THE STATUS OF A SINGLE INDIVIDUAL

He couldn't become king without marrying **into** a royal family.
She married **into** a petty-bourgeois family.
She said she had married **into** the establishment.

35. A CHANGE IN A PHYSICAL STATE/MATURING

The larva changes **into** a butterfly.
You help them grow **into** decent, well-mannered adults.
She blossomed **into** a great beauty.
Some young men develop even **into** their early 20s.
More people live **into** their ninth or tenth decades.

36. CHANGING VIEWS, OPINION/BEING MISLEAD

How did she transform herself **into** a radical poet?
They may buy **into** some of the wrong concepts.

37. CHANGE IN THE EMOTIONAL STATE

I was <u>stunned **into** silence</u> for a second.
We <u>lapsed **into** despair</u>.
It can <u>grow **into** a</u> tormenting <u>mystery</u>.
<u>Her brow puckered **into** a frown.</u>
<u>Shape life's chaos **into** meaning.</u>

38. CHANGE OF THE PHYSICAL STATE

That will <u>put</u> you **into** <u>a deeper sleep</u>.
Her words <u>twisted</u> my stomach **into** <u>knots</u>.
<u>Translate your feelings and needs **into** short sentences.</u>

39. A CHANGE IN THE SHAPE, SIZE/CONDITION IN AN OBJECT

<u>The ice turned **into** water.</u>
Cold air <u>dropped temperatures **into** the teens</u>.
At last <u>things seemed to be settling **into** a routine again</u>.
Many tried <u>to turn copper **into** gold.</u>
<u>Fold paper **into** a</u> usable paper <u>cup</u>!
<u>Shrink</u> all windows **into** <u>icons</u>.

40. BEGINNING OF AN ACTION

Only <u>one month **into** the new year</u>, and
you'd be seeing big changes.
<u>Baby New Year isn't even **into** training pants yet.</u>
<u>Half an hour **into** the flight</u>, and they realized
something was wrong.

41. CONTINUING AN ACTION WITH THE TIME LIMITS

They <u>talked</u> long **into** <u>the night</u>.
They would <u>drink **into** the late afternoon.</u>
<u>It will be well **into** the week</u> before the snow melts.
The action began in the past but is <u>continuing **into** the present</u>.

42. BEING AHEAD OF ANOTHER EVENT

Planes only beat helicopters **into** the air by 35 years.

43. CONFIRMING AN ANTICIPATED RESULT

I am already **into** him for $10.00.
Edie was already **into** that horse for $25.00.

Synonyms: *in, to*
Antonyms: *from, out of*

LESS indicates:

BEING SUBTRACTED

Seven **less** five is two.
Ten **less** ten makes zero.

Synonyms: *minus*
Antonyms: *plus*

(UN) LIKE indicates:

1. COMPARING/BEING SIMILAR, THE SAME WAY, RESEMBLING

There's many **like** us.
It's more **like** an advance briefing than a magazine.
Like private universities, UC officials do want diversity.
Like many other concepts, she presents it as obligatory.
It wasn't supposed to happen **like** this.
It's not **like you** to be sad.
Like his mother, he played the piano beautifully.

2. INTENSIFYING A COMPARISON

He works **like** a beaver.
Nothing brings people together **like** travel.
I've always slept **like** a log, but recently I developed insomnia.

He was a sleep walker, and once he <u>ran</u> **<u>like</u>** **<u>hell</u>**
in the streets while asleep.
His memory <u>is</u> **<u>like a computer</u>**.
You are <u>spending</u> **<u>like there's no tomorrow</u>**.
<u>It's a city **unlike** any other</u>.

3. REPEATING WHAT HAS BEEN SAID, QUOTING

    <u>Like</u> <u>I said</u>, I was very ignorant and naïve.
    <u>Like</u> <u>Jack says</u>, you never know.

4. EXPLANING/GIVING AN EXAMPLE

    He <u>composes</u> a variety of <u>music **like** songs</u>, country, and jazz.
    His aunt <u>collected things</u> **<u>like dolls</u>**.
    He liked <u>cooking mushrooms</u> **<u>like shitaki</u>**.
    They <u>grow</u> <u>vegetables, **like** beets</u> and <u>carrots</u>.

5. BEING IN A MOOD/DISPOSED/INCLINED TO DO SOMETHING

    I <u>feel **like** going</u> to bed.
    Gerri <u>feels **like** staying</u> inside today.
    We <u>feel **like** eating out</u> tonight.

6. APPEARING TO BE PROBABLE

    <u>Looks **like**</u> <u>a bad weather</u> for skiing.
    <u>It looks **like** it's going to snow</u>.

    Synonyms: alike
    Antonyms: unlike

    NEAR indicates:

1. A PROXIMITY IN SPACE/BEING NOT FAR, CLOSE

    Their dormitory is **<u>near his house</u>**.
    They <u>live **near** each other</u> (a few blocks apart).

We'll refer you to a center **near** where you live.
The Theater is **near** here.

2.   MOVING CLOSE TO, TOWARD

Sit **near** me, OK? And they will sit **near** each other.
They relocated the post office **near** the station.

3.   A PROXIMITY IN TIME/WITHIN A SHORT TIME

Our agency opened **near** the beginning of the year.
We sometimes shop **near** closing time.

4.   BEING CLOSE TO A CERTAIN CONDITION, STATE

They are **near** an agreement.
They consider the trial **near** close.
The author described feelings of the people **near** death.
Our state ranks **near** the bottom, compared to other states.
In October, she was **near** breakdown.

Synonyms: *at, beside, close*
Antonyms: *far from*

NEXT TO indicates:

1.   BEING AT THE SIDE/IN THE NEAREST POSITION

His house is **next** to mine.
A wastebasket **next to** my desk is never empty.
I was trapped on a train **next to** a very talky girl.
I sit **next to** Alice in math class.
No, it was his **next to** last book.

2.   BEING CLOSEST IN RANK, ORDER, VALUE

I'm **next to** him in physics, he got 92 on the exam, and I got 91.
Next to French cooking, I like Northern Italian best.

I might have <u>bought</u> an apartment <u>**for next to** nothing</u> then.

Synonyms: *at, by, close, near*
Antonyms: *far from*

NOTWITHSTANDING indicates:

BEING OPPPOSITE TO/HAPPENING NEVERTHELESS

<u>**Notwithstanding** the prediction of rain</u>, they went hiking.
<u>**Notwithstanding** her bad cold, she had to do her tax returns.</u>
<u>**Notwithstanding** his anger, Jack spoke</u> to the stranger
in a quiet manner.
<u>**Notwithstanding** her old age, she was very active.</u>

Synonyms: *0*
Antonyms: *0*

OF indicates:

1.   A PART, COMPONENT, ELEMENT OF A NATURAL PHENOMENON

<u>A drop **of** rain</u>, is it much?
The wind <u>blew</u> <u>a grain **of** sand</u> into my eye.
I look at <u>the glistening leaves **of** the tree</u>.
What is <u>called</u> <u>'The Garden **of** Eden'</u>?
<u>If only we knew the size **of** the hill.</u>

2.   A PART OF THE BODY

The doctor <u>held the back **of** my head.</u>
The drug <u>changed</u> <u>the particles **of** the blood</u>.
I do <u>remember the voice **of** my Mother</u>.
I will study <u>mini-maps **of** the body</u> in our feet.

3.   A PART, COMPONENT, ELEMENT OF A MECHANISM/DEVICE

<u>The door **of** the car</u> was smashed.
<u>Some rungs **of** the ladder</u> need repair.

4.   A PART, COMPONENT, ELEMENT OF FOOD

Two pieces of bread are enough.
I took a sip of my drink.

5.   A PART, COMPONENT OF A SYSTEM

Learn the elements of a winning strategy!
There are elements of truth to that way of thinking.
It's important to study those patterns of English grammar.
Do each of the following.

6.   A PART, COMPONENT, ELEMENT OF TIME

I will never forget my first day of school.
Make decisions about what is left of your life.
Give of your time to the homeless.
What will you be doing on the first of May?
You can buy CDs with the music of the thirties.

7.   A QUANTITY, AMOUNT/FREQUENCY

She did most of the work.
Learn to make the most of it!
Most of the cases deal with women.
I won't see much of her in future.
Save 10% of your gross income per month.
Some of the information is missing.
One of the two uncles perished in the war.
I love all the animals, all of them.

8.   A CONNECTION/CONTINGENCY

He tries to be completely independent of his parents.
It's impossible to be fully independent of circumstances.

9.   A CONNECTION WITH A PLACE

My friends are natives of India.
The population of the globe is enormously huge.

He <u>is a citizen **of** two countries</u>.
<u>The names **of** many streets</u> were changed recently.

10. BELONGING/HAVING, POSSESSING

<u>All the land was property **of** the state.</u>
<u>All the toys **of** the kids are in those</u> five <u>boxes</u>.
<u>She's started a business **of** her own.</u>
I want <u>to hear about those plans **of** yours</u>.

11. AN AUTHOR, AUTHORSHIP

Did you <u>read any novel **of** this writer?</u>
How many <u>sonnets **of** Shakespeare</u> do you <u>know</u>?

12. A BASIC NATURE/ESSENCE

They resort to any <u>form **of** supernatural intervention</u>.
Hard as I try, I don't <u>see the point **of** it</u>.
I am worried about <u>the diet **of** soft drinks</u>.

13. A STRUCTURE/COMPOSITION/LOCATION OF A PART OF A WHOLE

<u>What</u> does this program <u>consist **of**?</u>
The committee <u>consisted **of** five experts</u>.
Human knowledge <u>admits **of** any possible level</u>.
This piece of <u>music is made up **of** three major parts</u>.
We know <u>all the words **of** this song</u>.

14. A MATERIAL/BEING MADE, COMPOSED OF

<u>A wall **of** red brick</u> separated our yards.
<u>That new dress **of** silk</u> costs $80.00.

15. A CONTAINER/HOLDER

At last, he brought <u>a bag **of** groceries</u>.
We had <u>a basket **of** wild strawberries</u> each.
Put <u>a box **of** cereal</u> on the table for kids.

16. AN ATTRIBUTE, QUALITY, FEATURE OF A MEDIUM/SUBSTANCE

The color of oxygen is blue.
I caught the smell of the mixture.

17. AN ATTRIBUTE, QUALITY, FEATURE OF AN OBJECT/EVENT

It was typical of a life there.
All this was symptomatic of the decay.
I like the smell of the fresh fish.

18. AN ATTRIBUTE, FEATURE OF A PERIOD OF TIME

He needs a day of rest.
Another year of famine, and they'll be gone.
You are giving him a chldhood of terror.
Teachers start their classes with a minute of silence.
The evening was an agony of waiting.

19. AN ATTRIBUTE, QUALITY, PROPERTY OF AN INDIVIDUAL

My uncle is a person of honor.
She is a woman of exceptional courage.
This woman of honor lived in the past century.
We need people of integrity like you.

20. A RESEMBLANCE, SIMILARITY

Swimming is more of a summer sport.
Build a business of your dreams.
It was more of a business translation than anything else.

21. A REDUCTION OF THE STATUS/CONTRADICTION

Those years mean that I am that much less of a sceptic.
I am not much of a line dancer.
He does not look the part of a fighter.

22. AN INTENSIFIED COMPARISON

That idiot of a driver did not stop.
He was a genius of a designer.
What a honey of a deal!

23. AN EVALUATION/APPRAISAL/OPINION

Very good of you to come.
Very nice of you to call me back.
It was stupid of me to think of them.
That was naïve of us.
It was cruel of her to treat him so.
Is it worthy of thought?
You are unconscious of what you lose.

24. AN ADVICE

Be wary of that acquaintance.
Beware of strangers in dark and unfamiliar places.
Think highly of her proposals.

25. AN ACCUSATION

She was convicted of conspiring.
They could not complain of us for that.
He was under suspicion of seditious activity.

26. A MEMBER OF A GROUP/INSTITUTION, ASSOCIATION

It was unexpected to all of us.
A patron of the library asked for advice.
He was the chairman of the Advisory Committee.
The voters of the city are uncertain about the taxes.
Many of his pupils work in this business.
One of us should go there again.

27. A CREED, BELIEF/VIEW

A man **of** this religion abstains from marriage.
They claim **to** speak for every person **of** faith.

28. A PERSON'S PROFESSION, OCCUPATION

She works as a teacher **of** biology here.
I was as an Assistant Professor **of** Russian.

29. AN ORIGIN, SOURCE/DERIVATION/BEING PRODUCED BY

Men **of** the North are special.
What are products **of** the vine?
Outside came the roar **of** planes.
The ringing **of** the bells reminds me of older days.
The risk **of** violence is not compensated.
Just think of the thrill **of** it all!

30. UNDERSTANDING/KNOWLEDGE/REMEMBRANCE

Few taxpayers are aware **of** this rule.
He accepted it in the same spirit, mindful **of** etiquette.
I have good memories **of** him and his family.
We learned **of** her sickness today.
He was abreast **of** the news.
John was thinking **of** me.

31. A CATEGORY, TYPE OF INFORMATION/GENRE

What kind **of** literature do we get?
After the lecture, I bought a book **of** songs.
He issued a new book **of** his poems.

32. A SOURCE OF INFORMATION

What I want to ask **of** you is this.
I asked all that **of** Carlo and his wife.
When asking questions **of** people, do it in a softened form.

One must not <u>beg anything of other people</u>.
He ignored <u>the plans of the leaders</u>.

33. A SPEECH ACT/COMMUNICATION

You have to <u>notify them of the delay</u>.
They <u>remind us of the schedule</u>.
It's hard to <u>convince you of that</u>.
She was <u>advised of the risks</u> of the surgery.
He <u>warned of something</u> but I didn't understand what specifically.
He <u>boasts of their adventure</u>.
You can <u>write of your childhood</u>.

34. A TYPE, KIND OF A DOCUMENT/CONFIRMATION, VERIFICATION

I was asked to send <u>certificates of birth and marriage</u>.
<u>A transcript of his academic record</u> was sent to Los Angeles.
<u>A statement of your account</u> will be issued in May.
<u>Records of our sales</u> are regularly issued.
You need <u>proof of residence and naturalization</u>.

35. A COPY, REPRODUCTION, DUPLICATE/REPLICA

He asked for that particular <u>picture of my family</u>.
He boasted of <u>having all the recordings of the singer</u>.

36. A FEELING/FAVORING, APPRECIATING/(DIS) LIKING

The parents <u>approved of this</u>.
Her father <u>disapproved of his drinking</u>.
Letters proclaimed <u>his hatred of technology</u>.
I am <u>an adherent of Verdi.</u>

37. A FEELING/AFFECTION

<u>Love of my son</u> was now the prime motive of my existence.
Her <u>love of horses</u> drives me mad.
<u>His adoration of her</u> was great.

38. A FEELING/CONCERN

Are you a little <u>jealous of a new baby</u>?
<u>His jealousies of other people</u> vanished.
I am <u>sick of all this ugly talk</u>.
He wondered <u>whatever became of her</u>.

39. A FEELING/BEING TERRIFIED

The government was <u>fearful of a drop</u> in productivity.
Overcome <u>your fear of public speaking</u>!
<u>Scared of stocks</u>?
He was <u>apprehensive of the imminent disaster</u>.

40. A STATE, CONDITION

I never <u>tire of tending</u> to my tulips.
He is <u>tired of working</u> day and night.
I am <u>sick of telling</u> you that.
He was <u>slow of speech</u>.
My vacation <u>was such a relief of burden</u>.

41. BEING CERTAIN, CONFIDENT/POSITIVE

I'm not so <u>sure of it.</u>
We have <u>no doubt of it.</u>
Are you <u>dubious of that</u>?
I call him to be <u>certain of his prospects.</u>

42. A POSITIVE ATTITUDE

They <u>have a love of learning</u>.
They <u>are respectful of the environment</u>
He <u>was</u> profoundly <u>wary of others</u>.
They <u>were</u> <u>supportive of his success.</u>
They <u>were</u> extremely <u>protective of her</u>.
My friends <u>are</u> very <u>considerate of me.</u>
She <u>was</u> too <u>respectful of her parents</u> to do it.
He is most <u>respectful of law and order</u>.

43. A NEGATIVE ATTITUDE

He was vain of his good looks.
Why are all of you so hard of hearing?
We suspected her of treachery.
He got sick of us.

44. A KIND OF BEHAVIOR

We never made an issue of it.
You don't know what's expected of you.

45. OBSERVING A RIGHT, A RULE, A REGULATION

In this street you, have the right of way.
Thom tells everyone what the right of way is.

46. A SEPARATION/RELEASING, RELINQUISHING

I've been relieved of my duties.
I got rid of my old books in March.
At last, he is rid of that nuisance.
They merely wipe their hands of the whole controversy.
How to let go of limitations?
You must let go of the past.
Let go of past regrets!

47. A FORCEFUL, VIOLENT SEPARATION

He was robbed of his watch.
The nation was robbed of its dignity.
I feel stripped of my right to be a kid.
He has been cheated of promotion.

48. MAKING FREE

Can they invent a simple device to relieve us of daily chores?
Is it possible to be cured of distemper?
Yet there is a way to relieve yourself of your anger.

Clear your yard of leaves.
Keep your drawers clear of old papers.

49. DEPRIVING

Don't drain the poor countries of their best brains.
We feel cheated of emotional satisfaction.

50. DEFICIENCY, ABSENCE

The teachers spoke about lack of interest.
I gave up the idea of buying a new house for lack of money.

51. A SPECIFIED TIME

It was five minutes of two.
They asked for some articles of recent years.
They might be called the most famous unknown of the century.
We arrived of an evening.

52. A SPECIFIED TIME AND LOCATION

Get together outside of work!
Use English outside of class, too!

53. A LOCATION/DIRECTION

Is Allentown west of New York?
The beach is a mile east of here.
South of the city is a nice plaza.

54. A DISTANCE/DEMENSION/SIZE, MAGNITUDE

The tower will be erected within a mile of the house.
For an animal like that, a depth of ten feet is not enough.

55. A CAUSE, REASON

Nobody has died of smallpox recently.

Hundreds of children <u>died</u> **<u>of hunger</u>**.
He got <u>sick because **of** you</u>.

56. A FUNCTION, OBJECTIVE

<u>Of</u> <u>what use</u> is this gadget?
<u>Of</u> <u>what purpose</u> is this statement?

57. AN ABILITY/SKILL

Is he <u>capable **of** lifting</u> 50 pounds?
We are <u>incapable **of** explaining</u> all the phenomena.

58. AN OBJECT AFFECTED BY AN ACTION

<u>Invasion **of** privacy</u> is out of control.
They provide <u>controlled practice **of** the structures</u>.
She knew nothing about the <u>learning **of** life's lessons.</u>
An advanced <u>learner **of** English</u> will do some extra work.
He had never been <u>an eater **of** sweets</u>.
<u>A one-day tour **of** the city</u> is quite enough.
An optician will <u>take care **of** your vision</u>.
She had little <u>control **of** her right hand</u>.
<u>Take charge **of** interviews</u> tomorrow.

59. A VALUE/BEING WORTH

I <u>asked</u> the saleswoman <u>the price **of** the toy</u>.
<u>The cost **of** living in California is too high</u>.

60. A METHOD OF DOING SOMETHING

Remember this graceful <u>way</u> I had **<u>of wearing</u>** my clothes?
Do you <u>know</u> <u>another way **of** doing</u> that?

Synonyms: *about, from, on, over.*
Antonyms: *0*

OFF indicates:

1.   MOVING FROM, AWAY

>   Come down **off** that ladder!
>   My niece fell **off** her bike.
>   Several boxes fell **off** the truck.
>   He has fallen **off** the roof or a horse.
>   The mirror fell **off** the wall
>   That man stepped **off** a safety island.
>   Go a few yards **off** the main highway.
>   Listen to the leaves falling **off** the trees.

2.   LEAVING A PLACE, LOCATION

>   He shambled **off** the room.
>   The squirrel hopped **off** the branch.
>   I jumped **off** my stool at the bar and ducked down.
>   This dress keeps sliding **off** the hanger.
>   Which way does the paper come **off** the roll?
>   He finally was **off** the sofa.
>   Get **off** the couch and into Club One Fitness!

3.   TERMINATING, STOPPING AN ACTIVITY/DESTROYING

>   Whole villages were wiped **off** the map.
>   The old version of the product rolled **off** the line.
>   They took her **off** the ventilator (in hospital).
>   Get **off** the phone, young lady!
>   He seemed ready to jump **off** a cliff just to fall in love.

4.   LEAVING THE WORKPLACE/NOT WORKING

>   I get **off** work at 5 o'clock.
>   He gets **off** work an hour early.
>   He said he is **off** duty on Wednesday.
>   She is **off** duty Fridays.

5. BEING RELIEVED FROM/GETTING RID OF

> It's **off** my mind now.
> You must marry her and take her **off** my hands.

6. REMOVING FROM A PLACE, LOCATION/TAKING AWAY

> They take criminals **off** the streets.
> I want to get that stuff **off** the premises.
> We must head them **off** the boats.
> He was taken **off** stage by paramedics.
> We can safely cross this visit **off** our list.
> I took the phone **off** the hook so that I could get some sleep.
> The district was lopped **off** their ruling.
> I'd give three years **off** my life if I could write that well.

7. WARDING AWAY, KEEPING AWAY/FENDING

> Please keep **off** the grass.
> Keep your dog **off** my lawn.

8. REMOVING FROM THE BODY

> She pulled the blanket **off** me.
> Take that wet thing **off** your head.
> The hairdresser took a little more **off** my top.
> Then he ripped his watch **off** his arm.
> Face aerobics will take years **off** your face.
> I can't take my eyes **off** her body

9. REMOVING FROM THE SURFACE

> Lift your legs quickly **off** the ground.
> I picked up the quarter **off** the sidewalk.
> She knocked the cup **off** the table.
> He grabbed the book **off** his desk.
> She took the quilt **off** the sofa.
> She whipped the cushion **off** the chair.
> She seized the kettle **off** the gas stove.
> Germs cannot be completely washed **off** china and silver.

She tore bed sheets **off** the mattresses.
He has torn uncancelled stamps **off** envelopes.
They ripped things **off** the ceiling.
I ripped the side branches **off** some sticks.
Wipe the dirt **off** your shoes.
She shook the rain **off** her raincoat.
He brushed a speck of dust **off** his hat.
The king dined **off** gold plate.

10. BEING *NOT* FAR FROM/IN THE VICINITY/CLOSE

He was born in a village **off** the main road.
She saw the Post Office not far **off** the road.
The show is in the International Center, just **off** 4TH Avenue.
Report what you see on and **off** the Avenue, OK?
The store is on Steiner Street, just **off** Broadway.
The Senior Center was just **off** Funston Street.
They saw him run in the alley **off** 12th Street.
I saw him at a furniture store **off** the freeway near my house.
The Opera House is just **off** the main square.
A whale is spotted **off** the starboard bow.

11. BRANCHING OUT FROM, EXTENDING

You can see three lanes **off** the highway.

12. STAYING AWAY/APART FROM

He could marry **off** America.
How to fend **off** an offensive joke?
Keep **off** the grass!

13. GIVING NO PERMISSION, NOT ALLOWING

Our interview was **off** the record.
Remarks and comments may be **off** record.

14. CHANGING THE DIRECTIION, COURSE/DEVIATING

I drove my car **off** the road.

Her car veered **off the highway**.
The streetcar went **off the tracks** again.
The train went **off the tracks** in May.
We seem to have <u>got</u> **off the straight track** somehow.
I apparently <u>was</u> **off course** driving at night.
If you stray **off course**, don't panic!
He's going **off course**, I am afraid.

15. BEING SEAWARD OF/AT SOME DISTANCE TO SEAWARD OF

It happened **off Cape of Good Hope**.
The ship was only <u>a mile</u> **off the coast.**
The cargo ship is <u>a mile and a half</u> **off that harbor**.
He was tossed by waves on a reef <u>a few hundred feet</u> **off shore.**
We found them <u>5 miles</u> **off the coast**.
Small boats appeared **off the city.**

16. AN ORIGIN/COMING FROM

The dissolved minerals in the oceans eroded **off the Himalayas**.
It's North America that 'came from elsewhere',
off Europe and Africa.

17. A SOURCE

I bought my car **off the showroom floor**.
Some customers walk in **off the street**.
The news would have to be **off the air**.
I should get the weather **off the web**.
You'll be able to order **off a menu**.

18. A SOURCE OF LIVING

I decided to live **off the land** like our ancestors.
Living **off my pension** is a challenge.
Few poets can live **off poetry**.
These birds live **off locusts and honey**.

19. TAKING ADVANTAGE OF SOMEBODY, SOMETHING

They have been making a huge profit **off** <u>me</u> for years.
Parasites <u>live **off** others</u>!
He lives **off** <u>his parents</u>.
States have taxed cigarettes and made millions
of dollars **off** <u>them.</u>

20. A SOURCE OF ENERGY

My portable TV works **off** <u>a car battery</u>.
He runs his lights **off** <u>a generator.</u>

21. CASTING LIGHT BACK

You can get sunburned from sun reflected **off** <u>sand</u>, snow and water.
The morning light glinted **off** <u>the facades</u> of the buildings.

22. EATING HABITS

Do you first bite **off** <u>the little narrow end</u> of the pear?
I <u>bit **off** the apple</u> only twice.

23. ABSTAINING, REFRAINING FROM

He went **off** <u>drugs</u>.
But is he's **off** <u>gambling</u>, though?
I want to lose weight, so I'm **off** <u>sweets</u> for a while.
Don't <u>skimp **on** the sunscreen</u>.

24. BEING NO LONGER IN CONTACT

I was **off** <u>connection</u> for a couple of hours.
Wait, she is **off** <u>the phone</u> now.
When I got **off** <u>the phone</u>, I felt relieved.
The phone <u>lay **off** the hook</u> near his table.

25. A NEGATIVE ATTITUDE

They <u>shrugged **off** his new Jaguar</u>.

What else did she <u>want **off** him</u>?
You do it <u>to keep me **off**</u> balance.

26. A STATE, CONDITION

It's one of <u>the **off**-price stores.</u>
<u>You're</u> a little flighty & <u>**off** your balance.</u>
<u>The kids are **off** school today.</u>

27. CHANGING A STATE/SITUATION

He was <u>**off** his game</u>.
He <u>went **off** the drugs</u>.
<u>I'll get **off** my butt</u> and go.
It'll <u>take the economy **off** the rocks</u>.
She tugged at my arm, <u>pulling me **off** balance</u>
It <u>carried</u> them clear <u>**off** their feet</u> with delight.
He was <u>placed **on** two years probation</u>.
<u>Put brakes **on** your emotions.</u>
<u>Get your life back **on** track!</u>

28. AN UNCOMMON, UNUSUAL STATE

They say you are <u>**off** the wall</u>.
His ideas are **off** the wall.
<u>Totally **off** the wall</u>, this wish made no sense whatsoever.
Some eccentrics might be <u>**off** center</u>.
Your sister <u>is **off** base.</u>

29. A LOWER PRICE, COST

I'll let you have the car at 10% <u>**off** the market price.</u>
You can buy it discount, a couple of dollars
<u>**off** the regular price.</u>
Take $5 <u>**off** the usual price.</u>

30. BEING ISSUED, PUBLISHED

His novel came **off** the press in November.
Jack's book on grammar will come <u>**off** the press</u> in May.

31. DISCLOSING A SECRET, TRUTH

Help blow the cover **off the latest threat** to the environment!
Her legend leaps **off the pages** of the books.

Synonyms: *from, beyond, close to, over*
Antonyms: *at*

ON indicates:

1. A LOCATION/BEING, STAYING IN A PLACE

See that dark line **on the horizon**?
Flowerbeds **on both sides** of the highway are well tended.
On each side of the lane there were bus stops.
The glass factory **on the edge** of town caught fire.

2. BEING AT A CERTAIN POINT IN THE SPACE

The Zoo entrance will be **on your left**.
The meadow is **on the right**, the grove **on the left**.

3. A GENERAL DIRECTION/PART OF THE WORLD

On the north there's a bridge, **on the south side**, a park.
Shall we sail **on the southerly course**?
His daughter lives **on** the East Coast, his son **on the West**.

4. BEING ON A LAND SURROUNDED BY WATER

He has an estate **on that island**.
The center of New York is **on Manhattan Island**.
An apartment **on Roosevelt Island** may cost $500 a month.

5. BEING IN THE MOUNTAINS

He lives in a cabin he built himself **on a mountain**.
Do you want a summer home **on Mount Shasta**?
There's a part **on Bear Mountain** that is especially romantic

6. BEING AT A BODY OF WATER

They swear they've seen you walk **on water.**
He dreams of <u>a house **on the lake.**</u>
There were disputes over <u>shipping **on the high seas.**</u>
The west end of the Panama Canal is **on the Pacific,**
and the east end is **on the Atlantic.**

7. BEING ASSOCIATED WITH A STREET/STREET NAME

Do you know that <u>store **on 19th Street?**</u>
Is the Club **on the same street?**
Public telephones are <u>located **on the streets, too.**</u>
The number 28 bus <u>stops **on** Taraval.</u>
In San Francisco, we <u>lived **on 44th Ave.**</u>
<u>Walking **on** Market Street</u> gives an idea
what downtown looks like.

8. BEING, STAYING IN THE VICINITY, NEIGHBORHOOD

A program includes skilled nursing and
<u>assisted living **on premises.**</u>
<u>Community **on campus**</u> is diminishing.
On the border you will pass by a village.
On the local level, some people take it seriously.
On lesser levels, we can relate to this dilemma.

9. BEING ATTACHED/BEING A PART

Learn to read <u>labels **on the items**</u> you buy.
Read the <u>instructions **on clothing tags**</u> first.
<u>Function keys</u> appear **on the menus.**
They changed <u>the legs **on four chairs**</u>

10. BEING ON A HORIZONTAL SURFACE/ON THE TOP/ABOVE

The snake lay **on the ground.**
I see my reflection **on the water.**
We were enjoying a few hours **on the beach.**
You see but few kids **on the playground.**

We were watching the signs **on highways**.
My skirt snagged **on the exposed tree roots**.
The topping **on your pizza** smells unusual.
You can smooth some paint **on canvas**.

11. BEING ON A VERTICAL SURFACE

That carpet is **on the opposite wall** now.
They will knock **on the door** of the store.
The flash **on the scoreboard** showed who won.
The door swung back **on its heavy hinges**.

12. BEING WITHIN

She stopped **on Chapter Two**.
Check your choices **on the form**.
The stress is **on the second syllable**.
Mark December 10th **on your calendar**.
Capitalize the D **on the word 'Disciples'**.
Check your answers **on page five.**
There are new names **on the list**.

13. A BASE, BASIS/FOUNDATION, SUPPORT/INTERIOR

We sat **on the armless chairs**.
I sleep under the covers with my head **on a pillow**.
I banged **on the desk.**
I didn't want him **on my doorstep**.

14. HAVING SOMETHING ON ONE'S BODY

It looks good **on you**.
Wear your ring **on your right hand**.
He did not have a gun **on him**.

15. POSESSING MONEY AT THE PRESENT TIME/FINANCIAL STANDING

Do you have any cash **on you**?
Jack had a couple of dollars **on him** at the time.

16. USING SOMEONE'S BODY FOR SUPPORT/REST

His head <u>rested</u> <u>on my shoulder</u>.
She insists on <u>sitting</u> <u>on her father's lap</u>.
<u>He was sound asleep</u> <u>on her lap.</u>

17. COMING, BRINGING INTO CONTACT/TOUCHING

She <u>planted a kiss</u> <u>on my cheek</u>.
A <u>pat</u> <u>on the back</u> is enough for her.
Her mother <u>patted</u> me <u>on the shoulder</u>.
He <u>puffed</u> <u>on his cigar</u>.
He <u>wiped</u> <u>his nose</u> <u>on his sleeve</u>.
She <u>wiped</u> her hands <u>on her skirt</u>.
<u>She wiped her hands</u> <u>on her thighs.</u>
He <u>heard a soft knock</u> <u>on the door</u>.
<u>Her mouth came down hard</u> <u>on his.</u>
<u>He stepped hard</u> <u>on the accelerator.</u>

18. ASSUMING A POSITION ON THE SURFACE

<u>On your mark</u>, get set, go!
They <u>congregate</u> <u>on the corner</u>.
She <u>knelt</u> <u>on the floor</u> by the tub.
He was <u>leaning</u> <u>on the chair</u>.
He put his head <u>on his pillow</u>.

19. MOVING IN THE DIRECTION

They decided <u>to march</u> <u>on the capital</u> in June.
<u>The march</u> <u>on Washington</u> is planned for January.

20. MOVING TO REACH A DESTINATION

She <u>stepped</u> <u>on the stage</u>.
We <u>walked out</u> <u>on the platform</u>.
My Dad <u>was</u> <u>on a trip.</u>
I decided <u>to go</u> <u>on a field trip</u> first.
<u>We are going</u> <u>on an adventure now.</u>
Agents <u>converged</u> <u>on his house</u> last week.

The coin landed **on** the sidewalk.
My eye falls **on** another picture.
The spotlight fell **on** the actor.
Try to land **on** your feet!
The cat gets **on** my lap.

21. AFFECTING THE WHOLE SURFACE OF AN OBJECT

The dust storm was **on** us.
The hurricane is **on** the village already.

22. PLACING/SETTING UP/STATIONING

Put the blanket **on** the baby.
Put the bins out **on** the curb once a week.
He threw the coin **on** the ground.
Sprinkle pepper **on** the meat!
Hang the towel **on** the hook.
I included tomatoes **on** my grocery list.
They put you **on** the waiting list.
I had to lay his tie **on** the line.
Write these words **on** your hearts.

23. A SOURCE OF LIVING/SUSTAINING LIFE WITH FOOD

Don't get hung up **on** feeding.
The longer babies feed **on** mother's milk, the better.
The crew ran out of food and subsisted **on** fish.
Thrive **on** a healthy diet of admiration honestly won!
Hawks thrive **on** other birds.
We got drunk **on** this wine.
He is drunk **on** wine.

24. A SOURCE OF LIVING/SUSTAINING LIFE WITH MONEY

Are you **on** a limited income?
Can you live comfortably **on** a such a salary?
Everyone will prosper **on** it.
I can live **on** $ 20 a week.
I had to get along **on** $5 a week.

25. A FUEL AS A SOURCE FOR RUNNING VEHICLES

The train <u>runs</u> <u>on diesel fuel</u>.
This car can run farther <u>on the other brand of gasoline</u>.
Not many automobiles <u>run</u> <u>on electricity</u> yet.

26. A WORKPLACE/FIELD OF ACTIVITIES

I <u>worked</u> <u>on a farm</u> last summer.
They cannot afford <u>to be</u> <u>on a jury.</u>
I didn't <u>see</u> him <u>on stage</u> lately.
Learn to <u>communicate</u> effectively <u>on the job</u>.
My students <u>are the best</u> <u>on this campus</u>.
Shall I <u>sacrifice fairness</u> <u>on the altar of science</u>?
She <u>sat in</u> <u>on major meetings</u>.

27. A TYPE OF AN INSTITUTION

Someone from <u>the American Society</u> <u>on Aging</u> left
a message for you.
For general information, call <u>the Department</u> <u>on Aging</u>.
She told me that she'd rather not <u>serve</u> <u>on the Committee</u>.
<u>There are nine judges</u> <u>on the Supreme Court.</u>
<u>A Coalition</u> <u>on Homelessness</u> project was started last month.
<u>The Commission</u> <u>on Teacher Credentialing</u> will decide it.
We need <u>members</u> <u>on our Board of Directors</u>.
She <u>serves</u> <u>on the Council of Directors.</u>

28. A STATUS ON THE JOB

I am <u>a baby-sitter</u> <u>on call</u>.
Is he still <u>a doctor on-call</u>?

29. A PLACE FOR TRADING, SELLING, SHOPPING

I decided <u>to take a chance</u> <u>on the stock market</u>.
There are <u>products</u> <u>on the market</u> that can control your hair.
Get <u>support</u> in the Word Processing Forums <u>on CompuServe</u>.

30. PARTICIPATING IN AN EVENT/SPECIAL TIME PERIOD

He went on the talk shows.
We will go on the auction block.
Ever since we met, my wife has been on a campaign.
The workers are on strike.

31. A LEISURE TIME, RECREATION/BEING AT REST

He had gone on a vacation.
She is on vacation this week.
Are you taking this book on vacation?
Is he on leave now?
She is on extended leave.

32. LABORING/DEALING WITH, HANDLING

I am working on an album of ballads.
They collaborate on a fictional novel.
They were collaborating on a piece of music.
No one in her office worked on the matter.
They work on multiple issues.
He has also worked on physical problems.

33. FIXING/ADJUSTING, REPAIRING

When will you work on our car?
Martin is working on the details now.
We will work on the yard.

34. A SOURCE OF KNOWLEDGE/ORIGIN

He draws on new material in this volume.
The speakers will draw on their 7-year experience in the field.
Did you catch it on the news last night?
They can access resources on any topic.
We'll reach our judgments on results.

35. CLARIFYING DATA, FACTS/REVEALING, MAKING KNOWN

Get information on that!
Provide information on the ethnic groups.
They have the latest news on medicines and techniques.
He can give us a prediction on technology.
The prognosis on debt sinks from 'stable' to 'negative'.
See below for details on how to claim your gift.
The book lifts the veil on that situation.
We'll let him in on the secret of how to sound smart.
I was suddenly clear on where I want to go.

36. A RECORD, PAPER, DOCUMENT, ACCOUNT

For documentation on how images were created,
see Appendix 1.
Provide a fact sheet on your program.
They checked out the prescriptions on her drugs.
Where is the practice material on American English?
Read numbers on public opinions.

37. A THEME, IDEA, TOPIC, POINT

I can write a book on anything in two weeks.
Videotapes on these subjects are very important.
More on the this diet you'll find on page two.
I must read up on cholesterol.
He reads tomes on medical history.
They speak out on issues that affect us all.
No one would elaborate on these differences.
It's the topic on which you may give advice to others.

38. A POINT/REGARDING, CONCERNING

On this question, history is mute.
Here is the deal on the application.
He tangles with thinkers on the question of ethics.
On home assignment, they were truly bridge-builders.
We got few answers on the repair of the computer.
He teams with John on the new set of bargains.

The book is vague on the subject.
We may phone on that tomorrow.
Hold off on mega-decisions just a bit longer.
We will challenge them on moral issues.
Similar patterns are evident on other issues.
More politics on that senator?

39. AN APPROACH, ATTITUDE TOWARDS *IN*ANIMATE OBJECTS

We took a position on ten propositions.
They took no position on the camera issue.
What's their policy on late work?
What do we know about their policy on donor organs?
We will follow up on any complaints or concerns.
The new study backs our stand on this.
They go easy on this case.
One of them was keen on the situation, too.

40. A PROBLEM/DILEMMA/LOST OPPORTUNITY

You may loose on that.
Calls from the public on complaints came the next day.
Two buildings fell short on security.
He missed out on a good party.
What's the rush on this?

41. COMMUNICATING/CONVERSING

Spread the word on the breast cancer to women of color.
They'll talk on perspectives of racism.
He narrates on Giotto marvelously.
Don't forget to compliment the host on the food.
I need you to elaborate on the advice you gave.
He quotes board members on the need to preserve the books.
I read the works of others and pontificated on them.
They dare to quibble on a couple of fine points.
He harps on everything negative.

42. A SPEECH FORM

I have a question on fire safety.
We can explain these questions on economics.
He gave a talk on first aid.
He'll be coordinating talks on health-related topics.
The report on the first item on the agenda was good.
We will report on these companies.
They reported on the conduct of the children.
I listened to the presentation on the device by the inventor.
They made an announcement on the sale of the company.
What are his critical remarks on the book based on?
He has no comment on the allegations.
His diatribe on the accident was articulate.
My recent column on the wonder and mystery was a success.

43. A GENRE/LITERARY FORM

I got top marks for my essay on wildlife.
It was a kind of satire on Nature.
It was a sermon on tolerance.
That story on beautiful women came from another source.
He will reveal inside stories on his family.
He mentioned an article on young writers.
We'll read this article on dolphins together.
You may search for rhymes on words here.
He gave feedback on a documentary TV Special.

44. ANALYSING, INTERPRETING, CLARIFYING

He wrote the book "Autopsy On An Empire".
Please give me some insight on this matter.
Secrecy is lifted on destroying chemical arms.

45. REGISTERING DATA/INFORMATION

She goes on the record.
This event is on record.
We have all the information on file.
All you could hear on playback was rushing water.

Best lectures are being <u>captured</u> <u>on</u> tape.
Can you <u>capture</u> the last moments of a person's life <u>on film</u>?
He minces no words <u>on paper</u>.

46. ASKING, DEMANDING/FORCING, PRESSING

Their <u>claims</u> <u>on the economy</u> were suspect.
Court rejected the immigrant's <u>plea</u> <u>on searches</u>.
Court rejects <u>the appeal</u> <u>on the eviction</u>.
The agency <u>bears down</u> <u>on the finance industry graft</u>.
She <u>grills him</u> <u>on the meaning</u> of his writing.

47. A GATHERING TO DISCUSS AN ISSUE/QUESTION

The group's <u>meeting</u> <u>on unemployment</u> is futile.
<u>A summit</u> <u>on voluntarism</u> is planned for June.
<u>A forum</u> <u>on the</u> language of Korea will highlight the event.

48. KEEPING INFORMED/BRINGING UP TO DATE

They <u>caught</u> my aunt <u>up</u> <u>on the news</u>.
Let me <u>catch</u> you <u>up</u> <u>on all the gossip</u>.
I <u>update</u> him <u>on our progress.</u>
Check Kate's door for a daily <u>update</u> <u>on her condition</u>.
Get<u> the latest</u> <u>on the scandal</u>.

49. A COURT PROCEDURE

The Court grants speedy <u>hearing</u> <u>on the veto</u>.
I wanted the committee's <u>hearings</u> <u>on</u> him open to the public.
Who'll testify at the Senate <u>hearing</u> <u>on welfare</u>?

50. A PURPOSE, AIM/MOTIVE OF AN ACTION

She is wanted <u>on charges of writing bad checks</u>.
He came to San Francisco <u>on a speaking tour</u>.
Her husband <u>went to jail</u> <u>on some financial matter.</u>
He's <u>leaving</u> <u>on a business trip</u> next Friday.
He was <u>booked</u> <u>on suspicion of murder</u>.

She had <u>to travel **on** business</u>.
I am here <u>**on** serious business</u>.

51. A REASON/CAUSE

Bonds <u>slide **on** budget fears</u>.
The ceremony was <u>cancelled **on** account of the downpour</u>.
The trip was <u>cancelled **on** account of the rain</u>.
He wasn't <u>tried **on** the other murder</u>.
She <u>faulted</u> for a moment <u>**on** the words</u>.

52. USING A TOOL, DEVICE

I don't <u>write</u> letters <u>**on** the Personal Computer.</u>
He <u>wrote the book **on** the computer</u>.
<u>Click **on** the icon with the mouse</u>.
I <u>clicked **on** the TV</u>.
<u>Step **on** the brake</u> after you release the gas pedal.
Who'<u>s **on** the switchboard</u> today?

53. USING MEANS OF COMMUNICATION—TELEPHONE

I was <u>talking</u> to him <u>**on** the phone</u>.
He <u>is **on** the phone</u> right now, please leave a message.
I'd rather not <u>discuss it **on** the phone</u>.
Promptly <u>reply **on** the telephone</u> when you get a message.
The driver was <u>chatting **on** the cellular phone</u>.
His secretary <u>buzzed him **on** the intercom</u>.
I'll go <u>call</u> them <u>**on** the hot line</u>.

54. A RECEPIENT OF THE CALL

He <u>called **on** her</u> but got no response.
I used <u>to call **on** Alex</u> often.

55. USING AUDIO-VIDEO MEDIA

I <u>saw her **on** television</u> last week.
<u>There are movies on wildlife **on** television.</u>
He <u>disclosed the details</u> of <u>her life **on** worldwide television</u>.

I've <u>seen commercials</u> for it <u>on</u> TV.
She wondered how she <u>looked on</u> TV.
He has been <u>featured on</u> TV movies.
Stay home and <u>watch it on the tube.</u>
<u>On</u> the evening news <u>on</u> channel 6, he quoted us.
We talked about the lack of <u>quality programming on cable.</u>
He <u>was different on</u> camera.
She might as well have <u>been on that show.</u>

56. USING MEANS OF COMMUNICATION—BROADCASTING

I heard big news <u>on the radio.</u>
We understand anger from callers <u>on talk radio.</u>
He could even <u>get Paris and Moscow on the radio.</u>
You <u>are on the air</u>, what's on your mind?
<u>This show</u> will <u>air on</u> ABC.

57. USING THE INTERNET, BEING ON-LINE/WORLD WIDE NET

They will hear <u>arguments on the Internet.</u>
You can <u>get this information on the Internet.</u>
I found the explanation <u>on the Internet.</u>
Try to find the answer <u>on Google.</u>
I <u>read</u> this story <u>on my e-mail</u>.

58. PLAYING A MUSICAL INSTRUMENT

He is <u>a jazz cat on saxophone</u> and <u>bass clarinet.</u>
He <u>blows on the old trombone.</u>

59. BEING AVAILABLE, OBTAINABLE, READY TO USE

We have plenty of envelopes <u>on hand.</u>
Keep spare batteries <u>on hand.</u>
They are always <u>on hand to help one.</u>
I have a great deal of information <u>on tap.</u>
We have too much work <u>on hand.</u>

60. A FINANCIAL DEPENDENCE

Not all of us <u>on welfare</u> are freeloaders.
People <u>on welfare</u> don't work because they lack skills.

61. A PREDICAMENT, STRAITS/CIRCUMSTANCE

Your marriage <u>is on shaky grounds</u>.
He was unemployed and <u>low on money</u>.
That's got to be <u>hard on her</u>.
It's really <u>hard on our mother</u>.
<u>Life on the edge</u> is the topic of the film.
<u>The oddities verge on flaws.</u>
Why are they <u>on the skids</u>?
The correspondent <u>stumped on that issue</u>.

62. AN INNER STATE OF A HUMAN BEING

He's always <u>on guard</u>.
His <u>hold on reality</u> was fragile.
She <u>is on her annual 'commitment' jag</u> again.
You're always happiest when <u>on the prowl</u>.
He has always <u>had a crush on her</u>.
The baby <u>is on the way</u>.

63. AN ACTUAL STATE/PARTICULAR SITUATION/STATUS

Everyone'<u>s on the move</u>.
The juvenile <u>lockup is still on loose</u>.
Now she <u>was on the run</u>, hiding out in LA.
We are adults and <u>we're on our own</u>.
All I could think of to do was <u>to stay on track</u>.
I <u>was</u> probably <u>on the right track.</u>
I <u>am a year</u> <u>behind on</u> home studies.
Words, like men, are ever <u>on the march</u>.
<u>The</u> new <u>technology is on display.</u>
Some pieces of <u>furniture are on order</u>.

64. A TEMPORARY CONDITION

> How long have they <u>been **on** strike</u>?
> He will <u>be **on** probation</u> for three years.
> The wedding <u>is **on** hold</u>, and so are the gifts.
> We appreciate your patience <u>while **on** hold</u>.
> The division <u>was **on** the defensive</u> on a wide front.
> The smoke means the car <u>is **on** fire</u>.
> How many buildings <u>are **on** fire?</u>

65. A CHANGE IN THE STATE/TRANSFORMATION

> He has <u>fallen **on** hard times</u>.
> You're <u>turning tradition **on** its head</u>.
> Some may have <u>to go **on** unemployment</u>.
> The chemical spill <u>put the city **on** alert</u>.
> I hope <u>to catch up **on** my sleep</u> next week.
> I <u>whirled **on** the class</u>.

66. A CURRENT STATE/PROCESS

> They <u>are **on** notice</u> now.
> The civilian jet <u>was **on** course</u>.
> She <u>is **on** the way home</u>.
> <u>**On** their way to class</u> they talked it over.
> I <u>was **on** the hunt</u> for compatible people.

67. A DECREASE/INCREASE

> Dog fights are <u>**on** the decline</u>.
> My fortunes were <u>**on** the wane</u>.
> The industry was <u>**on** the rise</u>.
> Eating disorder <u>is **on** the rise</u>.

68. A PSYSICAL STATE/MENTAL STATE

> <u>His insecurity verges **on** panic.</u>
> I was <u>chickening out **on** that</u>.
> Do you <u>get all tongue-tied **on** the terms</u>?
> Her eyes were flashing, she <u>seemed **on** fire</u>.

They are always <u>high **on** dope</u>.
He is **on** <u>drink</u> again.

69. AN EMOTION

<u>He knitted his brows **on** him.</u>
I <u>pride myself</u> **on** <u>being savvy</u> about wine.
Her parents <u>prided themselves **on** her joyful spirit</u>.
Please accept <u>my sympathy</u> **on** <u>the loss</u> of your beloved son.
There were <u>mixed feelings</u> **on** <u>the garbage contract.</u>
She <u>wasn't keen</u> **on** <u>going out</u> with a minister.
I think everybody <u>had a crush</u> **on** <u>her</u>.

70. A DESIRE, LONGING, WANTING

She was <u>intent</u> **on** <u>pursuing her career</u>.
He was <u>intent</u> **on** <u>finding a way out</u>.
Her eyes are <u>fixed</u> **on** <u>Broadway</u>.

71. AN AGE/CHANGING AGE

She <u>is</u> **on** <u>the young side</u>, but experienced.
She <u>was 29 going</u> **on** <u>30</u>.

72. HAPPENING VERY SOON/AT THE SAME TIME/IMMEDIATELY

On <u>arrival at the church</u>, they realized they were late.
On <u>reaching my office</u>, I went to the Fellowship Hall right away.
On <u>entering the barn</u>, I saw it.
Mom fainted **on** <u>hearing the news</u> from Dad.
As her ex-husband <u>says</u> **on** <u>his exit</u>, 'See you, honey.'
Some teachers prefer not <u>to correct</u> **on** <u>the spot</u>.
Results were not <u>available</u> **on** <u>the autopsy</u>.
Cash for your <u>pizza</u> **on** <u>delivery</u>.

73. A TIME/AN EXPECTED TIME FRAME/*AT* THE INDICATED MOMENT, INSTANT

I am always **on** <u>time for class</u>.
Be sure <u>to arrive</u> **on** <u>time</u>.

Here comes the train, <u>right **on** time</u>.

74. A TIME/AN INDICATED MOMENT

I asked her for <u>a kiss **on** our first date</u>.
<u>**On** dinner dates</u>, these problems always come up.
I can't work <u>**on** the night shift</u>.

75. A TIME/A WEEKDAY/A PARTICULAR DAY

She <u>stays </u>with us <u>**on** the days</u> when her mother works.
He would do it <u>**on** every occasion</u>.
I planned to do a lot <u>**on** the weekend.</u>
Is your routine the same <u>**on** weekends</u>?
What do you do <u>**on** Tuesday</u>?
The car broke down <u>**on** that day</u>.
Recently, <u>**on** a very hot day</u>, I saw a dog left in a car.
<u>**On** the very first day</u> of class I learned what it meant.
<u>**On** the same day</u> they arrived on time.

76. A HOLIDAY

We're are going to have our exam <u>**on** the 4th of May</u>.
What'll you do <u>**on** July Fourth</u>?
We usually get together <u>**on** Thanksgiving</u>.
Exchange presents **on** Christmas Day, never <u>**on** Christmas Eve</u>.

77. A PART OF THE DAY

I was reading <u>**on** a brisk fall evening</u>.
It happened <u>**on** a night</u> in November.
We'll have our meeting <u>**on** a morning</u> next week.
<u>**On** that morning</u>, I would cross into Texas.
The parcel was delivered <u>**on** a Monday morning.</u>
<u>**On** a gorgeous morning</u> like this, I am happy.
<u>**On** this May afternoon</u>, I met him.

78. A SPECIAL EVENT, HAPPENING/A PARTICULAR CIRCUMSTANCE

I <u>met</u> them <u>**on** only a few awkward occasions</u>.

He visited her on two occasions.
My teacher took up the matter with my mother
on open school night.
I entertain at home with no time limit on my parties.
She took her first flight on her 6th birthday.
At that time, we were on our honeymoon in Europe.
Congratulations on your graduation.
You expect justice on this trial?
He asked them to sit in on his photo sessions.
We went out to dinner on our wedding anniversary.

79. A POSSIBLE EVENT/PREPARING FOR AN EVENT

What's on the agenda?
Twelve topics will be on the program.
It is on the cards that he will win.
She keeps on schedule by skiing 10 miles a day.
Are you planning on being home?
When do they plan on going home?

80. BEING ON THE ROAD, TRAVELING/GOING THERE

We're going on an incredible journey.
On my last trip home, I decided to drop in.
We'll rent a van and go on one giant grocery trip.
I bought my dress on one frustrating shopping expedition.
He was out on a day hike, they're going on a hike, too.
You'll have lots of fun on this excursion.
What do you think of a romance on excursions?
She talked with me on her visit to New York.
On my visits to the office, I always asked about Jim.
Friday we will go on a retreat.
I hate going on picnics in the fall.

81. AN EVALUATION, ASSESSMENT

On average, delays are shorter.
On the whole the trip was a success.
We have been tested on basic English skills and civics.
I gave him a little test on literature.

You can <u>check</u> <u>on admission fees</u>.
We'll <u>check</u> <u>on</u> <u>that</u>!
He <u>did well</u> <u>on any assignments</u>.
We will <u>rank</u> her <u>on the IQ scale</u>.

82. INSPECTING

<u>One exam</u>, I think, I will <u>do OK on</u>.
She <u>got 92</u> <u>on the exam</u>.
How did you <u>do on your big math final</u>?
They love to put <u>"trick questions"</u> <u>on multiple choice-test</u>.
It'll help the students' <u>scores</u> <u>on examinations</u>.
<u>Scores</u> <u>on</u> written and oral <u>examinations</u>
may be standardized.

83. STUDYING, TAKING A COURSE

I need <u>to brush up</u> <u>on my mathematics</u>.
<u>A quiz</u> <u>on the talk</u> will be tomorrow.
It's <u>a workshop</u> <u>on cultivating mushrooms</u>.
They need <u>to bone up</u> <u>on that law</u>.

84. TEACHING, INSTRUCTING

I'll <u>give a briefing</u> <u>on what we've accomplished</u>.
She's <u>lectured</u> <u>on physics</u> at a State University.
He <u>lectured</u> <u>on topology</u> for a couple of years.
He has <u>consulted them</u> <u>on casino games</u>.
See <u>instructions</u> <u>on initializing</u> a hard disk.
We make the <u>courses</u> <u>on vital subjects</u> available to you.
The course offers <u>techniques</u> <u>on preventing injuries</u>.

85. LAYING DOWN A CONDITION, PROVISION

We would <u>help only</u> <u>on request</u>.
<u>On joining us, you can take advantage</u> of many bargains.
Your credit is <u>pre-approved</u> <u>on your first order</u>.
<u>On the chance she misses this column,</u> find it for her.

86. A MEMBER OF AN EXCLUSIVE GROUP

> They were proud of being on a team.
> My son-in-law is on the basketball team.
> Everybody on the team knew it.
> Now she is a nurse on the hospital staff.
> He is a veteran agent on the task force.
> She has been on the commission for 3 years.
> Three teachers are now on the staff.
> He was the kidnap specialist on the force.

87. RELYING/ADHERING

> Can I count on your vote next year?
> You can count on me.
> Don't get hung up on feeding.
> She depends on her friends.
> Don't get stuck on him, please.
> He has no hold on me.
> Choose a purpose and follow through on it.
> I feel so much on my shoulders now.

88. SUPPORTING, MAINTAINING FINANCIALLY

> I am living on a limited income.
> How to thrive on a limited budget?
> How to eat well on a small budget?

89. RESTRAINING, CONFINING

> Is there a time frame on this?
> The statute of limitations ran out on that.
> The cultural limitations placed on women are ridiculous.
> The first limit on the population of the city might be water.
> Restrictions on evictions apply only to seniors.
> We need stricter restrictions on gun sales.

90. REGULATIING, GOVERNING, CONTROLLING

> Legislation on environment covers the creation

of special areas.
Lawmakers propose a bill on Irish history.
They alter rules on welfare.
There are some rules on capital gains and losses.
The court is to rule on the fate of the president's aide.
The judge is expected to rule on the issue by Friday.
He defied the court order on tests.
A new strategy is needed in the war on drugs.
The government is getting tough on drugs.
The judge will get you on contempt of court.
The court system should be tough on criminals.

91. POSSESSING A MONOPOLY

Neither party has a corner on all the good ideas.
Writers, musicians, artists have a corner on creativity.

92. PREVENTING/FORBIDDING/TABOO

It was a permanent prohibition on corporal punishment.
A ban on some abortions is desirable.
He is delaying the ban on admissions preferences.
We could have a moratorium on legal immigration.

93. MAKING MISTAKES, BEING WRONG/LACKING, NEEDING

Make sure you don't miss out on this exciting offer!
They are missing out on their granddaughter.
I realize I miss out on all of the bonus merchandise.
But they miss out on the nuances.
I would miss out on a fulfilling relationship.
Is it fair that they miss out on all the fun?
We are low on paper towels.

94. A CHARACTERISTIC FEATURE, AN ATTRIBUTE

He had a quick mind, quick on the pickup
with puns and jokes.
I certainly love who he is on the inside.
He was weak on that.

Those who are <u>easy on the eye</u> aren't often seen here.
Are they <u>on the level</u>?

95. AFFECTING ONE'S BODY/INJURING

They examine estrogen's <u>effects on the skin</u>.
Tell about <u>the effect</u> of the eruption of
the volcano <u>on health</u>.
I bent down and <u>my back locked up on me.</u>
You know about <u>the effect of sugar on teeth</u>.
He came here to have <u>surgery on his nose</u>.
He <u>took a tight grip on her hand</u>.
She had <u>a deep cut on her leg</u>.

96. A CAUSE OF MISHAP

His baby <u>cut</u> her finger <u>on grass</u>, I believe.
The kid <u>cut</u> his foot <u>on the broken glass.</u>

97. AFFECTING ONE'S PERSONALITY NEGATIVELY

It can <u>backfire on us</u>.
Don't experiment <u>on</u> me any more.
That sound grated <u>on my nerves</u>.
His habits <u>get on my nerves</u>.
Memory <u>plays</u> strange <u>tricks on the heart</u>.
She <u>honed in on him again</u>.

98. AFFECTING SOMETHING BY AN ACTION/INFLUENCE

Who says we can't <u>improve on nature</u>?
By the time I <u>catch up on all those things</u>,
it will be May.
It'll <u>exercise an impact on everything</u>.
We try <u>to act on the abuses</u> in the area.
You have <u>to work</u> overnight <u>on it</u>.

99. TAKING FOOD/EATING HABITS

<u>Chew on this</u> a little.

Protect your teeth, don't chew on hard substances.
Nibble on fresh fruit instead of candy.
I was sitting munching on an apple.
We usually lunch on fruit.
They were feasting on buffalo, wild turkey and natural foods.
We feasted heartily on a veggie burger.
We lunched on a cheeseburger.
They might choke on something solid.
I survive on very little food.

100. (MIS) USING MEDICATIONS, DRUGS

I've had that patient on antibiotics for several days.
He overdosed on the prescribed drug.

101. PERCEIVING THROUGH THE SENSES

He gazed on the vista.
You can gaze on the scene, not me.
You get to listen in on the conversation.

102. A MENTAL ACTIVITY/REMEMBERING

He is always on my mind.
It will be on her mind forever.
I was gaining on him.
Reflect on everything that was positive
about the last year.
As I reflected on this, I realized he was right.

103. AN OBJECT OF CONTEMPLATING/THINKING

Looking back on it, I understood more of the problem.
Your mind is on higher things, like responsibilities.
Dwell heavily on your relationships.
He never dwelled on his suffering.
I meditated on his actions.
Speculations on the intelligence of mammals are
in the journal.
You'll find my musings on the origin

of the universe in the book.

104. EXPLORING, INVESTIGATING

There's not much <u>research **on** pollution</u>.
Actually there's some new <u>research **on** that</u>.
I've done no profound <u>research **on** this</u>.
<u>Studies **on** the effects</u> of the drug prove effective.
They presented <u>a study **on** deaths</u> from heart attacks.
For a decade he's <u>been **on** a quest</u> to find it out.

105. RATIONALIZING/A DEDUCTION, SUMMARY

Diners <u>decide **on** dressing</u>.
I'll get in touch with you so we can <u>decide **on** the time</u>.
<u>A decision **on** whether</u> he should go for broke was painful.
The teachers will <u>vote **on** a strike</u> tomorrow.
I know how <u>to get a grip **on** the problem</u>.
<u>Conclusions **on** the project</u> are to be made on Monday.
<u>He came **on** the answer</u> by accident.
I've <u>set my mind **on** that.</u>
We scheduled a meeting for final casting <u>approval
on a movie</u>.
I am <u>determined **on** a few alterations</u>.

106. PROVIDING ASSISTANCE

It has <u>worked **on** thousands of patients</u>.
She liked <u>to wait **on** some customers</u>.
They <u>make e-mail easier **on** the eyes.</u>
We cannot <u>close the door **on** needy people</u>.
I had <u>the door locked **on** them all.</u>

107. GETTING SUPPORT

You can get <u>help **on** the feature</u> you are using.
You need <u>help **on** this type of call</u>.
Companies nationwide get big <u>breaks **on** those fines</u>.

108. APPROVING/ACHIEVING AN ACCORD ON AN ISSUE

There is definite consensus on many points
A deal is reached on the salmon run.
They couldn't agree on the price.
All parties agree on the results of the studies.
They agree on the important issues.
They agree on everything, from politics to pumpkin pie.
All can agree on the answer to this question.

109. BEING *NOT* IN AN ACCORD/CONFLICT, DISPUTE

Two agencies are still apart on that issue.
We're split on the decision.
They were divided on the worth of X-ray screenings for us.
They clashed on news leak.
My parents can't agree on anything.

110. DEALING WITH FINANCIAL PAPERS, DOCUMENTS

I was late with a payment on my car insurance.
You could make a down payment on that car.
I get a bill for the insurance on the remains of my car.
She pays the insurance on his truck.
Rates on stocks and bonds changed dramatically.
These are great deals on used computers.
Great deals on casual and expensive looking apparel!
Checks written on his bank accounts he keeps here.

111. AN INCOME INCREASE/GAINING WEALTH

They make money on this.
They think they can make some money on it.
To save on costs, schedule your trip beforehand.
Save money on unnecessary repairs.
Cashing in on special offers is challenging.
We got a good buy on our boat.

112. A REDUCTION, SUBTRACTION

The child is not taxed on your gift.
They pay taxes on income after expenses.
Why must you pay taxes on funds that lose money?
She used him to pay the mortgage on her home.
You can cut back on your spending.
We can cut down on our use of water.
This measure has cut down on truancy.

113. BEING LOST, MISSING/MISSPENT

Some people think, youth is wasted on the young.
Some systems of work are wasteful on labor.

114. MISUSING, ABUSING MONEY

They blow this money on gambling.
She wastes her money on a lawyer.
You start maxing out on your credit cards.
Benefits are gambled away on the stock market.

115. GIVING FREE/TREATING AT ONE'S OWN EXPENSE/ONE WHO PAYS

Tonight dinner is on me.
I hope drinks will be on the house.
Well, free lunch will be on us.
Are the peanuts on the house, too?

116. BEING KNOWLEDGEABLE, EXPERIENCED, ADEPT

He's an authority on the French Revolution.
Become an expert on achieving positive results!
An expert on these techniques is needed ASAP.
The parents are the real experts on the child.
He called him his coach on the population issue.
He offers his own experience on ways to handle it.

117. A BELIEF/OPINION/CONSIDERATION

We don't know their views on public matters yet.
We'll provide a thoughtful voice on public policy.
There'll be an exchange of views on a variety of topics.
Artists offer a unique visual 'take' on the world.
There is no point in judging this art on its aesthetics.
Here are some of his thoughts on teaching music.
There could be no doubt on such a subject.

118. AN APPROACH, ATTITUDE TOWARDS LIVING BEINGS

I completely rest on him.
Peasants do have pity on the animals.
His actions haven't turned him off on politicians.
The attention he lavished on her was gratefully accepted.
Please go a little easier on the young people of today.
Make a business travel easier on your family.

119. A NEGATIVE ATTITUDE TOWARDS LIVING BEINGS

My curse will be on you.
He takes his wrath out on the people.
The idea of a revenge on him is absurd.
The teacher is much too easy on the boys.
This tone shouldn't be used on animals either.
I would've hung up on him and never seen him again.
Please don't fall asleep on me while I am talking to you.
Yet I have no wish to be hard on you.
He's been drawing on my credulity.

120. A MISTRUST

You are banking on him too heavily.
Would anything cast suspicion on her?

121. OBSERVING A RULE/VALUE

I bring up my children on this principle.
On my honor, it was so.

122. A NEGATIVE ATTITUDE TOWARDS OBJECTS

Several companies <u>were negligent **on** toxins</u>.
<u>Silence **on** this subject</u> is agreement with bigots.
Taking shots, the photographer <u>intruded **on** the ceremony</u>.

123. CRITICIZING, REPRIMANDING/CONDEMNATION

Did I <u>blame it **on** the dog</u>?
Can I <u>blame it all **on** the guy</u>?
Experts <u>blame rash **on** mushrooms</u>.
I <u>laid a guilt trip **on** him</u> for having neglected the rules.
They <u>blamed</u> the authorities <u>**on** impasse</u>.

124. MISLLEADING, DELUDING, DECEIVING, SWINDLING

This doctor <u>cheated **on** his clients</u>.
He <u>cheated you **on** this</u> several times.
<u>Cheating **on** the income taxes</u> is common practice.
How about <u>lying **on** a bank loan application</u>?
He was trying <u>to sell</u> <u>you **on** a proposition</u>.

125. A TYPE OF BEHAVIOR

The forts <u>opened up **on** the troops</u>.
Some people <u>model their lives **on** his</u>.
I am <u>trying my ideas out **on** my friends</u>.
You expect them <u>to back off **on** controls on guns</u>?
That experience made me <u>slow down **on** dieting</u>.
<u>I was now going **on** the defensive</u>.
They <u>played the same joke **on** him</u>.
He <u>tried the joke **on** me</u>.

126. A NEGATIVE BEHAVIOR

He is free <u>to cash in **on** his fame</u>.
She was <u>capitalizing **on** her tragic story</u>.
He <u>capitalized **on** the shortage</u> of essential commodities.
He could <u>eavesdrop **on** sensitive conversations</u>.
Her failure <u>to follow up **on** promises</u> frustrated us.

You may have <u>over-promised</u> <u>on that</u>.
He failed <u>to make good</u> <u>on his promise</u> to release us.
<u>Kids are going out</u> <u>on the edge</u> during this time of year.
He <u>closed the door</u> <u>on the achievement</u>.
He <u>overdosed</u> <u>on drugs</u> and died.
Some people <u>go</u> <u>on the offensive</u>.

127. AN AGGRESSIVE BEHAVRIOR/MISTREATING A LIVING BEING

Why do <u>they prey</u> <u>on kids</u>?
They <u>were defiant</u> <u>on captives</u>.
You don't <u>tell</u> <u>on friends</u>, right?
Her <u>playing pranks</u> <u>on him</u> was mean.
It means, in effect, <u>spying</u> <u>on people</u>.
I <u>was</u> too <u>rough</u> <u>on my brother</u> a week ago.
<u>Breathing garlic even</u> <u>on the enemy</u> is not nice.
She likes the boys but <u>picks</u> <u>on the girls</u>.
Some kids <u>pick</u> <u>on other children</u>.
She <u>is</u> <u>on me</u> like a tigress.
She <u>turns</u> balefully <u>on him</u>.

128. ATTACKING SOMEONE PHYSICALLY

The robber <u>clubbed her</u> <u>on her head</u>.
The dog <u>bit</u> the bull <u>on the nose</u>.

129. A VICTIM OF AN ATTACK

He ordered <u>the hit</u> <u>on her</u>.
<u>Attempts</u> <u>on her life</u> were numerous.
They <u>set</u> <u>on me</u> with daggers.
He is in jail for <u>the attack</u> <u>on his rival</u>.
The rate of <u>assaults</u> <u>on women workers</u> is high.
The army <u>advances</u> <u>on the rebels</u>.
A lion <u>pounces</u> <u>on antelopes</u>.
A cat <u>pounces</u> <u>on mice</u>.

130. AN OBJECTIVE/REACHING AN OBJECT

You are <u>right</u> <u>on target</u>.

A reconnaissance run was <u>made **on** each target</u>.
<u>The raid **on** the police station</u> started in the daytime.
<u>The attack **on** the building</u> was ineffective.
<u>To get in **on** all prizes</u>, you need to be 18.
They <u>concentrated fire **on** the beaches</u>.
They marched <u>**on** my city at dawn.</u>
Don't <u>trample **on** our soil</u>!

131. A GUIDANCE/RECOMMENDATION/WHAT IS RECOMMENDED

Get <u>tips **on** how to do it!</u>
Here are <u>the tips **on** getting the most of your trip.</u>
Learn <u>the tips **on** applying make-up</u>!
I always give <u>advice **on** that</u>.
Get <u>advice **on** love</u> in general!
Get <u>advice **on** buying your car</u>!
Who <u>advised you **on** that</u>?

132. PAYING A SPECIAL ATTENTION/WATCHFULLNESS

<u>Shower praise **on** the bride!</u>
<u>Be **on** the lookout for moles</u>!
<u>Concentrate **on** pleasing yourself.</u>
<u>Work **on** healing rifts in the family</u>!
Somebody will <u>keep an eye **on** the old woman.</u>
He wants <u>to spend</u> more <u>time **on** his music.</u>
<u>Emphasis **on** trade espionage</u> is the key issue.
Always <u>focus **on** one idea!</u>

133. A MANNER OF DOING THINGS

<u>Meeting him **on** a blind date?</u>
They have <u>acted **on** conviction.</u>
He was <u>released</u> early <u>**on** parole</u>.
Please <u>help me **on** ways to stop it.</u>
The village can be <u>reached **on** foot</u>.
They <u>did</u> the window <u>repairs **on** the cheap.</u>
He rides up to the bar and <u>drinks **on** horseback</u>.
Stocks ended up <u>**on** a positive job report</u>.
<u>His mother raised him **on** her own.</u>

This thing worked on paper only.
Fold the paper on the diagonal!
It's best to finish on a high note.
I wrote to you on the chance.

134. AN INAPPROPRIATE, UNDESIRABLE MANNER OF DOING THINGS

They did it on purpose, I know.
Kids are often unable to behave on reason.
Never buy things on impulse!

135. A METHOD OF DOING THINGS

Students are admitted on grades.
The trains will operate on regular schedules.
His tragedy is written on the model of Greek plays.
I've lost weight on bacon and eggs for breakfast.
I bought the piano on credit.

136. BEING (IN)DEPENDENT

He did all the work on his own.
The niece lives on her own.
Acting on her instructions was an ordeal.

137. REPEATING AN ACTION/EMPHASIZING

I heaped error on error at that time.
We listened to the news every hour on the hour.

138. MEANS OF TRANSPORTATION/CONVEYANCE

I've flown on a plane many times.
I am going to put you on a plane.
But I can't sleep on the plane.
I see him on the planes sometimes.
He made journeys on horseback.
They went on the train to San Francisco.
We sometimes ride there on a train or bus.
Usually I'm reading or writing on the bus.

He goes to work on the bus.
He sent a messenger on a bicycle.
I go on board tonight for India.
All the passengers are on board now.

139. BEGINNING DOING SOMETHING

They will go on duty soon.
This policeman goes on duty at four o'clock.
Start on your new career today!
We'll go right on doing what we normally do.
There is exultation in starting off on a new life.
He set off across Europe on a passionate adventure.
She embarked on her memoir of him.

140. CEASING, TERMINATING, DISCONTINUING

I give up on sleep in the tent tonight.
She had almost given up on his sense of humor.
We have given up on freedom then.

Synonyms: *about, into, upon, against, near, over, above*
Antonyms: *off, out*

ON TOP OF indicates:

1.   BEING AT THE UPPERMOST LEVEL

When he proposed, she was on top of the world.
I bought her a puppy, and she was on top of the world.

2.   AN ADDITIONAL CIRCUMSTANCE/FOLLOWING CLOSELY

On top of all his troubles, he had an accident last week.
Her illness came on top of her bitter disappointment in him.
On top of everything, she broke her leg in May.

3.   BEING IN CONTROL/FULLY INFORMED ABOUT

My husband <u>is</u> always <u>**on top of** all political events</u>.
When asked about the new project, he <u>was **on top of**
the situation</u>.

Synonyms: *above, beyond, over*
Antonyms: *down*

ONTO indicates:

1.   EMPHASIZING THE IDEA OF MOVING TOWARD A PLACE

He <u>walked **onto** the platform</u>.
We all hopped <u>**onto** the train</u>.
They don't want our truck <u>pulling **onto** the property</u>.
He <u>drove **onto** the sidewalk</u> incidentally.
My <u>room opens **onto** a</u> large <u>balcony</u>.
The girl <u>is jumping **onto** the chair</u>.
The cat <u>leaps **onto** my shoulder</u>.
The baby stirred gently and <u>shifted **onto** his side.</u>
Once more, <u>**onto** the beach</u>!
The electrician <u>climbed **onto** the roof</u>.

2.   EMPHASIZING THE IDEA OF PLACING AN OBJECT IN A PLACE

<u>Tie cans **onto** the back bumper</u> of the getaway car!
The bull <u>slammed him **onto** his back</u>.

3.   EMPHASIZING THE IDEA OF STAYING IN THE SAME STATE/SITUATION

The dog <u>hung **onto** that bull</u> for a few seconds.
She steadfastly <u>held **onto** her privacy</u>.
His efforts to <u>hold **onto** adolescence</u> were ridiculous.
We both <u>hung **onto** our commitment</u>.

4.   INSTILLING, IMPLANTING, FORCING IDEAS

She hadn't <u>imposed her definition of a good life **onto** me</u>.

Parents often try <u>to ingrain their ideas **onto** their kids</u>.
<u>Please pass it **onto** your folks.</u>

5.   BEING INFORMED, AWARE OF

We <u>were **onto** that group</u> since October.
The police <u>are **onto** that gang</u> about the missing money.
The authorities <u>were **onto** the opposition's plans</u>.
I <u>am **onto** his tricks</u>.

Synonyms: *on, in, into*
Antonyms: *from*

OPPOSITE indicates:

1.   BEING ON THE OTHER SIDE, ACROSS/FACING

<u>There is a mirror **opposite** the door.</u>
Our house <u>is **opposite** the theater</u>.
<u>Park your car **opposite** the gate!</u>

2.   PLAYING ROLES IN A SHOW TOGETHER

He <u>played **opposite** her</u> in many films.
She used<u> to play **opposite** many celebrities.</u>

Synonyms: *across, facing, with, contrary*
Antonyms: *next to*

OUT indicates:

1.   MOVING OUTSIDE

He <u>fell **out** the window</u>.
They just <u>leaned **out** their windows</u> as if watching
the late show.
He <u>peered **out** the window</u>.
She <u>raced **out** the door.</u>
Every time we <u>walk **out** the door</u>, the cat follows us.

He <u>strode **out** the door</u> without saying anything.

2.   PLACING AN OBJECT, A PERSON OUTSIDE

<u>Toss your book **out** the window!</u>
The worst they can do is <u>to</u> <u>escort us **out** the front door</u>.

3.   BEING, STAYING OUTSIDE, AWAY

<u>**Out** this door is</u> the orchard.
<u>**Out** his home</u> he stepped into the world.

Synonyms: *away from, from, out of*
Antonyms: *in, inside*

OUT OF indicates:

1.   MOVING OUTSIDE FROM INSIDE AN ENCLOSED SPACE AT A GIVEN
     MOMENT

I saw a fox <u>coming **out of** the wood</u>.
One boy <u>storms **out of** the room</u>.
<u>The girls filed **out of** the room</u>.
I <u>ran **out of** his office</u>.
She <u>walked **out of** her parents' house</u>.
In a minute he <u>was **out of** the house</u>.
Stiffly, Mom <u>got **out of** the car</u>.
A guy <u>leaned **out of** his car</u> and asked me something.
<u>Tears sneak **out of** my eyes.</u>
The words tumbled **out of** her mouth in a flood
of stammering.

2.   MOVING AWAY/BEYOND/OUT OF SIGHT

<u>Get **out of** here!</u>
He <u>stepped **out of** the shadow</u>.

3.   LOOSING ONE'S FOOT/DROPPING

He fell **out of** a tree and broke his neck.
I rolled **out of** bed.

4.   LEAVING FOR A PERIOD OF TIME

He moves **out of** her parents' home.
I moved **out of** my mother's house and back in again.

5.   AVOIDING

Try to stay **out of** debt.
They tried to get **out of** jury duty.
Stay **out of** the sun from 10 am to 2 pm.
Stay **out of** debt for the rest of your life!
He will stay **out of** trouble.
It gets you **out of** trouble.
How will I ever get **out of** this?

6.   ESCAPING/BREAK OUT/EVASION

I would sneak **out of** bed at 6 o'clock in the morning.
He managed to sneak **out of** town.
Let's get **out of** the wind and rain.
Take anxiety **out of** stressful encounters!
I've been trying to stay **out of** petty office politics.
Things fly **out of** control.
Crime has shot **out of** control.

7.   GETTING FREE, FREEING

I extricated myself **out of** the tangled seaweed.
DNA testing has sprung innocent people **out of** jail.
I squirmed **out of** his arms and pushed him away.

8.   QUITTING

Why do the people drop **out of** exercise programs?
The youngster wanted **out of** 11th grade.

To back **out of** the menu, press Escape.

9. PLACING, POSITIONING OUTSIDE/AWAY

Empty the oatmeal **out of** the packets.
Don't toss cigarette butts **out of** the car window.
She put the toy away, **out of** his reach.
I wanted to keep emotions **out of** my heart.

10. REMOVING USING FORCE/WITH EFFORT

They were bombed **out of** the their cities.
The dog took a bite **out of** an angry bull just
in time to save her life.
She ripped the sheet **out of** my hands.

12. BEING AWAY/STAYING OUTSIDE A CLOSED SPACE

I was, alas, **out of** town.
She was **out of** the country at that time.
We'll be **out of** the office this afternoon.
He called me once when I was **out of** the house.
Kids don't stay too often **out of** doors at this time.
I was **out of** doors when it rained.
His head stuck **out of** the blankets.
One hand was clutchng a teddy bear,
the other hanging **out of** the bed.

13. BEING BEYOND THE BOUNDARIES, LIMITS

It's a snapshot, a little **out of** focus.
She was already **out of** sight, **out of** hearing.
It was **out of** the question.
Those sentiments sounded **out of** place.
The results will be **out of** this world.

14. STAYING INSIDE, NOT LEAVING

She works **out of** the main office.
He worked **out of** his home.

15. BEING ABSENT/PLAYING TRUANT/DISMISSING

> The kids <u>were **out of** school</u> for three days.
> If you miss your class four times, <u>you'll be **out of** class</u>.

16. GRADUATING FROM A SCHOOL

> We plan to be married once <u>we are **out of** college</u>.
> She'll move to Mexico as soon as she <u>is **out of** college</u>.
> My cousin is just **out of** law school.

17. USING UTILITIES FOR TAKING FOOD, DRINK

> They will <u>drink only water **out of** a cup</u>.
> I can't <u>drink **out of** a dog dish</u>.

18. A PARTICULAR STATE, CONDITION/CURRENT SITUATION

> He's <u>been **out of** work </u>for two months.
> I <u>am **out of** practice</u>.
> Good manners never <u>go **out of** style</u>.
> Your skirt <u>is **out of** fashion</u>.
> The fire was extiguished, we <u>were **out of** danger</u>.

19. PSHYCHOLOGICAL STATE/STRONG EMOTION

> She <u>is **out of** her mind</u> with grief.
> The guy is <u>bored **out of** his mind</u>.
> She <u>is **out of** touch with reality</u>.

20. BEING IRRITATED/FRIGHTENED

> Loud noises made me want <u>to jump **out of** my skin</u>
> <u>My heart was about to burst **out of** my chest</u>.
> I lay still <u>scared **out of** my wits</u>.
> You used to <u>startle the daylights **out of** me</u>.
> She was <u>shocked **out of** a passive trance</u> back
> into reality.

21. CHANGING THE STATE/SITUATION

I was coming **out of** a dream and in a half awake state.
She woke **out of** a sound sleep.
Did they fall **out of** love?
His mind ran **out of** control at once.
Snap **out of** it! Get back to reality!

22. CHANGING PEOPLE

Make honest people **out of** yourselves.
He will make positive thinkers **out of** them.
His music charmed his listeners **out of** themselves.

23. PERSUADING

You can't knock it **out of** him.
It's wasted time to try to argue her **out of** her illusion.

24. HAVING NO MORE/LACKING/ABSENCE

He was **out of** fresh fruits and vegetables.
You're **out of** bread and milk and the lettuce is wilting.
Why do I keep getting "**Out of** Memory" messages?
I am **out of** ideas.

25. A MISHAP/GOING WRONG/NOT FUNCTIONING PROPERLY

The plane went **out of** control.
The elevator is **out of** service today.
But it's way **out of** whack.

26. A MATERIAL FOR MAKING A PRODUCT/CARVING

We made two castles **out of** sand.
I used to carve figurines **out of** bark.
The dress is made **out of** wool.

27. AN ORIGIN, SOURCE

He made extraordinary stories **out of** ordinary lives.

Come learn how <u>to get more **out of** your life</u>.
You walk out of the theater wondering if people
<u>got more **out of** the movie</u> than you did?
<u>Get the most **out of** every meeting!</u>
He had learned <u>to gather facts **out of** the newspapers</u>.
I <u>got</u> <u>little **out of** him</u>, he struck me as stupid.

28. A CAUSE/REASON

He <u>did it **out of** ignorance</u>.
She <u>did it **out of** a desire</u> to re-shape her garden.
<u>I held my bouquet up high **out of** a fit of shyness.</u>
She agreed <u>to meet him **out of** courtesy</u> to her friend.
I am <u>acting **out of** respect</u> for their moral values.
Out of <u>anger</u> I do everything I can to frustrate him.

29. CHOOSING, PICKING, SELECTING

<u>Take any ten paintings **out of** twenty.</u>
<u>Two **out of** three votes</u> belong to elderly people.
Those are just <u>two guys **out of** hundreds</u>.

30. DEPRIVING SOMEONE

They've <u>cheated me **out of** promotion</u>.
He <u>cheated her **out of** her money</u>.

31. A WAY, MANNER OF DOING THINGS

His mother <u>bore him **out of** wedlock</u>.

32. A FRACTION/RATIO

You <u>scored seven **out of** ten</u>.
I <u>got 80% **out of** the answers correct</u>.

Synonyms: *from, from inside, from within, from out,
of, beyond, outside, without*
Antonyms: *into, in, within*

OUTSIDE (OF) indicates:

1. BEING ON THE EXTERIOR/NOT WITHIN

> My dog is never **outside** the house.
> We <u>saw someone **outside** the window.</u>
> I want <u>to see him **outside** the office</u> someday.
> He didn't <u>work **outside** the home.</u>
> <u>**Outside** my window,</u> the street lies empty.
> <u>Beneath the hills **outside** of Rome</u> galleries
> have been tunneled through rock.

2. BEING BEYOND THE LIMITS

> <u>Find some little place **outside** the city.</u>
> <u>Nothing lies **outside** the margin of error.</u>
> Some people <u>exist **outside** the social contact.</u>
> They should <u>say no to sex **outside of** marriage.</u>

3. BEING EXCEPTIONAL, EXCLUSIIVE

> **Outside of** Thursday, I won't be free any day this week.
> They had <u>no other information **outside** these statistics.</u>
> He <u>has no interests **outside** his hobbies.</u>

4. MOVING FROM THE INTERIOR TO THE EXTERIOR/FORTH

> When the dog <u>gets **outside** the fence,</u>
> he tries to chase cars.
> That stuff <u>goes **outside** the door.</u>

5. PLACING SOMEWHERE

> <u>Push the reader further **outside** the story.</u>
> Encourage her to <u>get **outside** her sense of guilt.</u>

> Synonyms: *over, beyond, except, but, besides*
> Antonyms: *inside*

OVER indicates:

1. BEING EVERYWHERE

   Lakes are <u>scattered **over**</u> Finland.
   Males <u>were wearing baseball caps all **over** the place</u>.
   There are <u>books all **over** the house</u>.
   Quiet finally <u>settles **over** the room</u>.
   A hush <u>falls **over** the crowd</u>.

2. BEING ABOVE

   A hang-glider is <u>flying **over** the sea</u>.
   The typhoon <u>lost force **over** the North Pacific</u>.
   <u>The sun was almost **over** the horizon.</u>
   <u>See the moon **over** Coit Tower?</u>
   <u>The moon is peering **over** the hills.</u>
   <u>The sign **over** the door</u> is gone.
   There is <u>a light **over** his desk</u>.
   <u>The song was **over** the heads of the listeners.</u>

3. BEING AT A HIGHER LEVEL/VERTICALLY HIGHER THAN

   Two towers <u>projected **over** the street</u>.
   <u>The water was **over** my shoulders.</u>
   The Great Pyramid is still <u>towering **over** the desert</u>.

4. PROTRUDING, OVERHANGING/COVERING AN OBJECT

   He <u>bent</u> slightly <u>**over** his car</u>.
   He <u>stooped **over** his car</u> slightly.
   I expect three meals a day and a <u>roof **over** my head</u>.
   <u>The barge struck the bridge **over** the Mississippi.</u>
   In the spring the honeysuckle <u>droops **over** the hillside</u>.
   Both of them <u>were bent intently **over** the chess board</u>.
   I <u>fell asleep **over** my book.</u>

5. BEING ON THE SURFACE/COVERING AN OBJECT

   <u>A mask **over** his face</u> indicated his intentions.

I smooth makeup over the fine lines to hide my age.
Did you have a net over your hair?
Jack wore a warm jacket over his shirt.
See the green leaves strung over the door for luck?
The cursor is over the button labeled 'Tutorial'.

6.   BEING ON THE OTHER SIDE, ACROSS/OUTSIDE, BEHIND

I'll choose a little town just over the border.
Can you see a village over the border?

7.   FACING/BEING OPEN TO

The room looks over the park.
I had a room looking over a courtyard.
Sitting over the campfire, they sang old ballads.

8.   MOVING ALONG/HERE AND THERE

I'll walk all over this floor leaving marks on it.
He walked over the grounds.
Your dog is walking all over the neighborhood again.
He roamed all over the world for many years.
She traveled all over Africa.
They chased that car over the freeways.

9.   MOVING THROUGHOUT/FROM ONE END TO ANOTHER/ACROSS

The letter was sent over a long distance.—no over?
We strolled over the Golden Gate Bridge on Sunday.
Go over the railroad tracks to the highway.
We head back home over the Noe Hill.
The road over the hills passes between corn fields.
We have to hike a mile over the hill.
We walked our dogs over the hill.
Strange lights appeared over certain locales.
Many over-the-counter remedies are available
in drug stores.

10. MOVING ABOVE/ABOVE AND DOWN

He hovered over an abyss.
The kid tripped over his toys.
The dog jumped over the fence.
He leaped over the bushes.
The ball fell over the cliff.

11. PLACING SOMETHING ABOVE/ABOVE AND DOWN

Hang it on a line over the dish-drainer to dry.
They installed some cabinets over the counter.
A plate shelf over the window was added later.
He tossed the tough end over his shoulder.

12. PLACING ON THE SURFACE/COVERING/HIDING

He stroked a hand over a shiny little car.
She put her hand over her mouth.
He put a hand over hers and waited.
He put his hand over my eyes.
I held my finger over the edge of the letter.
Put a coat of varnish over all woodwork.
He threw a shawl over her shoulders.
Throwing the blanket over the dog's face will help, too.
Put the new tablecloth over the table!
Put some rocks over the cave entrance.
Put your cursor over the icon.
They put a veil over this dismal case.

13. OBSERVING, VIEWING SOMETHING ABOVE THE LEVEL

She was looking at me over her glasses.
He peered gravely over the broad rims of his glasses.
She gave me a grin over her glass.
The papers on your desk get so high that you can't see
over them anymore.
In the picture, my face is just visible over her shoulder.
Open the windows and look out over the rooftops.
I can't see over the wall.

She glanced at it **over** the top of a twin sheet.
I glanced **over** my shoulder once again.

14. PREPARING MEALS ABOVE THE SOURCE OF HEAT

She will be cooking it **over** a campfire.
It's a pot for cooking beans **over** the flames
in the fireplace.
Cook beef **over** low heat for an hour!
Heat oil **over** medium heat until hot.
I first melt chocolate **over** hot water.

15. AN AGGRESSIVE BEHAVIOR/PHYSICALLY ABUSING, INJURING

They dumped a pot of glue **over** his head.
Hitting the dog **over** its head, isn't it disgusting!

16. SCRUTINIZING/CHECKING, EXAMINING, INSPECTING

He ran his eyes unwillingly **over** the letter.
They went **over** the proposition with him.
She goes **over** his homework with him.
Jack went **over** all the examples I used.
Look **over** your corrected papers.
I've looked **over** your report.
We looked **over** the features of the new car.

17. A MENTAL ACTIVITIY/MUSING, CONTEMPLATING

They said they'll think **over** my advice.
I sat ruminating **over** his rebuff.
They puzzled **over** such things as eclipses.
Concentration is difficult as you mull **over**
a weighty issue.
He was wistful **over** a treasure like this.

18. REFRENCE TO AN OBJECT OF INTEREST/REGARDING, CONCERNING

He filed a grievance **over** the firing.
They'll sue the company **over** an oil pipeline

Cabbies <u>strike **over** proposed rules</u>.
They <u>resign **over** the crisis</u>.
They <u>lose the fight **over** donations</u>.
The current <u>rage is **over** children</u> and <u>smoking</u>.
We have to have another <u>meeting **over** the budget</u>.
<u>Questions arose **over** whether he moved too quickly.</u>
They loose <u>the verdict **over** the deal.</u>
The government <u>punishes companies **over**</u>
<u>ecological abuse.</u>
<u>The deal collapsed **over** money.</u>
They denounce the <u>delay **over** our plan</u>.
Few people were <u>losing sleep **over** the news</u>.
Do you sometimes <u>scratch your head **over**</u>
<u>this statement?</u>
They <u>cry foul **over** the rules change.</u>

19. PROVIDING AN ADVICE

<u>Don't cry **over** her singing.</u>
Don't <u>get paranoid **over** polite questions</u>.
<u>Talk **over** you questions</u> with your parents.
But don't <u>worry **over** this overmuch</u> because
it never ends.
Don't <u>go gaga **over** rutabaga</u>.

20. A TOPIC OF COMMUNICATING/SPEAKING

He <u>talked **over** some point</u> of the music program.
To <u>say prayers **over** him</u> was not easy.

21. AN OBJECT OF AN OPINION, IDEA, ASSUMPTION, CONSIDERATION

Different <u>views **over** whether to ban it have opened</u>
<u>a new forum in the debate **over** censorship.</u>
We expressed <u>disbelief **over** his alleged involvement in that</u>.

22. AN APPROACH, ATTITUDE

His mother <u>doted **over** him</u>.
He <u>knitted his brows **over** this difficulty</u>.

<u>Concern **over** a shift</u> in view brought
the market off its high.
We share your <u>concerns **over** the jokes</u> he made.
He <u>is nuts/crazy **over** her.</u>

23. BEING SPLIT, IN DISCORD/OPPOSITION/AN OBJECT OF CONFLICT

They found themselves in <u>disagreement **over** the details</u>.
The most important <u>divide is **over** ways of worship.</u>
<u>The controversy **over** the picture</u> attracted our attention.
We <u>differ **over** ways</u> to reach the clients.
They <u>argue **over** a controversial law.</u>
There has always been <u>an argument **over** methods</u>.
Kids <u>forked **over** money</u> for their driver's ed lessons.
<u>The debate</u> <u>is **over** who shall have access</u> to it.
We've <u>broken up several times **over** this.</u>

24. A STRONG DISAGREEMENT ABOUT AN OBJECT

Mom was sick of <u>fighting</u> with me **over** <u>every outfit</u>.
There was <u>a battle **over** the old site.</u>
They <u>battle **over** whether it should be up or down.</u>
<u>The battle **over** art</u> would not be <u>fought **over** content</u>.
Are you always <u>struggling **over** money</u>?

25. AN OBJECT OF A POSITIVE EMOTION

We all are <u>enthusiastic **over** these prospects</u>.
They <u>rejoiced **over** a good hunt</u> and bountiful harvest.
People were <u>jubilant **over** the successful test</u>.
Girls were <u>giddy **over** movie stars</u>.
My husband <u>raved **over** lamb shanks</u>.
They <u>go into ecstasy **over** artichokes</u>.

26. AN OBJECT OF A NEGATIVE EMOTION

They are <u>angry **over** the new taxes</u>.
<u>Passions flare **over** that case.</u>
They felt <u>outrage **over** his negativism</u>.
It caused <u>an outrage **over** videotaped assault by them.</u>

The letter reflects <u>dismay **over** the latest developments.</u>
I <u>became excited **over** this failure.</u>
<u>Mania **over** the new issue</u> is no fairy tale.
What do you think about <u>that uproar **over** the photo</u>?
Parents are in an <u>uproar **over** the new</u>
<u>methods of education.</u>
<u>The hullabaloo **over** that party</u> won't die down.

27. A SOURCE OF A STRONG EMOTION, STATE

We're are <u>in despair **over** the girl</u>.
He was <u>despondent **over**</u> financial <u>troubles.</u>
She was so <u>distraught **over** what she had done.</u>
Students were <u>upset **over** a headline in a recent editorial.</u>
He <u>was in despair **over** his inability</u> to find any pleasure in it.
He feels <u>depressed **over** her mother's criticism.</u>
They <u>anguished **over** his arrest, **over** the shame.</u>
They are still <u>moping **over** the end of that show.</u>
She <u>frets **over** mistakes</u> that only she could notice.
Don't <u>fret **over** finding a girlfriend.</u>
It was a new kind of <u>grief **over** our repeated failures.</u>

28. A KIND OF BEHAVIOR/NEGATIVE BEHAVIOR

They're <u>stepping all **over** themselves.</u>
They aired their <u>grievances **over** new regulations.</u>
He doesn't <u>lament **over** the</u> hopeless urban <u>landscape.</u>
He <u>gloated **over** the spectacle</u> of so much food.
They <u>laughed **over** the pages.</u>

29. ADVANCING AGAINST/DISCONTENT/DEMONSTRATION

There was <u>a protest **over** the plan</u> to open a store on that avenue.
Workers <u>went on strike **over** medical benefits</u> and job securities
They <u>are on strike **over** benefits and wages.</u>
There were <u>riots **over** price increases.</u>

30. CHANGE IN THE STATE/BEHAVIOR

<u>Fear swept **over** me.</u>

I cannot describe the feeling that came **over** me.
The change that came **over** the lad surprised the family.
Every rasp of it tore **over** his raw nerves.
Panic sets in **over** severing of benefits.

31. OVERCOMING A DIFFICULTY, A PROBLEM

I think I am **over** the worst of the flu.
Her love of life triumphed **over** tragedy.
It was a sign of our success **over** the challenges of life.
Get **over** it!

32. EXCERSIZING POWER, AUTHORITY/DOMINATING

He rules **over** his family like a tyrant.
The kid had no control **over** himself sometimes.
I've no control **over** my life.
The library has no control **over** the information accessed.
It's a fight for control **over** television.
We had a strong influence **over** her, I believe
They watch **over** us day and night.
We kept watch **over** the ballot process.

33. A SUPERIOR POSITION, DEGREE IN AUTHORITY

People **over** me in the chain of command have Masters Degrees.
There was no one **over** him in the department.
The new supervisor who was put **over** them had a nice family.

34. MANAGING, DIRECTING

The director presides **over** the meeting.
When presiding **over** the case, he represents the judicial system.
The territory **over** which he rules is small.
Basic mastery **over** the computer is OK
He turns up the volume so he can hear the television **over** all the noises

35. PREVAILING, COMING OUT ON TOP/GAINING THE UPPER HAND

In the film, god usurped authority **over** the man.

My job is <u>taking **over** my life.</u>
<u>I gain a measure of triumph **over** Nick.</u>
It was <u>a distinct advantage **over** our competitors.</u>
<u>He wins **over** the shareholders.</u>
<u>He scores one **over** Richard.</u>
She <u>won a narrow victory **over** her rival</u>.

36. FAVORING, PREFERRING

<u>He picked a job in a small town **over** all the other opportunities.</u>
They may <u>choose him **over** me</u> for the promotion.
They <u>selected her **over** all the others.</u>
There must be <u>ambition **over**</u> and above <u>just making money.</u>
Her parents prized <u>knowledge **over** material possessions.</u>
<u>Mind **over** mood?</u>
They favor <u>prayer **over** sex education.</u>

37. BEING SUPPLEMENTARY

Over <u>and above her secretarial duties</u>, she is the office manager.
Over <u>and above my salary</u>, I get commission.

38. CROSSING SOME AGE/GOING BY IN YEARS, PAST

<u>He is now **over** a year old.</u>
He was <u>a</u> fine <u>man **over** thirty years</u> of age.
The company doesn't <u>promote people **over** a particular age.</u>

39. BEING HIGHER, MORE THAN EXPECTED/EXCEEDING

The temperature didn't <u>go **over** freezing</u> all day.
They had <u>to walk **over** ten miles.</u>
<u>My rampage may have been</u> **over** the top.

40. BEING HIGHER, MORE THAN EXPECTED/EXCEEDING FINANCIALLY

The software <u>cost **over** $100</u>.
The sum <u>comes out a hundred or so **over** the mark.</u>
<u>Expenses are a</u> little **over** income this month.

41. LASTING/GOING ON/CONTINUING

Over time, everything changed.
Over the summer, she took a waitressing job
I had money enough to tide him **over** the hard years.
The skill has been developed **over** long practice.

42. THE PRECISE PERIOD OF TIME OF AN EVENT

The stocks increased **over** the year by more than 3%.
The use of gas has multiplied many times
over the last year.

43. DURATION/FROM THE BEGINNING TO THE END

He had not seen us for **over** a week.
She has been sick **over** the last three weeks.
They stayed with us **over** night.
The meeting lasted **over** an hour.
He has been gone for **over** an hour.

44. LEISURE TIME/DAYS OFF

She'll stay with us **over** the weekend.
The kids stayed with us **over** the holidays.
We're planning to go there **over** the holidays.
They decided to read the papers **over** the holidays.
I'll be in New York **over** Christmas.

45. AN ACTION THAT HAPPENS DURING A MEAL

I made that suggestion **over** coffee.
It was a chat **over** coffee, you know.
She looked at him lifelessly **over** her cup.
Lisa took to doze at her whist and **over** her dinner.
The men and boys could linger **over** the meal.
I asked her about it **over** our evening martini.
Parents were seated **over** their wine.

46. USING A TELECOMMUNICATION DEVICE

Information is transmitted over
a communications channel.
He calls your name over a microphone.
They address the children over the loudspeaker.
The laser printer is accessed over the network.
The program will be provided to people over the Internet.
The products are sold over the Internet.

47. USING TELEPHONE

He is being interviewed over the telephone.
I can't discuss this over the telephone.
The sound of her voice over the phone was unusual.
See if you could set up an interview over the phone.

Synonyms: *beyond, past, throughout, for, outside, across, above*
Antonyms: *under*

OWING TO indicates:

1. A CAUSE, REASON

Owing to the flood, they had to move.
Owing to power outage, we were without
electricity for an hour.
Did she quit owing to public pressure?

2. ACTING ON ACCOUNT OF

Owing to the donations, repairs of the roof
were conducted fast.
Owing to his high blood pressure, he could not
continue the experiment.

Synonyms: *thanks to, because of, on account of*
Antonyms: *0*

PAST indicates:

1. TIME DIVISION AFTER AN *HOUR*

    Somebody knocked on my door <u>at a quarter **past** one</u>.
    It <u>was **past** two</u> by the time I had finished everything.
    We had to work **past** 9 o'clock.
    I consider it unhealthy <u>to stay up **past** 11</u>.
    It <u>was nearly</u> <u>an hour **past** midnight</u>.

2. HAPPENING LATER THAN, AFTER

    He <u>worked from sunup to **past** sundown</u>.
    The fun begins and <u>continues till way **past** midnight</u>.
    It was **past** dinnertime.

3. AFTER AN AGE DIVISION/LATER IN YEARS

    Another lady <u>was **past** middle age</u>.
    <u>A swarthy man was **past** the prime of life</u>.

4. LATER, LONGER THAN EXPECTED/SURPASSING

    You <u>are **past** the age</u> of adventure.
    He was told he would not <u>live **past** 40</u>.

5. BEING TOO LATE TO TAKE ACTION/STATE OF THINGS, SITUATION

    The drawings in the cave <u>were **past** recovery</u>.
    The books <u>were **past** saving.</u>
    Things were <u>getting **past** a joke.</u>

6. A STATE/NO LONGER ABLE TO DO SOMETHING

    Even adults, <u>long **past** adolescent sensitivities</u>,
    get excited about it.
    My father <u>is</u> bitter now and **past** caring.
    We kept over old horses when they <u>were **past** work</u>.
    <u>This is **past** all bearing.</u>

He <u>is</u> beyond drinking from the bottle and
past <u>sucking his thumb</u>.

7.   BEING FATHER THAN

My house <u>is</u> **past** <u>the next corner</u>, his **past** <u>the first stoplight</u>.
In that snapshot, my eyes are <u>focused</u> **past** <u>her</u>.

8.   MOVING BY, BEYOND A PLACE/OUTSIDE

The car rolls swiftly **past** the meadows.
The hot wind <u>swept</u> **past** <u>us.</u>
A bird <u>swept</u> **past** <u>them</u>.
Farmers <u>led dairy cows</u> **past** <u>streams</u>.
A snake was <u>moving</u> **past** <u>you</u>.
We <u>walked</u> **past** <u>a hole</u> in the sidewalk.
<u>Sneak</u> **past** <u>the masses of files</u> on the table.
He <u>walked</u> **past** <u>her</u> into the office.
Young guys <u>squeezed</u> **past** <u>us</u>.
<u>I ran</u> **past** <u>the library.</u>

9.   BEING MORE THAN, BEYOND POWER/SCOPE

<u>It's</u> **past** <u>belief.</u>
<u>The problem is</u> **past** <u>the point of resolution.</u>

10.   OVERCOMING AN OBSTACLE, DIFFICULTY

You'll discover <u>how to work</u> **past** <u>your nervousness</u>.
<u>Work</u> **past** <u>your fears</u> through interaction and feedback!
<u>You'll get</u> **past** <u>your blocks</u> and learn to draw.
She <u>looked</u> **past** <u>all the labels</u> put on him.
People couldn't <u>get</u> **past** <u>his looks.</u>

Synonyms: *by, beyond, beside, besides*
Antonyms: *0*

PER indicates:

1. AN ASSESSMENT, ESTIMATION

    It cost $4.00 **per** pound.
    They pay <u>me $5.00 **per** hour.</u>
    Is it <u>a dollar **per** foot?</u>
    Gasoline costs <u>$1.50 **per** gallon.</u>

2. A MEASUREMENT, RATIO, BALANCE

    They traveled 400 miles **per** day.
    You have <u>to walk 5 miles **per** day</u> to remain fit.
    The agency will charge <u>$7.00 **per** person.</u>

3. BEING AVAILABLE/DISTRIBUTION

    The school has <u>one computer **per** student.</u>
    <u>More people **per** household</u> rent movies here now.
    Only <u>one application will be accepted **per** household.</u>

4. BEING IN ACCORDANCE WITH, CORRESPONDING

    Payment is <u>overdue as **per** our agreement</u> of July 12.
    As **per** <u>the terms of the contract</u>, the job is
    to be done by May 1st.
    They sent it by air as **per** <u>the customer's request.</u>

    Synonyms: *for each, as such, via*
    Antonyms: *0*

IN PLACE OF indicates:

SUBSTITUTIING/PREFERRING

    <u>I studied Spanish **in place of** Italian.</u>
    <u>They cooked catfish **in place of** salmon.</u>

    Synonyms: *instead, as, because, for*
    Antonyms: *0*

PRIOR TO indicates:

1. PRECEDING IN TIME

Undergo a medical evaluation **prior to** the use of this card.
They met **prior to** the ceremony.
I need your time sheet three days **prior to** payday.
You should sign it **prior to** applying for a loan.
The box office will open one hour **prior to** performances.

2. PRECEDING IN IMPORTANCE, ORDER/PREFERRIING

We had their invitation **prior to** yours.
Cancellation notice was received five days **prior to** departure.
Prior to the help by the agency, there'd been
a fight between them.

Synonyms: *before, ahead of, in front of*
Antonyms: *after*

RE indicates:

REFERENCE/REGARDING

Re our telephone conversation, I want to emphasize
the importance of the meeting.
Re the new trash container, submit your opinion to her.

Synonyms: *concerning, as to,*
Antonyms: *0*

REGARDLESS OF indicates:

1. THINKING/ACTING WITHOUT CONSIDERING THE CONSEQUENCES

Regardless of the money he'll have to spend,
he is ready to help her out.
Regardless of the consequences, they'll continue their research.

I understand <u>the gift is mine</u> **regardless of** <u>whether or not I keep my order.</u>
<u>All abusers,</u> **regardless of** <u>gender,</u> should be liable for their actions.

2.   NOT MINDING, WITH NO HEED TO

We provide help to everyone **regardless of** <u>race or creed</u>.
He tried to accomplish the assignment, **regardless of** <u>the</u> <u>effort.</u>
<u>He sat on the stone</u> **regardless of** <u>the dust.</u>

Synonyms: *against, despite, notwithstanding*
Antonyms: *0*

RESPECTING indicates:

REFRENCE TO AN OBJECT OF INTEREST/REGARDING, CONCERNING

He is going <u>to make a statement</u> **respecting** <u>his candidacy</u>. (regarding)
<u>Talk about our plans</u> **respecting** <u>the new fiscal year.</u> (regarding)

Synonyms: *concerning, of, in regard to, about*
Antonyms: *0*

ROUND indicates:

ENCIRCLING/ON ALL SIDES

A ribbon <u>tied</u> **round** <u>her hair</u> matched the color of her blouse.
<u>An iron belt ran</u> **round** <u>his waist.</u>

Synonyms: *around*
Antonyms: *0*

SAVE indicates:

BEING AN EXCEPTION/NOT INCLUDED

Everyone was <u>rescued **save the captain**</u> of the ship.
<u>They all voted **save** me</u> against that candidate.

Synonyms: but, except
Antonyms: including

SINCE indicates:

1. A POINT IN TIME/THE BEGINNING OF A STATE

   <u>**Since** high school</u>, he knew what he would do.
   They've been <u>friends **since** childhood</u>.

2. AN ACTION THAT LASTS FOR SOME TIME BEGINNING AT A CERTAIN POINT

   <u>We have been discussing it **since** the meeting.</u>
   They've been <u>working on the budget **since** June</u>.

Synonyms: because
Antonyms: 0

IN SPITE OF indicates:

CONTINUING ACTING REGARDLESS CIRCUMSTANCES

We kept listening to him **in spite of** <u>the late hour</u>.
I insisted on buying those things **in spite of** <u>high prices</u>.

Synonyms: despite, nevertheless, notwithstanding
Antonyms: 0

THAN indicates:

COMPARING OBJECTS

> He disliked <u>no one more **than** me</u>.
> Nobody is <u>more knowledgeable in this field **than** she</u>.
> She is <u>an administrator **than** there's none better</u>.

Synonyms: *as*
Antonyms: *0*

THANKS TO indicates:

THE RESULT OF AN ACTION DUE TO A CERTAIN ATTITUDE

> <u>**Thanks to** your column</u>, I am now aware of the situation.
> <u>**Thanks to** Jack's call</u>, the firemen acted promptly.
> <u>**Thanks to** the new coupons</u>, you can save on your expenses.

Synonyms: *0*
Antonyms: *0*

THROUGH indicates:

1. ENTERING/PENETRATING/MOVING TO THE OTHER END

> Did he <u>climb in **through** the window</u>?
> He <u>hurries **through** the gate</u>.
> He <u>disappears **through** the door</u>.
> I <u>crept **through** a break</u> in the ruined building.
> Sunlight barely <u>pierced down **through** the dense foliage</u>.
> <u>The</u> cold <u>wind</u> was <u>blowing in **through** the cracks.</u>
> A terrible <u>thought crept **through** John's brain.</u>
> <u>He ran one hand **through** his hair.</u>
> A pain<u> shot **through** her arm</u>.

2. PASSING/GOING IN AND OUT

> The cat is <u>coming **through** the door</u> now.
> The street car <u>went **through** the tunnel</u> in one minute.
> They <u>drive **through** a toll-booth</u> without stopping.
> <u>Her back was scraped **through** her shirt.</u>

3. MOVING AROUND, HERE AND THERE

> A fire <u>ripped **through** a chemical plant</u>.
> Children <u>tore **through** the house</u>.
> You have <u>to travel **through** several countries</u>.
> <u>I took my journey **through** the wood.</u>
> <u>Walking **through** the store</u> is fun to do.
> The librarian <u>went **through** the overdues</u>.

4. MOVINGG WITHOUT OBSTACLES/ACROSS

> Picture yourself <u>running **through** an airport</u>.
> We were <u>driving **through** California</u>.
> <u>A tour **through** Italy</u> costs $500.00 per person.
> I've not <u>been **through** the city yet.</u>
> Her application <u>went **through** our office</u>.
> The <u>bill has been passed **through** Parliament</u>.

5. OVERCOMING OBSTACLES

> He <u>saw her **through** the iron bars</u> of the gate.
> The dogs <u>went on **through** the icy cold water</u>.
> The horse <u>carried him **through** the darkness</u>.
> **Through** <u>the dusk I could see</u> the light of TV sets.
> He would <u>crawl **through** broken glass</u> for it.
> We <u>walked home together **through** the snow</u>.

6. MOVING IN THE MIDST/BETWEEN, AMONG

> The monkeys were <u>swinging **through** the trees</u>.
> There he <u>was lumbering **through** the trees</u>.
> We enjoyed that <u>walk **through** the flowers</u>.
> Coming down the hill, we walked <u>**through** rags of fog.</u>

Not much <u>money will pass **through** your hands</u>.
Get out of here, <u>she hissed **through** her teeth</u>.

7.   MOVING WITHOUT STOPPING/PAST, BEYOND

He <u>drove **through** a red light</u>.
Our body and mind <u>go **through** changes</u>.
<u>He floats **through** life.</u>
You'll <u>course **through** your days</u> without a
care in the world.
I'd been driving for hours, <u>racing **through** the night</u>.

8.   SPEEDING BY/FLASHING BY

They <u>rush **through** breakfast and lunch</u>.
He <u>rushed **through** all the procedures</u>.

9.   PEOPLE AFFECTED BY A CHANGE/TRANSFORMED

<u>Influenza runs right **through** her whole family</u> every year.
The idea <u>sent shivers **through** neighborhood groups.</u>
His death <u>sent shock waves **through** the intellectual world.</u>

10.   CONTINUING THE ENTIRE PERIOD OF TIME

The economy <u>grew **through** the 1940's</u>.
They have <u>known him **through** the years</u>.
Her aunt didn't <u>last **through** the summer</u>.
<u>Length of Office is from January 5th **through** July 17th.</u>
That film will <u>run **through** May</u>.
I <u>slept **through** the whole morning</u>.
The nurse <u>stayed up **through** the night</u>.
She <u>sat **through** entire show</u> without saying a word.
<u>I had no friends **through** high school.</u>

11.   EMBRACING THE ENTIRE OBJECT

<u>The answers to questions 2 **through** 8 are listed below.</u>
I need <u>the volume that covers A **through** D</u>.
The life <u>went boiling **through** my veins</u>.

12. EXPERIENCING A DIFFICULTY, PROBLEM

> She <u>went</u> **through** <u>a lot of humiliation</u>.
> I am <u>going</u> **through** <u>with the divorce</u>.
> We've <u>been</u> **through** <u>a lot together</u>.
> You don't have <u>to struggle</u> **through** <u>distribution</u>.

13. SURMOUNTING DIFFICULTIES/NOT GIVING UP

> They can <u>maneuver</u> **through** <u>difficult situations</u>.
> Her anger will not <u>help her</u> **through** <u>her ordeal</u>.
> Learn how <u>to cut</u> **through** <u>red tape</u>.
> <u>Cut</u> **through** <u>the misconceptions</u> about it.
> She <u>was midway</u> **through** <u>her pitch</u>.

14. FINISHING AN ASSIGNMENT, PROCEDURE/ACCOMPLISHING

> <u>What time is he</u> **through** <u>work?</u>
> We <u>take you</u> **through** <u>the entire process</u> by
> providing information.
> I <u>went</u> **through** <u>high school</u> and <u>college</u>.
> I have <u>to get</u> **through** <u>school</u> before I can get married.
> <u>To go</u> **through** <u>therapy</u>, you need give us
> your permission.

15. ACHIEVING RESULTS/SUCCEEDING

> Many young people <u>work their way</u> **through** <u>college</u>.
> <u>We are</u> **through** <u>the initial testing period</u>.
> <u>Make a decision and follow</u> **through.**

16. ACHIEVING A RESULT BY APPLYING EFFORT

> I <u>acquired my possessions</u> **through** <u>years</u> of
> working and saving.
> <u>I succeed</u> **through** <u>hard work.</u>
> He <u>achieved</u> <u>success</u> **through** <u>hard work</u>.

17. USING SOMEONE'S HELP, ASSISTANCE/MEDIATOR

You got your job **through** a friend.
I heard the news **through** friends
She met him **through** mutual friends.
We bought our car **through** a dealer.
The vitamins are sold **through** drug stores.
The witness was examined **through** an interpreter.
I know most of the Greek classics **through** traslation.
Children changed all **through** this course.

18. THE WAY OF DOING THINGS

This is made possible **through** the cooperation
of our groups.
We would help **through** concerted efforts.
She achieved everything **through** her own efforts.
He constructs fiction **through** a process of collage.
Don't lose your daughter **through** rejection.
Each point is presented **through** a variety of exercises.
We don't live entirely **through** our work.
Success permits no letdown or release
except **through** failure.

19. A MEANS OF ACHIEVING A RESULT

Accomplishments come **through** education.
I learned everything **through** reading.
Share your ideas **through** writing and speaking.
He made his living **through** writing and acting.
Try to loosen up a bit **through** benign and
innocent behavior.
It was taken from her **through** force, fear, or intimidation.
Through my belief in the program, I restored
my life to sanity.

20. A TOOL FOR OF ACCOMPLISHING SOMETHING

We kept in touch mainly **through** Christmas cards.
They teach me every day **through** their letters.

The constellation was <u>familiar</u> **through** <u>the</u> photographs.
<u>Bring the images into your life</u> **through** <u>art.</u>
<u>Explore</u> your inner world <u>**through** dreams.</u>
<u>One experiences the reality of the world only</u>
through <u>his body.</u>
They <u>communicate</u> with each other <u>**through** news groups.</u>
<u>Get</u> maximum <u>earnings</u> **through** <u>maximum</u> <u>fun</u>.

21. USING A DEVICE/MEDIA

He <u>glanced</u> **through** <u>the periscope</u>.
It's like <u>studying an ant-hill</u> **through** <u>a magnifying glass</u>.
<u>Jack ran all the figures</u> **through** <u>the computer.</u>
He <u>ran her name</u> **through** <u>the computer</u>.
I've no <u>control over the information accessed</u>
through <u>the Internet.</u>

22. GLANCING OVER/SCANNING/REVIEWING

You can <u>read</u> **through** <u>the lecture titles</u>.
When <u>reading</u> **through** <u>this agreement</u>, I made notes.
As you <u>read</u> **through** <u>this guide</u>, you'll
understand the terms.
Be sure to retrieve files and <u>read</u> **through** <u>them</u>.
My boss quickly <u>glanced</u> **through** <u>the orders</u>.
I <u>scroll</u> **through** <u>my messages</u> every morning.
<u>Work</u> **through** <u>the remaining chapters</u>.
<u>Work</u> **through** <u>this guide first.</u>
I was <u>sorting</u> **through** <u>my memoirs</u>.
He <u>leafed</u> quickly <u>**through** the pages</u>.

23. CHECKING, INSPECTING/ANALYZING

They <u>went</u> **through** <u>his pockets.</u>
<u>Thumbing</u> **through** <u>the encyclopedia</u>, we tried
to find that name.
<u>Comb</u> **through** <u>the ads!</u>
Men <u>sort</u> **through** <u>the different meanings</u> of masculinity.
I need <u>to work</u> **through** <u>my feelings</u> with a therapist.
All is <u>filtered</u> **through** <u>the self</u>.

24. UNCOVERING/DETECTING INSINCERITY

People see **through** Dorothy's lies.
I could see **through** you right away.

25. A CAUSE, REASON

He declined the honor **through** modesty.
I ran away **through** shame.
It was **through** no fault of our own.
They died **through** violence.

Synonyms: *via, by way of, around, over, in, round, throughout, thanks to*
Antonyms: *0*

THROUGHOUT indicates:

1. BEING IN ALL PARTS OF A PLACE, EVERYWHERE

A variety of exercise types are used **throughout** the book.
He succeeded by making changes **throughout** the company.
The weather forecast predicted rains **throughout** the area.

2. PUTTING OBJECTS HERE AND THERE/EVERYWHERE

I put extension cords **throughout** the entire apartment.
Place smoke detectors **throughout** the house.
They put the signs **throughout** the entire neighborhood.

3. GOING ON FOR A WHILE/ALL THROUGH

These tales have been told **throughout** time.
The world has suffered terribly **throughout** history.
They'll remind us of important events **throughout** the year.
Visitors kept coming **throughout** the year.
It snowed **throughout** the weekend.
Keep a front porch light on **throughout** the night.

We had <u>to work</u> **throughout** <u>the night.</u>
<u>She maintained her composure</u> **throughout** <u>the ceremony.</u>

Synonyms*: across, all over, inside and out*
Antonyms: *0*

TILL indicates:

1.   GOING ON DOING SOMETHING UP TO A POINT

Let's <u>wait</u> **till** <u>morning</u>.
She will be <u>talking about it</u> **till** <u>dawn</u>.

2.   THE EXACT TIME BEFORE AN *HOUR*

The meeting <u>started at 10 minutes</u> **till** <u>10</u>.
I'll <u>set the alarm clock at 25</u> **till** <u>7 a.m.,</u> OK?
They <u>met at five minutes</u> **till** <u>eight</u>.

3.   SHOWING THE LIMIT/RESULT

They claimed they would <u>**fight** **till** **death**</u>.
I had <u>forgotten</u> about it<u> **till** <u>that moment</u></u>.

Synonyms: until
Antonyms: 0

TO indicates:

1.   MOVING IN THE GENERAL DIRECTION

Shall we drive **to** <u>the north or</u> **to** <u>the south?</u>
<u>The tropical storm formed</u> **to** <u>the west </u>of Guam.
That window was <u>open</u> **to** <u>a starry sky</u>.
Three people were <u>swept out</u> **to** <u>sea</u>.
<u>I pointed</u> **to** <u>the darkness</u> all around us.
Look **to** <u>the right</u>, then **to** <u>the left</u>!

2.   MOVING TO A DESTINATION/LOCATION/COUNTRY/CITY

British immigrants to Australia knew little about it.
She was an Irish emigrant to Canada.
He is off to Russia for a week.
He was ambassador to Haiti for three years.
This was stated by a visitor to the city last year.
They flew to the city of Samara in the summer.
He has been to his father's grave.

3.   MOVING IN THE DIRECTION OF A BUILDING/CHAMBER/FURNI-
TURE/DEVICE

My first trip to the hospital lasted one hour.
We head off to baggage claim hastily.
We dash to a telephone booth to call a cab.
The doors open to an inside hallway.
He retires to the basement room.
We crossed to the door in silence.
I was able to make it to my back door.
He himself got to the phone to talk to her.
The cats trail me upstairs to bed.
I darted to the TV to learn the news.
Her brother gets to sit next to you on the couch.

4.   ENTRANCE, PASSAGE/PENETRATION

I entered the gates to the park.
The bridge gave access to the castle.
There's no admittance to the hall.
The approaches to the town are blocked with the cars.

5.   GOING TO EVENTS/PARTICIPATING

I've been to two meetings.
They read the flyer on their way to class.
He went out to dinner.

6. GOING TO AN ENTERTAINMENT CENTER

They <u>walked **to** the theater</u>.
I never <u>go **to** modern plays</u>.

7. STARTING DOING/TAKING AN ACTION

<u>Get right down **to** it</u>.
<u>I went straight **to** the subject.</u>
Why not <u>put your spare time **to** good use</u>?

8. RESUMING AN ACTION/COMING BACK

<u>I returned **to** my customary work</u>.
<u>Thinking back **to** it,</u> I saw no hope.
<u>Think back **to** the Middle Ages!</u>
<u>I reverted **to** the question of prices.</u>

9. THE CLOSING OF AN ACTION/TERMINATION

<u>He finally ground **to** a halt.</u>
The Oakland <u>bus hissed **to** a stop</u>.
The enemy <u>fell back **to** their lines</u>.
It's the perfect <u>end **to** the best trip</u> I've ever been on.
<u>The banquet drew **to** its close</u> at midnight.
<u>I knew the page numbers and flipped **to** them.</u>
There's <u>a bottom line **to** all this</u>.
<u>That's all there is **to** it</u>.
<u>It has come **to** this.</u>

10. REACHING AN ULTIMATE POINT/RESULT/LIMITS

<u>We read it cover **to** cover.</u>
We <u>grew **to** five feet</u> in a year.
<u>The cream rose **to** the top of the pot.</u>
He suddenly <u>rose **to** his feet</u>.
He <u>flipped the paper open **to** a</u> large <u>picture</u>.
The water was <u>clear all the way **to** the bottom</u>.
He didn't <u>turn the radio **to** his station.</u>

My heart flew **to my throat.**
Tears rose **to my eyes.**

11. PLACING AN OBJECT SOMEWHERE/TRANSFERRING

He delivers the mail **to the school**
Bring **to** class simple drawings!
She will take the boots **to** her shoe repair guy.
The command on the menu copies all **to** where you like.
Don't plant potatoes too close **to** tomatoes.

12. BEING BESIDE, NEARBY/IN ADJACENT LOCATION

The border runs parallel **to the river.**
We lived close **to Golden Gate park.**
She could see three men seated **to her right.**
They were sitting back **to back.**
We silently stood for a while, face **to** face.
The language function is lateralized
to the left hemisphere of the brain.

13. ASKING, SOLICITING

Refer me **to a good dictionary.**
Help yourself **to some coffee.**
Call **to** order (At a meeting).
He turned **to a variety of experts.**
I am turning **to you for advice.**

14. AN OFFER, PROPOSAL

We welcome you **to our banquet.**
You are invited **to our potluck party.**
The officer motioned **to me** to open the trunk.

15. PERMISSION/SANCTION/INTRODUCTION

I have no access **to his archives** now.
Do you have access **to those newspapers?**

16. ACHIEVING A DESIRABLE OUTCOME, EFFECT

He <u>was on the fast track to success.</u>
The book <u>went straight to the bestseller list</u>.
It <u>contributed to</u> their <u>progress to higher attainments</u>.

17. A WAY TO ACHIEVE A DESIRABLE RESULT

Do you know <u>shortcuts to success</u>?
Who knows <u>the secret to success</u>?
<u>Is there a secret to a happy marriage</u>?
Variety is <u>key to your good health</u>.

18. FAILING TO ACHIEVE A DESIRABLE OUTCOME, RESULT

I am not <u>living up to what she wants me to be</u>.
My performance doesn't <u>measure up to my expectations</u>.
We find all the other avenues to distinction <u>closed to us</u>.

19. BEING CAPABLE, COMPETENT, EFFICIENT

<u>Is he up to the challenge</u>?
<u>No words would come to me.</u>

20. AN ADMISSION, REGISTERING, ENROLLMENT

He has been <u>accepted to Stanford.</u>
He had been <u>accepted to a small school.</u>
He was <u>admitted to a writing course</u> at City College.
<u>He received a full scholarship to Yale University</u>.

21. A PHYSICAL STATE OF A LIVING BEING/TENDING

I <u>am prone to motion sickness</u>.
He was <u>inclined to obesity</u>.
He is <u>subject to nervous fits</u>.
Kids are now less <u>vulnerable to polio</u>.
Pets are <u>vulnerable to the heat</u> of summer.
He <u>felt sick to his stomach</u>.

22. CHANGING A PHYSICAL STATE

I wake up to the noise of the city.
Wake up to feelings and dreams!

23. A CURRENT SITUATION/POSITION

I am not even close to ready.
Though very busy, he is very easy to access.
I got used to working late.

24. BRINGING LIVING BEINGS TO AN EXTREME PHYSICAL STATE

They nursed the premature twins to health.
I cry myself to sleep.
The wind chilled me to my core.
The kids were wet to the skin.

25. AN EXTREME EMOTIONAL STATE

Now I am scared to death.
That's very embarrassing to me.
The breakup of her marriage was quite a shock to her.
It was a great surprise to me.
To my horror, I saw him standing there.
He may be vulnerable to suggestions from families.
It was repugnant to him.

26. BRINGING LIVING BEINGS TO AN EXTREME EMOTIONAL STATE

She drives him to distraction.
My job stretched my nerves to the breaking point.
He has been moved to tears.
She brings audiences to tears by her performing.
Every scratch scares me to death.
They laugh themselves to death.

27. AN EXTREME ACTION/CONDITION

He took to his bed with the cold.

Some animals <u>starved to death</u>.
<u>The cat jumped to his death.</u>

28. BRINGING LIVING BEINGS TO AN EXTREME CONDITION

Foxes were <u>hunted to death</u>.
Love may <u>blind you to possible consequences</u>.

29. BEING LIABLE/OPEN

The project is <u>subject to revision</u>.
They are <u>exposed to other cultures</u>.

30. BEING CHARACTERISTIC, TYPICAL/AN ATTRIBUTE

There are <u>some oddities to the book.</u>
<u>The song has a real cruelty to it.</u>
There was <u>a slightly Victorian tinge to the whole thing</u>.
There's a bit of <u>a brisk chill to the morning air</u> today.
He discovered a sarcastic <u>side to the author.</u>
There're many <u>advantages to this program</u>.
Here is <u>a dark side to some Internet products.</u>
<u>There is more to the Internet</u> than browsing.
Isn't <u>there more to life than work?</u>
There's <u>a history to this project.</u>
Some patients <u>have horrible crimes to their names</u>.

31. BRINGING AN OBJECT/A SITUATION TO AN UTTER CONDITION

He <u>tore her letter to pieces</u>.
The civilized world had been <u>bombed to ruins</u>.
Buildings are <u>dashed to pieces</u> before their eyes.
<u>If it comes to war</u>, many changes may be necessary.
<u>Develop your idea to the point</u> where I get interested in it.
I <u>yelled words to the effect of 'Never do that again!'</u>
<u>Don't push your arguments to such extremes.</u>
<u>Calculate the height of the tree to within an inch.</u>
I decided <u>to do something radical to my hair</u>.

32. SETTING CONDITIONS/INSTRUCTIONS IN COOKING

   Beat cream to a butter.
   Cook meat to a temperature of 160 degrees Fahrenheit.
   Bring water to a boil.

33. PERFORMING A FINANCIAL TRANSACTION

   She makes no deposits to the account.
   Bring the money order made payable to the Fund.
   Make checks payable to Tenants Rights.

34. TOUCHING A SURFACE/PHYSICAL CONTACT

   I pressed my palms to the frozen window.
   Keep cords in hard-to-reach areas.
   Hold the disk to a light and you'll see many scratches.
   Overexposure to the sun is dangerous.
   The comet is becoming visible to the naked eye.

35. ADHERING/CLASPING

   The boy, still in bed, clung to the sheet.
   Babies hold on to a chair or to their parents' hands.
   Her eyes traveled over me to my hands.
   He turned to us in surprise.
   He snuggled closer to her.
   The white substance binds to this site.
   A yellow leaf sticks to his arm.

36. STAYING IN THE SAME SITUATION

   I'll just stick to my present occupation.
   You have to stick to studying if you want to succeed.
   They have stuck to low-calorie diets.
   Learn how to hang on to your hard-earned dollars.

37. ATTACHING, CONNECTING, LINKING

   He pinned the badge to my lapel.
   Sew new buttons on to the vest.

38. AN ADDITION, SUPPLEMENT/FOLLOW-UP

It was a perfect <u>complement to our costumes</u>.
History provides a powerful <u>perspective to the conflict</u>.
The film is <u>the sequel to Star Wars.</u>

39. A PART OF AN OBJECT/A COMPLEX

Is it <u>an end to the name</u> or a part of the field name?
I lost <u>the key to my front door</u>.
Have you seen <u>the jacket to my</u> new <u>suit</u>?

40. A RESTRICTION/CONTROL/DISCIPLINE

Mom <u>limited him to four meals</u> a day.
They <u>confined her to jail</u> for theft.

41. A RESTRAINT DUE TO THE PHYSICAL CONDITION

He was <u>confined to a plaster body</u>.
He was <u>confined to his hospital bed.</u>
She is <u>bound to a wheelchair</u>.

42. SIGNING UP FOR A PERIODICAL/RECEIVING A PERIODICAL

<u>How many newspapers do you subscribe to?</u>
I have been <u>subscribing to Harper's</u> for two years.
The <u>subscribers to *The Washington Spectator*</u> were angry.

43. A PREDOMINANCE, PREPONDERANCE

These results are <u>inferior to last year's results</u>.
He feels his skills <u>are inferior to the skills of others</u>.
The new principles <u>are superior to the previous ones</u>.
I think d<u>ogs make far superior pets to cats</u>.
Eating ice cream is <u>preferable to eating hot spinach</u>.
Back pain is <u>second only to the common cold</u>.

44. CHANGING THE SITUATION

As <u>afternoon turned **to** evening</u>, they left.
<u>A switch **to** a new day-care provider</u> is another possibility.
Why is skepticism<u> turning **to** cynicism</u>?
We made <u>an upgrade **to** your product design</u>.

45. REGAINING THE POSITION/RECOVERING

He<u> returned **to** his feet</u> right away.
Your emotions will all <u>settle back down **to** normal.</u>
I was <u>back **to** my regular self</u>.
He<u> restored his life **to** sanity</u>.
<u>She is back **to** working</u> full time.

46. BEING SIGNIFICANT, ESSENTIAL

Money has always been <u>central **to** politics</u>.
Ideas must be <u>central **to** progressive </u>reform.
It's <u>critical **to** what happens</u> with our values.
It's <u>crucial **to** our ability</u> to provide quality service.
Every reply is <u>crucial **to** me</u>.
He <u>meant too much **to** him</u>.
Your satisfaction is very <u>important **to** us</u>.
We know what Newton was<u> **to** the physical universe</u>.

47. BEING VALUABLE, PRECIOUS

<u>What it means **to** me!</u>
You <u>mean the world **to** me</u>.
These feelings <u>give meaning **to** existence</u>.
Love is what should <u>matter **to** us</u>.
You <u>are heroes **to** all the young people</u> out there.

48. A PROSPECT/GOAL

<u>There might be a point **to** it.</u>
<u>There isn't any point **to** my life.</u>
She no longer saw <u>a purpose **to** her life</u>.
Some thinkers try <u>to look **to** the past</u> for traditions.

49. AN EXPECTATION/ANTICIPATING AN EVENT

> They looked to us with hope.
> We are looking forward to seeing you.
> Are you looking forward to college?
> Look forward to surprises.

50. REACHING SOMEONE

> The past caught up to him this week.
> The program reaches out to the community.
> Did it take long to get through to the secretary?
> It first came to the public attention last year.

51. PROVIDING A SERVICE

> We provide different services to the community.
> Reach out to people who support your goals.

52. EXTENDING HELP

> He came to their aid shortly.
> Parents do it to kids all the time.
> The ranch has become home to abused children.
> He was elected to be responsive to the electorate.
> Try to be attentive to their needs.

53. RECIPIENT OF A SERVICE/BENEFICIARY

> It was a comfort to him.
> A caregiver will be assigned to you.
> The access to benefits is denied to them.
> Don't deny treatment to legal aliens.
> She sneaked a kiss to her husband.
> He would always be special to her.
> I never tire of tending to my tulips.

54. BEING OBTAINABLE, SERVICIBLE/AT HAND

> This course is accessible to everyone.

This workshop is free and <u>open **to** the public</u>.
The program is <u>geared **to** low income individuals.</u>
The Campus is <u>convenient **to** all modes of transportation</u>.
Schedule the hearing at a time <u>convenient **to** all.</u>
They will be <u>available **to** the participants</u>.
These goodies <u>are available **to** you</u>.

55. THE EFFECT OF AN ACTION ON THE RECIPIENT

Their dedication is <u>inspiring **to** us</u>.
Counseling could be very <u>helpful **to** him</u>.
The daughter is <u>a credit **to** her mother</u>.

56. SUPPLYING VICTUALS/PROVISIONS/SUSTANANCE

<u>Special rations were issued **to** refugees</u>.
Large amounts of the corn <u>we feed **to** cattle</u>, pigs
and poultry.
I plan on <u>serving this lively feast **to** guests</u> soon.
The store had 45 <u>people to cater **to** the mannequins</u>.
They should stop <u>catering **to** the corporations</u>.

57. A PROMOTION, ADVANCEMENT

She has been <u>nominated **to** a high-level post</u>.
He was <u>raised **to** the position of the manager</u>.

58. A RECEIVER OF AN OBJECT

<u>I've already sent a fruitcake **to** them.</u>
<u>She handed a magazine **to** me.</u>
He hasn't <u>returned the books **to** us</u> yet.

59. POSSESSION, OWNERSHIP

<u>He didn't have a dime **to** his name.</u>
<u>He had a plane **to** himself</u> before the stroke.
I loved <u>having her **to** myself</u>.
Two <u>awards so far are **to** his claim</u>.

60. A SOCIAL STATUS/OCCUPATION, CHOSEN WORK, JOB

He's <u>a consultant **to** the industry</u>.
<u>The aides **to** the President</u> disagreed with him on that.
She <u>is a new secretary **to** the chairman</u>.

61. AN EXCLUSIVE RELATIONSHIP/A MARITAL STATUS

She was <u>wed **to** another man</u>.
I am <u>married **to** a mathematician</u>.
She <u>married twice **to** his father</u>.

62. STARTING A FAMILY

She <u>gave birth **to** three wonderful kids.</u>
These children are <u>born **to** teen mothers</u>.
She was <u>born **to** a family</u> with old traditions.

63. WITHSTANDING/DURABILITY/ENDURANCE

Individuals could <u>stand up **to** the forces</u> of history.
His books have <u>stood up **to** the passage of time</u>.
Vitamins increase <u>resistance **to** bacteria</u>.
Fresh air increases <u>the resistance **to** decay</u>.

64. A BEHAVIOR/ACTING IN THE RIGHT WAY

We <u>react **to** different people</u> differently.
City officials <u>reacted swiftly **to** the article</u>.
<u>What is the appropriate response **to** this?</u>
<u>I rose **to** the occasion and shook his hand.</u>

65. A BEHAVIOR/ACTING IN THE WRONG WAY

She easily <u>fell **to** tears</u>.
They <u>bow **to** my command</u>.
Should women <u>bow down **to** men</u>?
<u>Acquiescing **to** her</u> was the strangest thing possible.
He <u>helped himself **to** the phone</u> without permission.
Don't <u>play up **to** the people's nostalgic feelings</u>.

He always <u>goes to the bad</u>.
It's a tremendous <u>overreaction to the problem</u>.
She <u>saw to it</u> that he was expelled.

66. TAKING PLACE/AN OBJECT AFFECTED/AN INDIVIDUAL AFFECTED

<u>It can happen to everyone</u>.
It <u>happened to me</u> on several occasions.
<u>Whatever happened to courtship rituals</u>?
Then <u>it would occur to someone else</u>.

67. A DAMAGING EFFECT ON A LIVING BEING

It's <u>poisonous to a baby</u>.
Drugs are all <u>toxic to the body</u>.
My actions could be <u>harmful to others</u>.
<u>Injuries account for many deaths to children</u>.
I watched cases such as <u>burns to witnesses</u>.
Don't forget history of <u>abuse to children</u>.
<u>What are we doing to society?</u>

68. DAMAGE/INJURY TO A PART OF THE BODY

He finished the bear with <u>a shot to its head</u>.
He died from <u>a blow to the back of the head</u>.
It was a gunshot <u>wound to the left arm</u>.
He suffered second-degree <u>burns to his face</u>.

69. A MORAL HARM

The only <u>damage was to his pride</u>.
The book is about <u>violence to the spirit</u>.
<u>The environment is hostile to me.</u>
It's not the weight of the world <u>that gets to me</u>.
<u>How could you do this to me</u>?
I knew you were <u>lying to me</u>.
You have <u>been cruel to us</u>.

70. A CAUSE OF THE PHYSICAL STATE

I am <u>allergic</u> <u>to feathers</u>.
Many people are <u>allergic</u> <u>to yeast</u>.

71. A CONSEQUENCE TO A HARMFUL SITUATION

We <u>lost the patient</u> <u>to drug addiction</u>.
He <u>lost his leg</u> <u>to a terrible road accident</u>.
He <u>lost sales</u> <u>to competitors</u> eventually.
He <u>fell victim</u> <u>to a</u> vicious <u>attack</u>.

72. INFLICTING A DAMAGE, HARM TO AN OBJECT

<u>The boy set fire</u> <u>to his toys.</u>
Any <u>damage</u> <u>to mail boxes</u> is a crime.

73. BEING APPROPRIATE, FITTING, MATCHING

<u>Some rules apply</u> <u>to everyone.</u>
Everything seems <u>to relate</u> <u>to</u> <u>ourselves</u>.
He looked for some <u>suitable tie</u> <u>to his new suit</u>.
<u>True</u> <u>to his word,</u> he found everything.

74. AN ACTION CAUSED BY A SOUND

John <u>danced</u> <u>to the rhythm</u> of the music.
They <u>danced</u> <u>to some romantic tune</u>.
I usually <u>do morning exercises</u> <u>to music</u>.
I <u>woke</u> <u>to the sound</u> of the smoke alarm.

75. THE TIME UNTIL/THE END OF A PERIOD OF TIME

Now I <u>work from 9 a.m.</u> <u>to 4 p.m</u>.
<u>To this day,</u> I refer to him by his original name.

76. THE TIME BEFORE SOME POINT

<u>Cathy came at five minutes</u> <u>to eight.</u>
A medical evaluation is necessary <u>prior</u> <u>to the use of the pills</u>.

77. AN EXACT POINT IN TIME/ON THE TIME

Set the alarm clock to the time you wish.
This salary adjustment is retroactive to May 1st.
The schedule was retroactive to the end of April.

78. A DEMAND, REQUEST/PRIVELEGE

There were five claimants to this estate.
He recognized her claim to a tragic destiny.
What are you entitled to?
His clients have the right to a fair trial.
He had a right to that.
Secure the legal rights to your idea.
Who purchased the rights to her interview?

79. ASSESSING, MATCHING

His work is comparable to hers.
They compared my style of writing to his.
They could see the parallel to the past events.
Tailor your material to a specific audience.

80. BEING EQUIVALENT, IDENTICAL, SIMILAR, DIFFERENT

He bears a resemblance to a certain character.
This was akin to making remarks about looks.
This does not correspond to my idea of a vacation.
In contrast to your proposals, his seem more realistic.
These demands are anti-ethical to our mission.

81. AN ASSENT, ACCORD/CONSENT

His word speaks to all our needs.
The tense used is appropriate to the meaning.
He found job responsibilities suited to her abilities.
He admits to being driven by rage and ego.
He will eventually accede to us.
She agreed to an interview.
Shall I agree to his terms?

82. A DISPUTE, CONFLICT

Such an action would be <u>contrary to our principles</u>.
There were important <u>dissents to the panel's findings</u>.
We couldn't <u>conform to his principles</u>.
Nobody could <u>conform to those conditions</u>.

83. PROVIDING A PROOF, A CONFIRMATION

My friends can <u>testify to its accuracy</u>.
Anyone can <u>attest to the importance</u> of this habit.
This is a sad <u>testimony to life</u> for them here.
We have become <u>reconciled to the truth</u>.

84. AFFECTION, PREFERENCE, DISPOSITION

<u>It's a spa to your liking</u>.
<u>We build lives to our own liking</u>.
It will be <u>appealing to adult readers</u>.
His behavior <u>appeals to the sense of the absurd</u>
in some people.

85. BEING FAMILIAR/DEFINITE

It will be <u>obvious to everyone</u>.
It was <u>clear to all of us</u> but him.
I was so <u>unaccustomed to the experience</u>.
<u>Unknown to me</u>, he's been collecting the same stuff.

86. A PROPORTION, DIMENSION, RATIO

<u>There are four quarts to a gallon</u>.
I <u>get 36 miles to a gallon</u> on the highway.
<u>Does twelve stand to a dozen?</u>—bad?
The score of the last game was nine to zero.
<u>Two to the second power is four</u> ($2^2 = 4$).

87. THE UPPER LIMITATION OF AN APPROXIMATION

<u>He is forty five to forty six years old</u>.

A fire grows to four times its original size.
I abbreviated the letter to three paragraphs.
She used the opportunity to the max.

88. REPEATING AN ACTION, DUPLICATION

Her father was alerting all people from door to door.
I will use side-to-side strokes in the massage on you.

89. A SOURCE OF OPINION

It sounds bad to her.
It looks small to us.
It is very rude to me.
Let us know how this plan looks to you.
To the casual observer, it might seem senseless.
To my husband, it's no big deal.

90. A SPEECH ACTIVITY/AN ADDRESSEE

Always refer to specific persons!
Speak to whoever answers the phone.
Explain it to us as soon as possible!
Allow us to break the news to you.
We'd soon be teaching to practically empty classes.
I've talked to the school board and principal.
Report suspicious activities to police.
I'll write to you again soon.
This suggests two things to me.

91. A SPEECH ACTIVITY/RESPONSE

Did you get an answer to your letter?
A child's answer to a mother may surprise you.
What will you say to this?
He responded to my message immediately.

92. EXPRESSING GRATITUDE, APPRECIATION

I'd like to extend a sincere thank you to everyone.
I want to extend my thanks to Ann and Betty.

93. A SOURCE OF HELP

I am indebted to her for everything.
He survived thanks to his friends.
All I ever attained in life I owe to my father!
I owe it to all of you.

94. PROVIDING AN ADVICE/INSTRUCTION, RECOMMENDATION

New students need a guide to marketing.
Buy 'The Complete Guide to Foot Reflexology.'
Read 'Foreword to the Present Edition' first.
They are mute testaments to a reform movement.

95. A WARNING AGAINST AN UNDESIRABLE SITUATION/DANGER

Never open the door to strangers.
Alert the victims to the attack!
We forced them to face up to the crime of child labor.
They've already introduced themselves to each other.
Alert your students to the need for improvement!

96. ADDRESSING SOMEONE ON A SPECIAL OCCASION/A SALUTE

Congratulations go out to Cassie!
Offer the first toast to the bride and the groom!
They made a toast to me, the hostess, first.
We drank to her health.

97. A RECEIVER OF AN EMOTION

My heart goes out to your son.
I feel my soul opening up to him.
He has a particular aversion to us.

98. AN ATTITUDE/A POSITIVE ATTITUDE

She was <u>committed to the civil rights cause</u>.
I think of his <u>commitment to young singers</u>.
You feel <u>devotion to Egypt</u> from reading her book.
We're <u>sensitive to issues</u> that might be incorrect.
Your <u>approach to this issue</u> will be simple.
They were not <u>averse to changes</u>.
He would never have <u>been treacherous to his friend</u>.

99. A NEGATIVE ATTITUDE

Do not <u>commit to anyone</u> at your age.
You can <u>find the downside to anything</u>.
The justices heard arguments in <u>a challenge to a law</u>.
<u>I said good-buy to my studies</u> because of my baby.
<u>My unhappiness was a comfort to him</u>.

100. YIELDING, CONCEDING, SURRENDERING

I will not <u>give in to my temper</u>.
It was impossible not <u>to succumb to the pandering</u>.
Americans are <u>warming to the idea</u> of studying abroad.
He <u>pleaded guilty to that crime</u>.

101. RESPECT

It was <u>a homage to silent film</u>.
<u>The courtesy of a child to an elder</u>—at such an age?

102. SEARCHING FOR A JOB, EMPLOYEMENT

Alex <u>applied to the</u> non-profit <u>organization</u>.
I am thinking of <u>applying to this company</u>.
She will <u>apply to the University</u> again.

103. STARTING A NEW OCCUPATION, CAREER, DEVOTING, DEDICATING

I must <u>apply myself to writing books</u>.

<u>Turning **to** music</u> was an interesting happening in his life.
I have <u>to go to class</u>, too (start studying).

104. STARTING USING EQUIPMENT/A DEVICE

They are <u>taking **to** their new tools</u> quickly.
The new university <u>takes **to** the Web</u> to promote itself.

105. A PROBLEM/ISSUE, QUESTION

The global warming <u>is a threat **to** our survival</u>.
<u>How to overcome the roadblocks **to** financial health</u>?
Were there any <u>impediments **to** their marriage</u>?
<u>The challenges **to** our liberties</u> are minor.

106. AN ANSWER TO A PROBLEM/SETTLEMENT

I think I've <u>discovered the secret **to** life</u>.
We'll help you work out fair and lasting <u>solutions **to** conflict</u>.
Help students <u>find new solutions **to** problems</u>.
<u>The solution **to** this problem</u> is not simple.

Synonyms: *into, towards, at, on, until, up, up to, upon, as far as*
Antonyms: *from, against*

TOWARD(s) indicates:

1. MOVING IN THE DIRECTION OF A PLACE/HEADING FOR

They jumped up and <u>ran **toward** the ocean</u>.
Passangers <u>hurried **toward** the plane</u>.
<u>We walked **toward** the house slowly.</u>
With fond memories, you'll <u>travel **towards** home</u>.
She had <u>started **toward** the door</u>.
<u>I tiptoed **toward** the telephone.</u>
He <u>ran **toward** the departing bus</u>.
<u>Work **toward** the other side</u> of the mouth.

2.   MOVING IN THE DIRECTION OF SOMEONE/FACING

The storm was coming toward us rapidly.
He came toward me twirling the car keys.
My mom shoved me gently toward my groom.
Standing with her back toward us, she tried to hide her tears.
I took another couple of steps toward them.
He bent toward her for a rapid kiss.

3.   ADDING/SHARING

I contributed $5.00 toward the bill.
We'll give our son money toward his medical expenses.
Jack gave money toward their education.
Volunteers contribute toward a new library with their time.

4.   A RELIEF, ASSISTANCE, SUPPORT

The money will go toward helping the family.
The aid will go towards the refugees.

5.   AN ATTITUDE TO SOMEONE, CONCERNING, REGARDING, ABOUT

His feelings toward me are too strong.
He is loving and affectionate toward her.
Animosity toward anybody is not justifiable.
They changed their policy toward senior citizens.
We follow a "don't ask, don't tell" policy toward
the adopters of the animals.
He didn't behave politely toward his mother.

6.   A DISPOSITION/MANNER/APPROACH

Her attitude towards work has improved.
He displayed an optimistic attitude
toward the future of our company.
We knew about his tough attitude toward discipline.

7. A PURPOSE, AIM, PROSPECT/THE DIRECTION OF ACTION

    We started <u>saving</u> **toward** <u>a new car.</u>
    We're <u>saving money</u> **toward** <u>a new house.</u>
    He is <u>saving money</u> **toward** <u>the time</u> when he retires.
    Do it before you <u>begin your steps</u> **toward** <u>citizenship.</u>

8. LOOKING FORWARD/EXPECTATION, HOPE

    He is known for his <u>efforts</u> **toward** <u>peace.</u>
    They are <u>heading</u> **toward** <u>an agreement.</u>
    We are <u>making slow heading</u> **toward** <u>parity</u> with men
    in the workplace.
    <u>I look</u> **toward** <u>Monday</u> without a sigh.

9. AN ANTICIPATED RESULT/PROGRESS

    Learn how to set and <u>work</u> **toward** <u>goals.</u>
    It's another <u>step</u> **toward** <u>the examination.</u>

10. DEVELOPING AN INTEREST/STARTING A NEW OCCUPATION

    She <u>turned</u> **toward** <u>religion</u> after her divorce.
    He <u>turned</u> **toward** <u>cubism</u> in the 1920s.

11. AN APPROXIMATE TIME BEFORE/CLOSE TO TIME, A CERTAIN
    POINT/AROUND

    <u>It happened</u> **toward** <u>evening.</u>
    <u>It started to rain</u> **toward** <u>sunrise.</u>
    They fell asleep only **toward** daybreak.
    <u>He watched the clock crawl slowly</u> **toward** <u>five.</u>
    I always <u>feel hungry</u> **towards** <u>dinnertime.</u>
    Toward <u>the end of her life</u> she wrote a book.
    <u>We slouch</u> **toward** <u>a millennium.</u>

    Synonyms:*, about, at, around, by, near, to*
    Antonyms: *away from, from*

UNDER indicates:

1. BEING BENFEATH, UNDERNEATH/BELOW THE SURFACE, PHYSICAL CONTACT

> The family has <u>an acre **under** potatoes</u>.
> He sat with one of <u>his legs curled **under** him</u>.
> I stopped <u>sweating **under** my arms</u>.
> With a snorkel, you can <u>swim **under** water</u>.

2. BEING COVERED/A PHYSICAL CONTACT

> <u>I slept **under** several blankets.</u>
> Never <u>leave your keys **under** doormats</u>.

3. AT A LOWER LEVEL, POSITION THAN

> The boys often <u>sat **under** those trees</u>.
> He was <u>looking at me **under** the light</u> of the moon.
> There's <u>a light **under** his desk</u>.
> We <u>lived **under** the same roof</u> for three years.

4. MOVING BENEATH, BELOW

> You have to <u>go **under** the bridge</u> first.
> <u>I reached **under** the bed</u> and pulled out my books.
> In the bedroom, I am <u>crawling **under** the covers</u>.
> The ball <u>rolled **under** the chair</u>.
> <u>I picked the cat up **under** her armpits.</u>

5. PLACING BENEATH, BELOW

> She <u>urged her son **under** the covers</u>.
> He <u>puts a thermometer **under** my tongue</u>.
> <u>Slip the keys **under** the door.</u>

6. A SMALLER AMOUNT, SIZE, DEGREE

> The temperature <u>stayed **under** freezing</u> all day.
> <u>The new pot's capacity is **under** a gallon.</u>

7.   A SMALLER PRICE, VALUE/EXPENDITURE/LESS THAN

Each book <u>cost **under** three dollars.</u>
<u>They lived well for **under** $25,000 a year.</u>

8.   A LOWER LEVEL IN SOCIAL STATUS/, BEING LESSER IN RANK

<u>I have several people **under** me.</u>
There <u>are only three people **under** him.</u>

9.   BEING BENEATH AN ASSUMED SURFACE/BEING CONCEALED/A GUISE

<u>He traveled **under** a false name.</u>
<u>She registered **under** her husband's name.</u>

10.   BELONGING TO A GROUP, CLASS/CLASSIFYING

<u>File these people **under** 'Smith'.</u>
<u>Find my name **under** 'Y'</u> in the telephone book.
The object was <u>listed **under** 'Heavenly Bodies'.</u>
<u>Look up 'butterflies' **under** 'Insects'</u> in the encyclopedia.
<u>Classify the ads **under** 'Employment' category.</u>

11.   A CURRENT STATE OF AN INDIVIDUAL

<u>She was **under** no pressure</u> now.
<u>I am feeling **under** the weather</u> today.
He <u>was **under** the impression</u> that they knew it.
We <u>bend **under** the heavy weight of our duties.</u>
The kid <u>muttered it **under** his breath.</u>

12.   A CURRENT STATE OF AN OBJECT/SITUATION

<u>How many boats are **under** sail?</u>
He will be <u>**under** house arrest.</u>

13.   A PROCESS

The child <u>will be **under** medical treatment</u> for a month.
The buildings <u>are still **under** construction or **under** repair.</u>

The matter is still under discussion.
The concept has come under increasing criticism.

14. A PROVISION/ACCORDING TO

Under the terms of the treaty, we'll withdraw our troops.
Under the contract, you have to deliver all goods by May.
Under the plan, they could have the clerk perform ceremonies.

15. A CURRENT STATE OF AFFAIRS/PREDICAMENT

I couldn't act otherwise under the circumstances.
Under no circumstances would I engage in that argument.
The doctors are unable to act under these conditions.

16. A RULE/CONTROL/BEING SUBORDINATE

The ship goes under the French flag.
You'll have to swear to the truth under oath.
Tests performed under rigorous laboratory conditions
yielded new results.

20. SUPERVISION

Her mom is 80 and needs to be under constant care.
Under her guidance, the toddler learned how to share his toys.
He toured Mexico under the auspices of the State Department.

21. INSPECTION/RE-EXAMINATION

New districts are under review now.
Traditional family values are under scrutiny.

22. CONDUCTING/PERFORMING

I will always remember singing under his direction.
He was the accompanist for the Chorus under J.Hallberg

23. AUTHORIZATION

> **Under** law, they are not liable for the damages.
> **Under** federal laws, the funds will be distributed between them.
> They did it on the basis of a letter **under** his signature.

21. A CONVENTIONAL TIME/EPOCH

> People wore those things **under** Henry the Eighth.
> **Under** this supervisor, the office was reorganized.

22. A SPECIFIC PERIOD/IN THE TIME OF

> **Under** the old regime, they dared not to write about that.
> I was born **under** Sagittarius.

23. BEING NOT OLD, MATURE ENOUGH

> She cannot vote because she is **under** age.
> He can't leave school because he is **under** age.

> Synonyms*: beneath, underneath, below, according to, in view of*
> Antonyms*: above, over*

UNDERNEATH indicates:

1. A LOWER LEVEL THAN/BELOW/COVERED

> You can see many treasures **underneath** the sea.
> Life continues **underneath** the snow.
> She keeps her pets **underneath** her bed.

2. PLACING SOMETHING/MOVING BELOW, UNDER

> Put the keys **underneath** a pile of cloth.
> I put a red napkin **underneath** each plate.
> He shoved the note **underneath** his binder.

3.   A HIDDEN, CONCEALED FEELIING

> **Underneath** her smile there is a lot of heartache.
> **Underneath** his uncle's smile is a mean nature.

Synonyms: *beneath, below, under,*
Antonyms: *above, over*

UNLIKE indicates:

BEING DIFFERENT, UNEQUAL, INCOMPATIBLE

> **Unlike** other supplements, Beta-1 triggers the immune response selectively.
> **Unlike** other kids, he wouldn't go out too often.

Synonyms: *0*
Antonyms: *like*

UNTIL indicates:

1.   A TIME BEFORE SOME SPECIFIED POINT

> He continued lecturing **until** a few years ago.
> I can't leave **until** Monday.
> They danced **until** dawn.
> He didn't return **until** the next morning.
> One must wait **until** the evening to see how splendid the day was.
> He always reads **until** late at night.
> I was allowed to be out **until** 10 p.m.
> He didn't know that **until** shortly.
> Nominations are open **until** then.

2.   REACHING A NEW STATE, CONDITION/ULTIMATE POINT

> Beat eggs and sugar **until** light.

Heat milk over medium heat **until** hot.
Cook the beans **until** tender.

Synonyms: *till, before, up to, up till, to, prior to*
Antonyms: *0*

UP indicates:

1. LOCATION/BEING AT A HIGHER POINT

School European II is **up** hill.
The old library was **up** the road.

2. LOCATION FURTHER ALONG THE WAY, AT SOME DISTANCE

The construction site is **up** the street.
Linda lived two blocks **up** the street.
Their motel is five miles **up** the road.

3. MOVING TO A HIGHER PLACE, LOCATION

We walked **up** a hill to get to the school.
Climb **up** these steps to get to the backyard.
The dog chased the cats **up** a tree.

4. MOVING TO A HIGHER POINT/LEVEL

Hike **up** Jack's Peak!
The water came halfway **up** the tires.

5. MOVING TO A POINT FURTHER ALONG A WAY

We will drive two more miles **up** the highway.
We went three more miles **up** the road.
He jogged **up** the path in the park for an hour.
He looked **up** the street toward the car.

6.   MOVING AGAINST A CURRENT OF WATER

> John swam **up** the river for exercise.
> He was unable to swim **up** the river.

7.   MOVING TO THE ORIGIN OF THE RIVER/HEADWATERS

> See those boats going **up** the Volga?
> First the fish will go **up** the stream.

8.   MOVING AGAINST THE WIND/CONTRARY TO

> How fast will we go **up** wind?
> I couldn't walk fast **up** wind.

9.   A HIGHER RANK, STATION

> His brother is well **up** the social ladder.
> He plays in a Teenage Ball League **up** there.

10. A LIMIT/EXTREME SITUATION

> Try not to use **up** every dollar we have.
> I used **up** every chance to get to the show.

11. A DESIRED RESULT

> He is trying to drum **up** support.
> You've been out and about networking **up** a storm.

12. PUTTING TOGETHER, COMPOSING, CONSTITUING

> We dreamed **up** a wonderful idea.
> I made **up** a great deal of stories for her.

13. A TIME TILL SOME POINT

> We'll stay with them **up** to Monday.
> My friend will stay with us **up** till May.

14. CUTTING INTO PIECES/SEPARATING, DISCONNECTING

> I chopped **up** the onions and peppers.
> They divided **up** all their father's money.

> Synonyms: *upward*
> Antonyms: *down, downward*

UPON indicates:

1. MOVING TO AN ELEVATED POSITION/END POINT

> The tourists climbed **upon** the elephant.
> Eventually we did get **upon** the top of the pyramid.
> The boy saw a bird alight **upon** a bough.

2. BEING IN AN ELEVATED POSITION, LOCATION

> My balloon was sitting **upon** the tree.
> The heavy shelf was resting upon two supports.

3. RESTING ON, BEING SITUATED ON

> The temple is high **upon** the hill.
> You know where Newcastle **upon** Tyne is?
> He was afraid even to stand **upon** the carpet.

4. THE TIME AFTER SOME POINT/SOON AFTER

> He said it **upon** meeting you.
> **Upon** her arrival, she made a statement.
> **Upon** arrival in Boston, you'll be met at the airport.
> Thank people immediately **upon** receiving presents.
> Once **upon** a time there lived a frog.

5. AN ATTITUDE

> Don't rely **upon** him!
> We relied **upon** our good luck.
> His manners were looked down **upon**.

6.   DISCREDITING/COMPROMISING

> <u>What a disgrace **upon** the house!</u>
> They are <u>an intrusion **upon** the dignity</u> of the occasion.
> Who can forgive <u>the slight you put **upon** her</u>?
> I long <u>to bring censure **upon** that man</u>.

7.   A STATE/CHANGING OF THE STATE

> This is <u>binding **upon** them</u>.
> He was as light-hearted as <u>a boy **upon** a holiday</u>.
> <u>A panic came **upon** him.</u>

8.   A BEHAVIOR

> I <u>took it **upon** myself</u> to finish the project.
> He responds by <u>acting **upon** the environment</u>.

9.   PREDOMINATING/CONTROL

> Extract the good from whatever <u>circumstances
> prevail **upon** you.</u>

10.   ADDRESSING SOMEBODY

> Bless the rings with one word that we would <u>wish
> **upon** the newlyweds</u>.

11.   BEING GROUNDED/ROOTED/ESTABLISHED

> These results are <u>based **upon** an incorrect assumption</u>.
> Improved scores <u>depend **upon** your being more knowledgeable.</u>
> There were sausages & cheese to make a lunch **upon**.
> <u>**Upon** the felony conviction</u> the right to vote is lost.
> <u>Now it depends entirely **upon** you.</u>
> <u>There are leads to follow **upon**.</u>

12. BEING ALIVE, SUBSISTING/SOURCE OF LIVING

    They prospered upon what they got from the farm.

13. AN UNEXPECTED ACTION, EVENT/HAVING DONE SOMETHING BY CHANCE

    He happened upon the two ladies.
    She happened upon the voice-mail messages.

14. THE BEGINNING OF A SEASON/EVENT

    Winter is upon us.
    The New Year will soon be upon everybody.

15. MOVING, COMING UP TO/AN EXPECTED EVENT

    Her birthday is upon us.
    The winds of change are upon us.
    Oh, yes, taxes are upon us.
    It will redound upon him sooner or later.

16. A NEGATIVE CONSEQUENCE, RESULT

    Pollution has a direct effect upon respiration.
    Fear has a paralyzing effect upon the body.
    The deception was practiced upon him.

17. BEING AGGRESSIVE, OFFENSIVE/ATTACKING

    The mosquitoes set upon the hikers.
    A great crisis is stealing upon my land.
    I deny the power of court to lay sentence upon me.
    Reality impinges upon our bodies.
    The company threw themselves upon the food.

18. PROVING, VALIDATING

    It's true, upon my word.
    We agree upon your plan.

19. REPETITION OF AN ACTION

Warriors, row **upon** row, were coming to the wall.
The crowd, row **upon** row, was pushing to the stage.
Row **upon** row of video movies, all the way back
to the time of black-and-white.

20. GLANCING, GAZING, STARING INTENTLY

Look **upon** your end and weep.
He fixed his black eyes **upon** me.

Synonyms: *up, on, after, in, next to, on top of*
Antonyms: *down, downward*

VERSUS indicates:

1. AN ALTERNATIVE/CONTRAST

Discuss advantages of the non-traditional medicine
versus traditional medicine.

2. ASSESSING, COMPARING IN LAW/SPORTS

They compared assets **versus** liabilities.
It's the situation "The plaintiff **versus** the defendant."

Synonyms: *against, opposite*
Antonyms: *0*

VIA indicates:

1. MOVING, PASSING THROUGH/BY WAY OF

She went from New York to Denver **via** Chicago.
They read all his plays **via** English translations.
They got the news **via** traveler.
We received the flyers **via** messenger.

2.   A WAY, MANNER OF DOING THINGS/MEANS

> **Via** hands-on activities I taught kids first aid techniques.
> This time she sent a letter **via** air mail.
> Taxicabs have wheelchairs accessible **via** ramps.
> I check my computer messages **via** modem.

Synonyms: *through, by, by way of*
Antonyms: *0*

IN VIEW OF indicates:

A REASON, CAUSE/CONSIDERATION

> **In view of** my deteriorating health, I shouldn't be working at all.
> **In view of** the rising costs, we're going to rise our prices.
> **In view of** your excellent credit history,
> you've been pre-approved for the MasterCard.

Synonyms: *because, considering, as regards*
Antonyms: *0*

BY WAY OF

1.   THROUGH, VIA/BY MEANS OF

> That flight doesn't go direct, it goes **by way of** Atlanta.
> They're planning to go to Florida **by way of** Washington.

2.   AN EXPLANATION/AS/METHOD

> He made no comment **by way of** apology.
> He drew some chart **by way of** example.
> **By way of** proof of the mushrooms being edible, I ate some first.

Synonyms: *via, through, around, over, throughout*
Antonyms: *0*

WITH indicates:

They wanted <u>to displace old thoughts **with** new</u>.
I <u>replaced that window **with** a double-panel window</u>.
He was <u>awarded **with** two medals for that.</u>
Many people have <u>concerns **with** the march</u>.
He doesn't <u>seek limelight **in/with** this case.</u>

1.   BEING TOGETHER/NEXT TO, ACCOMPANYING/INSEPARABLE

Are you <u>easy to be **with**</u>?
She is <u>pregnant **with** twins</u> and due next month.
<u>She is here **with** her five kids</u> for a week.
<u>It makes your time **with** the family more enjoyable.</u>
I had a special <u>bond **with** my grandfather.</u>
<u>He is **with** anyone who searches for truth.</u>
<u>He studied in Moscow **with** her</u> for a year.
You always <u>see Betty **with** her dogs</u>.
<u>The computer came installed **with** several programs.</u>

2.   COMING TOGETHER, MEETING

<u>Get in contact **with** the right people.</u>
<u>Meet **with** the counselor</u> to decide what to do.
It was her second <u>brush **with** a genius</u>.
They <u>join **with** groups</u> such as 'Housing Council'.
He told me he <u>had someone else to go **with**.</u>
<u>Get in touch **with** your intuition!</u>

3.   STAYING AT SOMEONE'S PLACE/IN THE COMPANY

<u>Join **with** those who dwell here.</u>
Who <u>lives **with** you</u> in the same house?
Did you enjoy <u>visiting **with** them</u>?
During his <u>visit **with** me</u> we talked about it.
<u>A visit **with** a pediatrician</u> lasts 15 minutes.
The boy can <u>move in **with** her.</u>
<u>He moved in **with** Debrah.</u>
<u>I became good friends **with** a girl next door.</u>
<u>I will go out **with** lots of boys.</u>

4. BEING SICK, HAVING A DISEASE

Individuals **with** visual impairment receive counseling.
I'm currently care giving for a lady **with** shingles.
Is John sick **with** the flu or pneumonia now?

5. BEING (IN) ATTENTIVE/FOLLOWING SOMEONE

Please repeat that, I'm not **with** you
You're not **with** me.
Then check **with** us to be sure it's acceptable.
Check your answers **with** the original.
I checked **with** my legal expert about it.
Check **with** the teacher when you should come.
It's good advice to check **with** the city.

6. QUITTING A RELATIONSHIP/MOVING AWAY

He broke up **with** Anne eventually.
I can't break up **with** him now.
I know that she parted **with** her second husband.

7. ESCAPING UNPUNISHED

You can get away **with** anything.
He did get away **with** it unfortunately.

8. LETTING AN INDIVIDUAL, OBJECT STAY IN SOMEONE'S CHARGE

She left her daughter **with** us for a day.
Leave the keys **with** the watchman.
He left his keys **with** his neighbors.
You can leave the letter **with** me.

9. LEAVING AN OBJECT RELUCTANTLY/AGAINST ONE'S WISH

I hate to part **with** my old books.
He didn't want to part **with** any of his possessions.
It was real hard to part **with** my past.

10. ABSENCE/BEING DISCONNECTED

He is <u>a man **with** no future</u>.
I am <u>a widow **with** no children</u>.

11. EXAMINING, INVESTIGATING

<u>Check it out **with** the Park Service.</u>
He <u>checked it out **with** the supervisor</u>.

12. STOPPING, QUITTING AN ACTIVITY

We <u>did away **with** typical hassles</u>.
He <u>did away **with** his old fu</u>rniture.

13. MOVING IN THE SAME DIRECTION

For a while, <u>they will be **with** the traffic</u>.
We <u>drifted down the river **with** the current</u>.
Being in the ocean, <u>swim **with** the stream</u> and never against it.
I increased the speed by <u>flying **with** the prevailing winds</u>.

14. MOVING ALONGSIDE

<u>The boundary **with** this country</u> runs for thousands of miles.
<u>The line of demarcation **with** their neighbor</u> was often crossed.
Please slow down, I can't <u>keep up **with** you</u>.

15. A CONCURRENT ACTION/SITUATION

<u>He always has his coffee **with** his dessert.</u>
<u>Gather momentum **with** each exchange of signals.</u>
Being overweight <u>brings many problems **with** it</u>.

16. PLACING TOGETHER/USING TOGETHER/ADDING

Why not <u>team your suit **with** a black shirt</u>?
It's a good idea <u>to match the color of the shoes
with your dress.</u>

17. BEING FULL/PACKED, CRAMMED

> He is <u>infused **with** radical thoughts</u>.
> The country is <u>exploding **with** dollars</u>.
> He'd <u>been so busy **with** his designing</u>.
> <u>Park in well-lit areas **with** plenty of traffic.</u>
> **With** <u>fond memories</u>, you'll travel towards home.
> She saw the room <u>crowded **with** strange people</u>.
> The refrigerator was <u>filled **with** bottles of wine</u>.
> They library system is <u>replete **with** high technology</u>.
> The basement <u>room was filled **with** smoke</u>.
> <u>His eyes welled up **with** tears.</u>

18. A CAUSE OF A STATE IN THE NATURAL ENVIRONMENT

> The branches of the trees <u>were heavy **with** snow</u>.

19. COVERING AN AREA/ADORNING

> I <u>planted the patch **with** red flowers</u>.
> He <u>decorated the walls **with** watercolors</u>.
> My <u>overcoat is lined **with** silk or nylon</u>.

20. BEING SUPPLIED, FURNISHED

> He <u>provided her **with** all the necessities</u>.
> The store is <u>stocked **with** swimming suits.</u>
> The lab is <u>equipped **with** modern technology.</u>

21. BEING BUSY, OCCUPIED/ABSORBED, ENGAGED

> I am pretty <u>swamped **with** the work</u>.
> <u>Laden down **with** knowledge</u>, we analyze every bit.
> I am still <u>awash **with** etiquette questions</u>.

22. PROVIDING INFORMATION

> <u>Fill in the blanks **with** an appropriate word.</u>
> <u>Fill out the form **with** the updated information.</u>

23. BEING EMPLOYED, A MEMBER/WORKING TOGETHER/A BUSINESS RELATIONSHIP

She is with the real estate company.
Thanks for your interest in becoming associated with our agency.
He has applied for employment with The Institute on Aging.
We may deduct fees from your accounts with us.
He served with the Army in the last war.
He has appeared as a soloist with the Bach Festival.

24. AN OUTCOME/CONSEQUENCE OF AN ACTIVITY

They came up with a new plan.
He came up with a great idea.
Come up with innovative ideas!
He has come up with a good solution.
He presented his boss with an ultimatum.

25. HANDLING A SITUATION

Some don't know how to cope with a failing life.
You'll learn how to cope with important challenges.
How to deal with awkward moments at this age?
Do you know how to deal with such a letter?

31. DOING SOMETHING UNSKILLFULLY

They tinker with the system that they believe has worked just fine.
He tinkers with the car engine so it works properly.

27. A NEGATIVE RESULT, CONSEQUENCE/BEING AT RISK, IN DANGER

The dog came down with a bladder infection.
She escaped with just a few scratches and bruises.
Some frogs are threatened with extinction.
Stretching the truth caught up with him.

28. A FINAL SELECTION

Eventually I <u>ended up **with** a white dress</u>.
He <u>ended up **with** a tough choice</u>.

29. BEING FINISHED, COMPLETED

I thought <u>you were through **with** it</u>.
I had to <u>go through **with** the haircut</u>.
Find courage <u>to go ahead **with** your dream.</u>
Don't break **<u>with</u> this tradition.**

30. A WAY OF ACHIEVING A DESIRABLE RESULT

She <u>made us laugh **with** her jokes</u>.
He knew how<u> to make her crazy **with** passion.</u>
It would make him <u>sweat **with** love</u> for me.

31. AN ACCOMPLISHMENT

<u>I had caught up **with** my peers in school</u>.
We wish you the best of <u>luck **with** your career search</u>.
<u>Be successful **with** voice mail!</u>
They ordered him <u>reinstated **with** back pay</u>.
He was <u>awarded **with** two medals for that.</u>

32. INTERACTING/SOCIALIZING

<u>I shook hands **with** each one</u>.
<u>I can serve as a mediator **with** your landlord</u>.
She always <u>mixes **with** the other guests</u> at a party.
<u>She kept a date **with** another flame.</u>
He has been <u>going **with** a woman</u> for a year.
<u>She is going **with** Bill</u> now.
They like <u>to play **with** the cat.</u>

33. AN ENCOUNTER/CONFRONTION/INTIMIDATION

We are all <u>faced **with** that question</u>.
He is <u>faced **with** eviction</u> again.

He was constantly <u>faced **with** problems</u>.

34. A COMPLAINT/DISAPPROVAL

The union <u>filed a grievance **with** the agency</u>.
They have <u>filed a protest **with** management.</u>
<u>She was already charged **with** auto theft.</u>

35. GIVING AWAY/YIELDING

<u>I've shared the books **with** several people.</u>
You usually <u>share a bathroom **with** other guests</u>.
She is <u>trading her pills **with** her friends</u>
Who's <u>to present him **with** the envelope</u> containing the fee?

36. A SUPPORT/COOPERATION/JOINT ACTION, COLLABORATION

<u>Can you help me **with** my luggage?</u>
He <u>presented me **with** the copy</u> of his latest album.
They spent many hours <u>proofreading **with** me.</u>

37. A REQUEST

<u>I pleaded **with** him to tell me.</u>
<u>He pleaded **with** his editor</u> to publish her poems.
Police are <u>pleading **with** the criminal</u> to come forward.
<u>Could I plead **with** them?</u>

38. A WARNING

<u>Be careful **with** your valuables.</u>
<u>Don't be taking photos **with** us.</u>

39. COMMUNICATING WITH SOMEONE/SPEECH ACTIVITY

<u>Talk **with** your doctor</u> as soon as possible!
You may <u>discuss it **with** college students</u>.
I've <u>corresponded **with** her</u> for seven years.

40. EXPRESSING ANGER VERBALLY

> I finally had it out with my boss.
> She had it out with her Mom at last.

41. ANNIHILATING, OBLITERATING, DESTROYING

> To hell with it!
> Down with the old system!
> Down with the old laws!

42. A VIEW, OPINION

> With him, it's of no importance.
> You can go now, fine with us!

43. EQUATING, BALANCING

> How do his values compare with yours?
> Match your interests with your career goals!

44. A CONFORMITY, ACCORD/INFLUENCE

> I certainly do agree with you.
> Go along with someone's suggestion.
> We had to comply with the instructions.
> The teacher's words carry a lot of weight with us.
> They were with me on the new rules.

45. A RESEMBLANCE, SIMILARITY, PROPORTION

> This side is not even with that side.
> The information is consistent with our data.
> Your situation is identical with mine.
> It was her world and she was in tune with it.
> His raise was commensurate with his efforts.
> Does this blouse go with my red skirt?

46. A DISAGREEMENT/BEING AGAINST/OPPOSITION

My husband never argues with me.
I differ with you almost on every topic.
His actions are in a sharp contrast with his words.

47. A CONFLICT, CLASH

Fantasy will collide with destiny.
At ten, I had my first brush with the law.
He had few brushes with tragedy in his life.
I don't want to fight with anyone.

48. A POSITIVE FEELING, EMOTION TOWARDS AN OBJECT

I am thrilled with the new program.
My supervisor was not thrilled with the idea.
I am fascinated with his mind.
He is pleased with his new assignment.
My boss is satisfied with my performance.

49. LIKING, AFFECTION, DEVOTION TOWARDS AN INDIVIDUAL

He was enraptured with a young girl.
She was in love with Mark, infatuated with him.
This dish is a favorite with our kids.

50. A NEGATIVE FEELING, EMOTION

Are you angry with me?
Everybody was angry with the senator.
He is not always at ease with his in-laws.
He wasn't affectionate with his new born brother.
I empathize with anyone who has lost a child.
He was always cross with the dog.
She is uncomfortable with all the gifts.
Are you dissatisfied with the service?
We can't worry ourselves with this.
I've lost my 'thrill' with homemaking.

51. AN ATTITUDE/RELATIONSHIP

How to break ice **with** strangers?
They don't have to bother **with** teenagers.
· He enjoyed enormous sway **with** his boss.
I am just fed up **with** relatives and friends.
Don't be impatient **with** your sister.
You've got to be real **with** people.
They are popular **with** voters.
I sympathize **with** your feelings.
My dog showered me **with** affection.

52. A KIND OF CONDUCT

He didn't get along **with** any of his employees.
He has no right to interfere **with** her education.
She may be testing you **with** her behavior.
Always pepper us **with** questions!

53. AN AGGRESSIVE CONDUCT

She threatened me **with** her finger.
If threatened **with** a weapon, don't resist.
He hit the table **with** his fist.

54. A SOURCE OF AN IMPRESSION

They dazzled each other **with** their charms.
Do you seduce your readers **with** your words?
I make them proud **with** my beauty.

55. A CAUSE OF THE PHYSICAL STATE

He was weak **with** hunger.
Our dog trembles **with** fear during the thunderstorm.
We stayed out of school **with** colds.

56. A PSHYCHOLOGICAL STATE

He felt utterly discontented **with** life.

Depressed **with** his career, he moved to another state.
I was happy **with the results** of the elections.
He feels the discomfort **with his Mom's decision**.
Are you comfortable **with the new camera**?
The child was bored **with** her books.
I was blessed **with a visit** from my son.
He is less confident **with his male characters**.

57. A CAUSE OF AN EMOTIONAL CONDITION, STATE

She was so out of her mind **with grief.**
I am warmed **with joy** with these words.
The boy squealed **with excitement and delight.**
Her voice was hoarse **with the pent-up passion.**
The body can melt **with love** or freeze **with fear.**
The newlyweds were beaming **with** happiness.
Why should one be green **with envy** because of that?
You could hear a voice choked **with emotion.**
I was almost paralyzed **with** enchantment.
He had to drop out **with stress.**

58. AN EMOTIONAL REACTION

I watched them **with pain.**
They reacted to our idea **with joy.**
He looked on **with nostalgia.**
They howled **with laughter.**

59. A CIRCUMSTANCE, SITUATION

We often had problems **with** our old car.
I am one month delinquent **with my payments.**
With the traffic in this city, it takes a long time to get home.
She was diagnosed **with breast cancer.**

60. USING A MATERIAL

He liked making things **with wood.**
I make things for kids **with clay** now.

61. A DEVICE, INSTRUMENT, TOOL

I can't unlock the door **with** this key.
I rub my runny nose **with** my handkerchief.
Try not to eat it **with** your hands, but **with** your spoon.
Flu can be treated **with** antibiotics.
Get the answers **with** the "Topics" button!

62. DOING SOMETHING WITH THE HELP OF/BY MEANS OF

You can sow it **with** large stitches.
Now step forward **with** the left foot.
We spoil our son by crippling him **with** kindness.
I bought a lottery ticket **with** that money.
Resolutions are made **with** the verb "will".
Begin a name **with** a capital letter.
Let's start **with** the most common.

63. AN ABILITY, EFFORT APPLIED

She performed **with** great skill.
He solved all the problems **with** ease.
He always does it **with** great care.
We'll teach you how to write **with** impact.
I love you **with** all my heart.

64. A WAY, MANNER OF DOING THINGS

Store the brush **with** bristles facing up.
With your permission, I can start my work now.
Don't confuse children **with** trick questions.
He always slept **with** his mouth open.
He sleeps **with** his bedroom door closed.
Reward accomplishment **with** respect and love.
I am sitting **with** my back straight.
Do you pay **with** a check or money order?
She graduated **with** distinction at age 20.
They started the show **with** a poem.
My parents spanked us **with** regularity.

Walk confidently **with** purpose.
She acquitted herself **with** dignity.

65. A SITUATION CONCERNING, REGARDING

It's common **with** the students here.
This is specially prevalent **with** old people.

66. A CONDITION ACCOMPANYING A GIVEN SITUATION

With proper treatment, depression can be lifted.
With gradual adaptation, kids can conquer any situation.
With all of the unemployment, there is a feeling of
being threatened.
With the extinction of some species, researchers lost the tracks
of some links in the organic world.
Crimes against people accounted for 28% of incidents, **with** battery
the most common.
Never leave your car unattended **with** the engine running.
Hold the child **with** an August birthday back a year before
starting school.
With better pain management, fewer sufferers might seek
other options.

67. AN EVENT HAPPENING IN SPITE OF

With all his talents, he's never been very successful.
With all my education and experience, I couldn't find a job.

68. AN OVERSIGHT, ERROR/INACCURACY

I might have confused cholesterol **with** fat.
We have done dumb things **with** money.

69. A SPECIFIC FEATURE/PECULIARITY/IDENTIFICATION

See that house **with** the big front porch?
The woman **with** gray hair is my mom.
People **with** pleasant personalities often get ahead easily.

They hired <u>an officer **with** a drinking problem</u>.
He is now <u>a lawyer **with** a $35,000 salary</u>.

70. A SKILL IN A SPECIAL FIELD, ACTIVITY

She <u>was a genius **with** design</u>.
He <u>is very good **with** calculus</u>.

71. TWO EVENTS HAPPENING AT THE SAME TIME

He <u>rises **with** the sun</u>.
My darling son <u>gets up **with** the birds</u>.
His <u>brows knit **with** a sudden frown</u>.
<u>Keep up **with** the times</u>.

72. CHANGING WITH THE TIME PROGRESS/GAINING A NEW QUALITY

Wines <u>improve **with** age</u>.
Loss of muscle <u>occurs **with** aging</u>.
Hormone production <u>drops **with** age</u>.
<u>We become more tolerant **with** age.</u>
<u>One grows older **with** the years.</u>
<u>Skills increase **with** experience.</u>

73. A REASON

<u>Make a sign **with** your fingers</u> to ward off evil.
<u>The past glows **with** the memories of those men.</u>

Synonyms: *by, among, at, along, beside, from*
Antonyms: *against*

WITHIN indicates:

1. BEING INSIDE, IN THE INNER PART/FIELD

I can't find <u>a decent place to go **within** the whole city</u>.
We'd like to investigate <u>some places **within** the castle</u>.

There's been a lot of <u>tension **within** the family</u> lately.
<u>**Within** my heart</u> I do believe in it.

2. HIDING SOMETHING

We <u>keep</u> the history of his disease **within** the family.
I try <u>to keep my feelings **within** me</u>, not expose them.

3. MOVING INSIDE

<u>Water from the sprinkle reaches plants **within** five meters.</u>
<u>We pulled to **within** two points of winning.</u>
<u>Try to defuse these emotions **within** your relationship.</u>
Look for <u>the jobs **within** existing organizations.</u>

4. TIME LIMITS/LESS THAN A PERIOD OF TIME

The committee will <u>convene **within** the week.</u>
The idea is <u>to give customers service **within** seconds.</u>
It'll be <u>built **within** a week.</u>
I am unable <u>to read all these books **within** my lifetime.</u>
I could <u>guess one's age **within** a year.</u>
They had <u>to leave the country **within** 24 hours.</u>
<u>**Within** a day of his departure,</u> the police arrived there.

5. A DISTANCE/LESS THAN A DISTANCE

<u>Is your job **within** walking distance?</u>
<u>My house is **within** a mile of the shopping mall.</u>
<u>She was still **within** sight</u> when I was waving good bye.
<u>The museum is **within** easy reach.</u>
<u>The ball is **within** your grasp.</u>
<u>I was **within** one point of a perfect score.</u>

6. A DEGREE/NOT EXCEEDING THE LIMITS

We are taught how <u>to live **within** our means</u>
<u>Live **within** your means, **within** your income.</u>
They will do <u>whatever is **within** their capacity.</u>

7. LIMITS, LIMITATIONS OF SPACE

It received favorable <u>response **within** the community</u>.
<u>People **within** modern society</u> are torn between private
and public claims.

8. ABIDING BY THE RULES, REGULATIONS

<u>If he'd kept **within** the law</u>, he wouldn't lose his reputation.
Whatever I wear <u>falls well **within** social norms</u>.

Synonyms*: in, inside*
Antonyms*: out, outside*

WITHOUT indicates:

1. THE ABSENCE OF AN EVENT, ACTION

It was <u>a day **without** major disasters</u>.
<u>**Without** eight hours' sleep you soon will get sick.</u>
Can't I <u>tell a story **without** being interrupted</u>?

2. THE ABSENCE OF AN INDIVIDUAL, PEOPLE

Should I allow <u>her to go to the movies **without** an adult?</u>
<u>**Without** my family</u>, my recovery would
have been less rapid.

3. LACKING CHARACTER

<u>He is apparently **without** scruple.</u>
<u>The kid is completely **without** fear.</u>

4. A WAY, MANNER OF DOING THINGS

They will <u>help us **without** a doubt</u>.
<u>I accepted his offer **without** hesitation.</u>
<u>Be here at four **without** fail.</u>

5.   BEING FREE FROM/NOT HAVING

Without truth there can be no justice.
He talked **without** a cough or a wheeze.
They call him a man **without** luck.

6.   AUTHORIZATION/RECOMMENDATION

He was ordered held **without** bond.
You cannot do it **without** permission.
Officers may enter homes **without** a warrant.
He was sentenced to life in prison **without** parole.
Some drugs are available **without** prescription.
We cannot do **without** better instructions.

7.   AVOIDING, OMITTING

They left the room **without** saying good buy.
He left **without** cleaning up his desk today.
Bring up these issues **without** giving advice.
Cut spending **without** major lifestyle changes.

8.   NOT USING

I did the crossword puzzle **without** a dictionary.
She cannot read **without** her glasses.
I have my teeth pulled **without** anesthetic.

9.   NOT PERFORMING AN ACTION

She passed the test **without** studying.
Disabled immigrants will become citizens **without** passing
English and civics tests.

10.   BEING OUTSIDE THE LIMIT, BEYOND

My husband's car and our visitors were **without** the gate.
There's a good water supply within and **without** the city walls.

Synonyms: *at, on, beyond, out*
Antonyms: *in, within*

WORTH indicates:

1. HAVING AN EQUAL VALUE

   <u>What is your house **worth**</u>?
   The plane <u>is **worth** $150,000</u> now.
   This dress <u>is **worth** one thousand dollars</u>.
   <u>Is a picture **worth** a thousand words</u>?
   <u>How much is my book **worth**</u>?
   <u>How much are you **worth**</u>?

2. BEING GOOD, IMPORTANT/DESERVING, MERITING

   It <u>is not **worth** the trouble</u>.
   <u>It is probably **worth** trying</u>.
   His idea <u>is not worth considering</u>.
   Collaborative abilities may <u>be **worth** implementing</u>.
   Personal recommendations <u>are</u> often <u>**worth** following up</u>.
   Are you sure the play <u>is **worth** seeing</u>?
   It <u>is **worth** drawing a distinction between the two</u>.
   This example **worth** discussing
   My Jack <u>is **worth** millions</u>.

3. A MEASURE OF THE FINANCIAL STATUS/HAVING WEALTH

   Her husband <u>is **worth** 500,000 dollars</u>.
   He <u>is</u> sure <u>**worth** 1,000,000 dollars</u> now.

   Synonyms: *0*
   Antonyms: *0*

APPENDIX

1. *Complex prepositions*

The list below presents language units or phrases that are called *complex* prepositions by some linguists. This list comprises two sets of word combinations: units that consist of two or more different parts of speech like *'in aid of,'* and the units that consists of only two prepositions like *'down from'*:

> according to, in accordance with, on account of, across from, in addition to, in aid of, along with, apart from, as for, as to, aside from, away from, in (on) behalf of, because of, but for, by means of, by way of, due to, except for, down from, (in) back of, on, behalf of, in care of, in case of, in charge of, in (the) face of, in favor of, in front of, in lieu of, by means of, next to, in need of, insofar as, owing to, in place of, in quest of, in, with regard to, regardless of, in relation to, in respect of (to), insofar as, instead of, for the sake of, in spite of, on top of, together with, in respect of, to, in view of, up to.

2. Examples with *omitted* prepositions:

> They're talking innovation here. (**about** innovation)
> They are talking control here. (**about** control)
> You are talking fame and fortune. (**about** fame and fortune)
> You don't just talk a good game. (**about** a good game)
> We're talking magic and mystery. (**about** magic and mystery)
> Almost half my paycheck is eaten up by taxes. (**of** my paycheck)
> Student enrollment in schools rose 1% the past two years.
> (**in** the past two years)
> The place you want most to be is the one that's farthest away.
> (**in** that you want to be)
> It's a rarity for a deaf kid her age. (**of** her age)
> He was emotionally in line with other children his age. (**of** his age)

Men and women do not always handle sickness the same way.
(**in** the same way)
The frigid winters were the least of the disconcerting
conditions she had to accommodate. (accommodate **to**)
He makes straight A's and plays sports competitively.
We'll also be having a used book sale the same days.
(**in** the same days)
By eating this you'll reap over a half your day's needs
for vitamins. (a half **of** your day's needs)
The first couple times I worked for him I went home and cried.
(The first couple **of** times)
The plant is too near the city. (too near **to** the city).
I go to the movie Sunday. (**on** Sunday).
Just give me a cup a coffee. (a cup **of** coffee).
I rode the subway. (**on** the subway).
You may want to fly the ocean in a silver plane.
(fly **across** the ocean).

3. Examples of the *separated* usage of the preposition and its governing/head
    word:

    What is this shirt made **of**? (of what)
    This will be a party you won't have to apologize **for**.
    (for a party)

    Start from the program you want to keep working **in**!
    (in what you want)

    She takes me places I dream about going **to**.
    (to the places)

978-0-595-37577-6
0-595-37577-4

Printed in the United States
50328LVS00003B/74

9 780595 375776